LONG-TERM CARE

Your Financial
Planning Guide

LONG-TERM CARE

Your Financial Planning Guide

Phyllis Shelton

LTCi PUBLISHING
http://www.phyllisshelton.com

LONG-TERM CARE: Your Financial Planning Guide is published by

LTCi Publishing
108 Rhoades Lane
Hendersonville, TN 37075-8084

Special book excerpts or customized printings can also be created to fit specific needs. For details, write or phone the office of LTCi Publishing, 108 Rhoades Lane, Hendersonville, TN 37075-8084. Attn. Bill Pomakoy. Phone: 1-888-400-1118

ISBN 978-0-9633516-6-1

Printed in the United States of America

INTRODUCTION

"So I close by saying that I might have had a bad break, but I have an awful lot to live for. Today, I consider myself the luckiest man on the face of the earth." -- Lou Gehrig (1903 - 1941)

This tenacious "never give up" attitude is representative of famous people in our generation who found themselves battling a long-term chronic condition at a young age. Lou Gehrig, Christopher Reeve, Michael J. Fox and Muhammad Ali had to channel their energy from being "Iron Horse", Superman, *Back to the Future* hero, and "The Greatest" to fighting a condition that threatened their ability to brush their own teeth. How can vibrant, strong icons of youth and strength become so impaired so quickly? The answer is something that baby boomers have yet to reckon with: almost 40% of people needing long-term care in this country are working-age adults, ages 18-64.[1]

Private health insurance doesn't cover long-term, chronic care for younger people and Medicare doesn't cover it for older people. Medicaid pays only if you spend most of your assets. So we have to take care of ourselves.

Are you a small business person, entrepreneur, or climbing the corporate ladder? If you are working 60+ hours per week as many of us do, and out of the blue, your spouse or parent or parent-in-law has an accident or stroke and needs long-term care, what will happen to your career? At an average of $68,000–$135,000[2] per year (depending on where you live) for daily home health care or nursing home care, most families don't know where to turn for help.

The average baby boomer now has more parents than children to care for.[3]

There's a solution, and a good one, for this dilemma, but it's not for everyone.

This book is dedicated to helping you determine if long-term care insurance is appropriate for you, your spouse and/or your parents. Many people want information such as:

1. "I've heard that it's much more difficult to qualify for Medicaid long-term care benefits – is that true?" (See Chapter 5, *The Medicaid Benefit for Long-Term Care*, p. 163.)

2. What are the tax advantages for long-term care insurance? (See Chapter 1, *Tax Incentives for Long Term Care Insurance*, p. 18.)

3. I've read several articles that advise me to wait until I'm 59 to buy long-term care insurance. Is this a good idea? (See Chapter 2, *The True Cost Of Waiting*, p. 82.)

4. I'm only 40. Wouldn't I be better off just saving the premium and paying for my own long-term care? (See Chapter 2, *Saving vs. LTC Insurance*, p. 83.)

5. I'm hearing about an insurance plan that would help me preserve my assets and still get help from Medicaid for long-term care if I use up my insurance benefits. That sounds too good to be true. How does it work? (See Chapter 4, *The Partnership for Long-Term Care*, p. 148.)

As an insurance consultant and former LTC insurance professional, I am especially committed to providing current, meaningful information about long-term care insurance that is not available in any other publication. This book also will explain the other major programs that are impacted by the issue of long-term care, such as Medicare, Medicare Advantage, Medicare supplement and the Medicaid benefit for long-term care. It also addresses alternatives such as life insurance/LTC policies, accelerated death benefits, viatical and life settlements, long-term care annuities, critical illness insurance, and in some states, a special Partnership program between private LTC insurance and Medicaid.

Please, let me caution you. This booklet is only a summary of the highlights of the various programs. It is not a legal description of benefits and should not be used as such. If you have questions about specific benefit features, you should consult an insurance professional you trust or your state's insurance department (See **Directory of State Insurance Departments, Medicaid and Aging Agencies**, p. 281), and any appropriate insurance policy contracts.

I hope you find this information helpful.

Phyllis Shelton
Nashville, Tennessee
May 2008

*Medi-Cal in California and MassHealth in Massachusetts

Table of Contents

LONG-TERM CARE

Your Financial Planning Guide

Chapter 1

Long-Term Care
and Your Financial Security

∿∿∿∿∿∿∿∿∿∿∿∿∿∿∿∿∿∿∿∿∿∿∿∿

The most devastating thing that could happen to your financial future is not a bear market. It's the need for long-term care--for yourself, your spouse, or your parents.[1]

-- Terry Savage, *Chicago Sun-Times*
Financial Columnist

I *was three when my grandparents moved in with us. My grandmother died unexpectedly two years later after gall bladder surgery. My grandfather was so sad. I still remember him crying after the funeral.*

Born in 1886, my grandfather was blind, a diabetic who had to have a shot every day, and most importantly, my best friend. He listened with endless patience while I laboriously read the adventures of Nancy Drew, Cherry Ames, the Dana Girls, and Trixie Belden, none

1

of which I ever finished. I think he also heard excerpts from Black Beauty and Beautiful Joe, my favorite animal books. Sometimes he returned the favor by telling me stories about his logging days in the East Tennessee mountains.

My mother was a nurse, worked nights while my father could be with us, and cared for my best friend almost ten years in our home, with my help of course. I didn't give him his daily insulin shot or plan his special diet or bathe him or dress him. But I gave him hours upon hours of my time, partially because I took the caregiving responsibility my mother assigned to me very seriously, but mostly because of how much I loved him. We had to be quiet while she slept, so I read him story upon story and fetched many glasses of water and led him to the bathroom when he asked me to. Sometimes I just crawled up on his lap to let him make whatever problem I encountered during the day go away. As I grew older, his room was my first stop when I got home from school.

My best friend went to a nursing home when I was 12. He never asked for help, but I knew my mother was struggling between giving him her best (he was incontinent by then) and caring for me and my three-year-old brother. She was also working double shifts at the hospital for extra money. We moved him to another nursing home once because she didn't think he was getting the best possible care. When he passed away two years later, I was devastated. My best friend was gone.

Twenty years later, my mother lost a two-year battle with cancer at age 54. I thought about my best friend and finally realized that what was a normal lifestyle for me as a child must have been a tremendous sacrifice for her.

Home and community-based care and nursing home care may well be the nation's greatest uninsured need.[2] It is the largest health care expense that is not covered by group and individual health insurance, HMOs, retiree health plans or Medicare, Medicare Advantage plans and Medicare supplements. This chapter presents information about why long-term care has become a national concern. Have you ever known anyone whose assets were totally destroyed by prolonged home health or nursing home care? A friend, a neighbor, a relative—or even you—could be one of the many, many Americans who face this plight each year.

Nationally, the average annual cost for semi-private nursing home care is about $68,000, or $187 per day, up to about $77,000 or $210 per day, for a private room, which many people prefer.[3] A ten-hour shift for a home health care aide through a home health agency costs an average of $190.[4] (In some parts of the country like New York City, the cost is an astronomical $380 per day, or over $135,000 per year, and home health care can easily cost $25+ per hour in some parts of the country.)[5] Using the growth rate of over 6 percent we have seen over the last 20 years for the period 1987-2007, these costs could at least triple in the next 20 years.[6] This means that the 50-year-old of today can expect to spend at least $300,000 per year (or over $600,000 in the highest cost areas) if he or she requires care at age 80. If both spouses need care, the figure grows astronomically.

Do you find these projections hard to believe? The average semi-private nursing home cost in a 1990 Nashville, Tennessee cost survey was $60. That figure today is $164 —an average yearly growth rate of 6%.[7]

The average caregiving time in a national home care survey was 4.3 years, but 29% have provided care longer than 5 years.[8] The most recent national nursing home survey showed that although three-fourths of nursing home stays were three years or less, 12 percent of the patients stayed longer than five years.[9] One in four family caregivers is dealing with an Alzheimer's or dementia patient,[10] and an Alzheimer's patient can live an average of eight years or as long as 20 years.[11] A recent study showed that the annual cost to U.S. businesses for Alzheimer's patients and their working caregivers is $88 billion.[12]

> *Shaun Mabry, an independent insurance professional in Atlanta, Georgia, knows these statistics firsthand. His grandmother spent 11 years in a nursing home with Alzheimer's until her death at age 83. His knowledge goes far beyond an extended duration of care, however. He also watched as his grandmother went from a "saintly, churchgoing person to a sailor"—Shaun's term for someone with very salty language and a totally unfamiliar, very unpleasant personality, a heartbreaking transition for Shaun's family.*

This extremely high incidence of Alzheimer's, coupled with the over 85 age group being the fastest growing segment of the population, make it easy to see why a national survey said that caregiving directly affects one out of four families in the United States, with just over 20% of all U.S. households containing at least one caregiver in 2003. Twenty-two percent of these caregivers provided care for two people and 8 percent for 3 or more![13]

> *Shaun Mabry's other grandmother provides an extreme example of multiple caregiving. At age 77, she is caring for her 78-year-old husband, Shaun's grandfather, who has Alzheimer's, her 50-year-old daughter who had a stroke last year, and three grandchildren, all two-years-old, born two months apart. Her mother is still alive in Florida at age 106!*

Combine this staggering volume of caregiving with a *Wall St. Journal* 2006 poll that showed that two in five U.S. adults do not think they will have enough money to pay for their long-term care needs as they age and another third aren't sure if they will have enough.[14] Given these statistics, it's no surprise that 37 percent of caregivers in a 2006 John Hancock survey reported that caregiving significantly changed their financial situation and more importantly, two-thirds of them said that caregiving had a significant impact on their entire family.[15] As you can see, **long-term care is a family crisis for the 21st century.**

The Odds Are 1 out of 2

If you don't need care at a younger age, the actual risk at age 65 for needing long-term care (either home care, assisted living or nursing home care) is **greater than 60%**.[16] For most of us, that won't be nursing home care, as most people will never be in a nursing home. But home care can cost just as much or more than being in a nursing home, depending on how much you have.

The increasing demand for long-term care is the result of several factors—the aging population, a shortage of caregivers in the home due to women working and children locating away from parents and technology. Sometimes technology that prolongs life for victims of heart attacks, diabetes and the like, only to make it that much more likely the survivor will experience a stroke and need long-term care. All these factors combine to make the need for long-term care escalate at a dizzying pace.

An Aging America

Consider this rapidly unfolding social phenomenon. In a little over 200 years, life expectancy has doubled in this nation: "two-thirds of all those who have made it to age sixty-five in the history of mankind are today walking the earth!"[17] Today, fifty-year-olds can expect to live until their mid-eighties.[18] Currently, there are 37 million people over 65, some 13 percent of the population. By 2030, the number will grow to 70 million, or one-fifth of the population.[19] And the real shocker? There are 70,000 Americans over the age of 100, and that number is expected to grow six times by 2030!![20]

You may have heard of Jeanne Louise Calment of Arles, France, who lived longer than any human since Bible times. She was 122 when she died August 5, 1997. She never lost her saucy personality, evidenced by a humorous anecdote from an interview she did at age 115. The reporter asked her how she saw the future, and she replied without hesitation, "Short, very short!" She was wrong, though, wasn't she? She still had another seven years to go![21]

One-third of all Americans (78 million people) were born between 1946 and 1964—a group we affectionately named the baby boomers. We are about to exchange that well-worn term for another. Instead of having a baby boom, we are on the verge of the country's first senior boom. One out of three people in the United States is over 50, and someone turns 60 every six seconds! Movies and television over the last twenty years reflect this phenomenon: *Space Cowboys, Grumpy Old Men, Grumpier Old Men, Diagnosis Murder, Murder She Wrote, Matlock,* and the Oscar-award winning *Driving Miss Daisy.* Magazines like *Senior Golfer* and *AARP: The Magazine* enjoy readerships of millions. You can frequently see 50+ models like Lauren Hutton in fashion magazines and talent acts like Paul McCartney, The Rolling Stones and Tina Turner are still rocking audiences around the world. And Rod Stewart? Well, you might have caught his interview in *Smiler* magazine, entitled "Do You Think I'm Sixty?"[22]

In Akron, Ohio you can go to work for Mature Services, a successful employment agency specializing in workers in their 50's, 60's, 70's and up to meet the community's demand for older workers. It's a win-win: Older workers tend to already have a pension and Medicare, so working part-time without benefits creates a low-maintenance, highly trained labor pool for grateful employers. *Wall St. Journal* reports that by 2012, workers 55 and over will comprise nearly 20 percent of the workforce.[23]

Ray Crist, a 102-year-old professor of environmental science at Messiah College in Carlisle, Pennsylvania was honored as America's Oldest Worker in 2002 by Experience Works, a national nonprofit organization that provides training and employment services for mature workers. Fifty-two other older workers over 100 years old were also honored.[24]

Or consider this excerpt from a recent *Business Week* cover story:[25]

Emma Shulman is a dynamo. The veteran social worker works up to 50 hours a week recruiting people for treatment at an Alzheimer's clinic at New York University School of Medicine. Her boss, psychiatrist Steven H. Ferris, dreads the day she decides to retire: "We'd definitely have to hire two or three people to replace her," he says. Complains Shulman: "One of my problems is excess energy, which drives me nuts."

Oh, one more thing about Emma Shulman. She's nearly 93 years old.

We have managed to prolong life by overcoming a variety of contagious diseases, by utilizing sophisticated technology with heart, cancer and other catastrophic health conditions, and by taking better care of ourselves with diet and exercise, etc. While our great-grandparents would have been glad to have reached 60 years old, Americans are now seeing ninth and even tenth decades. Dr. Robert Goldman, founder of the National Academy of Sports Medicine and the American Academy of Anti-Aging Medicine predicts that "quantum leaps in medical technology will see many baby boomers and their children reach the grand old age of 120!"[26] Unfortunately, we may be buying ourselves a slow death, because long life doesn't guarantee long quality of life. In reality, the longer we live, the greater the chance we will need long-term care. And the people who take care of themselves the best will probably need long-term care the most, because they probably wont die suddenly of a massive heart attack or stroke—they'll just wear out slowly!

All Ages Need Long-Term Care

Since long-term care is defined as care that simply takes care of people who are enduring chronic conditions with little or no progress, it can happen to people at any age. Few people realize that regular health insurance will not pay for a thirty-two-year-old who winds up in a coma with no progress after an automobile accident. A tragic example is "Superman" actor Christopher Reeve who was almost totally paralyzed after a horseback riding accident at age 43 for ten years before his death. After almost a decade of battling Parkinson's disease, thirty-eight-year-old actor Michael J. Fox announced his departure from his popular television series *Spin City* to spend time with his family and raise money to search for a cure. This adds him to the list of well-known victims of Parkinson's disease—a list that includes Muhammad Ali, former three-time world heavyweight champion, and former U.S. Attorney General Janet Reno.

Fifty-three-year old accountant Bill Chambers will never walk again after a body surfing accident left him paralyzed from the waist down. "I didn't do anything stupid. It wasn't like jumping off a bridge. I surfed a wave no differently than I'd done thousands of times, so it was more like getting hit by a bolt of lightning. It just happened. Why me? Because I was there. Accidents happen to a lot of people."[27]

It's very important to realize that long-term care is not just an issue that affects older Americans. Almost 40 percent of Americans receiving long-term care are *under* 65 years old.[28] Less than fifteen percent of nursing home patients are in this younger age category[29] —the rest of the younger people are cared for in the community, mostly at home. Younger people need long-term care for automobile and sporting accidents, disabling events such as brain tumors, and disabling diseases such as muscular dystrophy, multiple sclerosis, Parkinson's and Lou Gehrig's disease. About 1.4 million Americans suffer some kind of traumatic brain injury each year—only 50,000 die, leaving many disabled for the rest of their lives.[30] Half of all traumatic brain injuries are due to transportation accidents involving automobiles, motorcycles, bicycles, and pedestrians.[31] One-third of the 700,000 stroke victims in the United States each year are under 60![32]

At 52, Marla Everett* leads a simple life in a one bedroom Airstream trailer on her sister's wooded property in Tennessee. Unable to drive or work fulltime, Marla still suffers residual damage from an aneurysm at age 30 that left her unable to care for her two young sons. Fortunately, her ex-husband kept the boys. She lived off and on with parents and friends for several years, then finally alone, until enough of her memory came back to support herself with occasional landscaping or domestic work. She tried a full-time job with the state food-stamp program once, but found the stress too much to continue. Combating a constant struggle to remember lyrics, her musical talent also landed her an occasional low-paying gig with local bands. Today she barely plays her guitar due to an increasing lack of concentration. She also battles agoraphobia.

*name has been changed to protect anonymity

Families In Transition

Another factor contributing to demand for long-term care is that the caregiving system in the home has experienced a significant decline. The bulk of caregiving is performed by women, and almost 60 percent of the caregivers are employed full or part-time.[33] In his best seller **AgePower,** Dr. Ken Dychtwald, an expert on the aging population, projected in 1999 that the average 21st century American will actually spend more years caring for parents than children, and in his newest book, **The Power Years,** he points out that the average baby boomer now has more parents than children.[34]

Often the need to care for aging parents coincides with the need to pay college tuition for dependent children. Even if college tuition needs are satisfied, the "empty nest" becomes filled with frail parents or in-laws and saving for retirement is compromised. The conflicting priorities for the ways both money and time are spent have to be carefully weighed. About 13 percent of Americans between ages 41 and 59 care for their children and parents at the same time, a Pew Research Center study said: [35]

Also, children now live extended distances from parents as our society becomes increasingly mobile. The impact of this mobility? Today, fewer than 15 percent of people over 65 live with relatives. The rest live independently, either alone or with a spouse.[36]

Of course, it is only fair to recognize that sometimes we simply cannot be cared for at home due to physical or mental conditions, even when someone is at home to provide the care. An Alzheimer's patient, for example, can require 24-hour care, which is extremely difficult for most families to manage.

Forty-one-year-old Julie Endert of Murfreesboro, Tennessee, quit a job she loved with the local school system to care for her aging father, who suffers from dementia. Her decision to quit was undoubtedly influenced by her husband and two teenaged children, one in college. Her only respite time to do grocery shopping and run other errands is made possible by an adult day care program that cares for her father three days a week.[37]

Even though you and your children may want you to live with them when you need long-term care, it's just not always possible when you need continuous caregiving 24 hours a day, as dementia is the most common reason why nursing home care becomes necessary.[38] On the other hand, if you require lighter caregiving, a home health aide may be able to stay with you for an eight- to ten-hour shift while your children work. This assistance can postpone and even eliminate entering a nursing home for some people.

But few Americans realize how precious a few hours a day of home health care can be to a distraught, exhausted caregiver until they are in the situation themselves. Even fewer Americans realize that those few hours which may mean the difference between sanity and insanity, to quote one caregiver, are not covered by health insurance. Consider these real-life situations:

A rare neurological disorder called primary lateral sclerosis has robbed Gary Nulty at age 43 of his ability to walk or feed himself. His 41-year-old wife and childhood sweetheart, Vivian, has lost 30 pounds in the past year trying to care for him and their two daughters. An environmental geologist, Gary had excellent health insurance, but just as with other health insurance plans, it will not pay for custodial care. Gary's mental capacity is excellent, but he cannot even pick up the telephone or right himself in his wheelchair if he slumps over. Vivian manages a part-time job, which she desperately needs since Gary can no longer work, so that he is alone only about two hours a day until their 11-year-old daughter gets home from school. Otherwise she provides him with constant care, since he can't even go to the bathroom by himself. Vivian is desperate for help. "There's 24 hours in a day," she said. "I'm willing to work 20. I'll take four [hours of help]. That's the minimum I need to not go insane." [39]

Actress Emma Thompson (Sense and Sensibility, Howard's End) *helped her mother and sister care for her actor/writer/ director father Eric Thompson, after his stroke in her teens. With a combined family effort, he was able to live until age 52, which meant about 15 years of caregiving. The good side, Emma notes, is it caused her and her sister to skip the normal teenage rebellion years because her mom needed so much help.* [40]

The Caregiver's Glass Ceiling

As of 2006, there were an estimated 7.7 million majority-owned, privately-held women-owned firms, accounting for 30 percent of all businesses in the United States. Women-owned firms in general employ 12.8 million people and generate $1.9 trillion in sales. Between 1997 and 2006, the number of majority women-owned employer firms (51 percent or more) achieved twice the growth rate of all employer firms! [41] It's fair to say, women have made monumental progress in the workforce in the last twenty or so years. What can stop them now?

Caregiving can slow and even stop many talented women. Since two-thirds of primary caregivers are women and over half of these women work outside the home,[42] caregiving may turn out to be the biggest threat to the women's movement in this century. The amount of time that caregivers spend caring for someone who needs help with two or more Activities of Daily Living (bathing, dressing, transferring, eating, etc.) is 40 or more hours per week. Eighty-three percent of these most intense caregivers had to make changes to their daily work schedule to accommodate caregiving. Ultimately, 35% had to give up work entirely, 12% took early retirement, 41% had to take a leave of absence, and 37% went part-time.[43]

How do you function in an executive position or grow your own business with those kinds of hours or work adjustments?

Technology and Lifestyle

A benefit from enhanced medical technology is increased survival from medical disorders such as heart attack, diabetes, brain tumors . . . things that 30 years ago people would have died from. A downside to prolonging life for these individuals is they may now be at risk of stroke. Stroke is the third leading cause of death in the United States, but is the #1 cause of disability.[44]

And as much as we like to think that we have healthier lifestyles, obesity is rampant in America. The risk of stroke is exacerbated when obesity is combined with one or more health problems such as high blood pressure or high cholesterol or lifestyle choices such as smoking or lack of exercise.

Competing with the highest demand for long-term care ever experienced in the United States is the low level of financing available for long-term care.

Together, conventional health insurance and Medicare pay less than a third of the nation's $200 billion annual bill for home health care and nursing home care. And, that small payment is mostly for short-term care that lasts less than three months, not long-term care which can last several years.[45]

Why Doesn't Private Insurance Pay More?

Conventional insurance, including individual and group health insurance for people under 65 or retiree health plans, restrict coverage to **SKILLED CARE**—and that's why conventional health insurance does not pay for long-term care, as illustrated in the real-life stories of younger people needing long-term care in the previous section, **Families in Transition.** HMOs, the new managed care programs for people of all ages, are even more restrictive than regular health insurance and pay very little for home health and nursing home care.

What is meant by skilled care? *Skilled care has nothing to do with how sick you are.* A person can be totally paralyzed or in a coma and still not be receiving skilled care, in which case private insurance will not pay. Skilled care is care to get you better—IVs, dressing bedsores, providing physical and speech therapy after a stroke, etc. Once progress stops, however, the care is "chronic" or "maintenance" and is no longer skilled. Daily cleaning of a colostomy drain or a catheter, or even oxygen or respiratory therapy needed regularly for an emphysema patient in a nursing home, are examples of care that is not skilled. Here's a real-life example of a family who did not understand the concept of skilled care at all:

> *The once-vibrant 39-year-old Guity Manteghi lies in a nursing home in Walnut Creek, California. Her heart failed with no warning in January, 1996, cutting off oxygen to her brain and sending her into a coma. After eight weeks, the insurance plan said she no longer needed skilled care and stopped payment to the nursing home the next day. With*

two young daughters, the 50-year-old husband, Maleck Manteghi, didn't know where to turn. "I thought I had the most adequate health coverage you could buy," he was quoted in the Contra Costa Times *as saying. "When you get insurance, who knows what custodial care is, what skilled nursing is?"*[46]

Why Doesn't Medicare Pay More?

Medicare can approve up to 100 days in a nursing home per benefit period but patients usually collect less. Why? Because Medicare pays only for *skilled care*, and the majority of nursing home care is not skilled. In fact, **the average number of days that patients collect from Medicare for nursing home care is only about 25 days,** because most people don't have very many days that qualify as skilled care under Medicare guidelines.[47]   Medicare pays nothing for eight-hour shifts at home and only pays home health care visits, when some skilled care is being provided. An Alzheimer's patient is a classic example of someone who needs little or no skilled care and would likely not benefit from Medicare. Medicare supplements and Medicare HMOs won't pay a dime unless Medicare pays first, so they won't pay either.

Due to recent legislation to promote cost containment in the Medicare program, restricted access to Medicare payments for home health care and nursing home care is expected to continue, which just serves to shift care back to the family.[48] (Also see **Medicare Benefits** in *Appendix A*.)

As you can see, a 30-year-old with private health insurance is not much better off for long-term care than an 80-year-old on Medicare.

You Can't Count on Medicaid

Medicaid, the federal and state welfare program for the poor, pays almost half of the nation's long-term care bill, and about a fourth comes out of private pockets—maybe yours.[49] And, a significant amount of the out-of-pocket money is coming from Medicaid patients who are required to give most of their income (including Social Security income) to a nursing home in order to receive Medicaid nursing home benefits as explained in Chapter 5.

You should beware of anyone who advises you to transfer assets to your children or trusts in order to qualify for Medicaid. Children may misuse or lose the assets (i.e., in the event of a lawsuit or divorce). Also, many nursing homes no longer accept Medicaid patients because a Medicaid patient represents a financial loss to most nursing homes. A Medicaid patient is at the mercy of the system and may have nowhere to go if nursing homes are full, or may have to go to a rural area if urban homes are full. It's not unusual for a Medicaid patient to be placed hours away from family members. Denise Gott, an Ohio insurance professional, shared this story of a family who found this out the hard way:

I conducted a workshop for a AAA Club in Canton, Ohio in September of 1999. I had finished the program and was taking questions. A young gentleman in his late thirties sitting with his wife raised his hand and asked if he could share a story. He proceeded to explain to the crowd of about 40 people that both his mother and father were in nursing homes; they had been there for 2 and 4 years respectively. Unfortunately for this family, they spent nearly all of their assets on the first two years of nursing home care for the father. When the mother went into the nursing home, the family home was sold, the remaining assets totaling $50,000 and the income that the mother was receiving from her retirement plan were all redirected to the nursing home to pay expenses.

All funds ran out after the first year and a half that Mom was in the facility. To make matters worse, both parents are now on Medicaid. The saddest part of this story is that due to the fact that there are very few available Medicaid beds in Ohio, Mom lives in a nursing home in Cleveland while Dad lives in a nursing facility in Toledo, a full two hours away. The couple lives in Canton, making visits to both nursing facilities difficult, both physically and emotionally.

Also, in most states, being on Medicaid often means being in a nursing home. Even with recent legislation passed in 2006 that allows states to use Medicaid programs for home care, the reality is there just isn't enough money in most state budgets to pay extensive home care, such as for eight- to ten-hour shifts. Currently, only a third of Medicaid dollars for long-term care are spent on home care.[50] To have options for home care, assisted living, adult day care, and to be able to choose any nursing home, a number of adult children are purchasing long-term care insurance policies for parents, even though financially the parents will either immediately or in a short time qualify for Medicaid.

A 69-year-old woman and her 30-year-old daughter certainly felt that way. When my client purchased her policy in 1993, her only asset outside of her home was a $30,000 annuity, and she was a widow. Her daughter attended the appointment and expressed how strongly she felt about keeping her mother off Medicaid if at all possible. We all cried around the kitchen table with the emotion of planning ahead for something no one wanted to happen, but if it did, that night's action of purchasing a long-term care insurance policy would make the way a lot easier by providing money to pay for choices that would make nursing home care a last resort.

Prospects for Government Help

Because of the serious nature of the long-term care crisis, some people advocate that a new benefit program be created by the federal government to pay for long-term care for everyone.

The answer to this question arrived January 1, 1997 with a new health care reform package that provides tax incentives for individuals and employers to purchase long-term care insurance. Basically, the government is saying there isn't enough money for any type of public program to pay for long-term care for everyone.

Consider that in 1945, in the early days of the Social Security program, there were 42 workers for each retiree. In 2000, the ratio was 3.4 workers for every Social Security beneficiary. By 2030, the ratio is projected to decline to 2 to 1.[51] With costs of home health and nursing home care over $200 billion per year and expected to increase at least five times in the next 30 years, from where will the taxes originate to pay the tab?[52] We are already spending over half of the total federal budget for the "Big Three" entitlements - Social Security, Medicare and Medicaid - and if we do nothing, the U.S. Comptroller General predicts it will be nearly 75 percent by 2040.[53] A long-term care program for the 79 million baby boomers could be a larger entitlement than these existing programs, which are already facing insolvency.

Tax Incentives for Long-Term Care Insurance

To encourage Americans to plan for their own long-term care needs and to ensure that long-term care insurance has great value for the future, the federal government passed legislation to provide tax incentives for long-term care insurance policies issued on and after January 1, 1997, and to standardize the benefits somewhat to offer the best value for the consumer.* For "qualified" policies that meet these criteria, the following apply for 2008:

▲   Benefits will not be taxable income, as long as benefit payments above $270 per day (or the monthly equivalent) do not exceed the actual cost of care. Conversely, benefit payments in excess of $270 per day that do exceed the actual cost of care will be taxed as income.

▲   A portion of a long-term care insurance premium based on the age of the policyholder now counts as a medical expense. Since medical expenses in excess of 7.5 percent of adjusted gross income are tax deductible, this means that a portion of your long-term care insurance premium will help you reach that threshold and may even put you over it to receive a tax deduction. Here are the amounts that count in 2008, and they are allowed to increase each year based on the medical Consumer Price Index:

Attained age before the close of the taxable year:	Amount that counts as a medical expense:
40 or less	$310
41 - 50	$580
51 - 60	$1,150
61 - 70	$3,080
71 and older	$3,850

Indemnity policies: Benefit payments above $270 per day that exceed the actual cost of care will be taxed as income.

* Policies purchased 12/31/96 and earlier were "grandfathered" and are considered qualified for the new tax treatment. Also, this section is not intended in any way to give tax treatment. Also, this section is not intended in any way to give tax advice. Please see your tax advisor for a final determination fo how this legislation applies to you.

While younger people generally don't have enough medical expenses to gain a tax deduction from long-term care insurance premiums, this provision may make it worthwhile for older Americans to itemize.

Let's look at an example. Bob is 74 and Martha is 71. Their long-term care insurance premiums are $3,900 and $3,400 respectively. Based on the above table for the year 2008, Bob gets to count $3,850 as a medical expense and Martha gets to count her entire premium, for a total of $7,250. They have an additional $4,500 in other medical expenses for retiree health insurance premiums and their deductibles and co-payments for that plan. Together with the $7,250 deduction for their long-term care insurance premium, they have $11,750 in total medical expenses. For tax purposes, they can count the amount of medical expense that exceeds 7.5 percent of their adjusted gross income. Their income is $50,000 and 7.5 percent is $3,750, so they can count $8,000 in medical expenses.

They also have $2,500 in charitable contributions and $4,500 in state income and property taxes, so their total itemized deductions equal $15,000. Since this exceeds the standard deduction for two taxpayers over age 65 of $13,000 for 2008, they are better off to itemize. Combined with the personal exemption of $3,500 per person that everyone is entitled to, their total deductions equal $22,000 ($3,500 x 2 = $7,000 + $15,000). Therefore their taxable income is lowered from $50,000 to $28,000. If they just took the standard deduction of $13,000 and didn't itemize, their taxable income would be $30,000 ($50,000 minus the standard deduction of $13,000 minus two personal exemptions of $3,500 = $30,000. The difference of $2,000 in a 15 percent tax bracket means they will save $290 in income tax by having long-term care insurance, which gave them a reason to itemize (see chart on next page).

Tax Impact of LTC Insurance Ages 74 and 71	With LTC Insurance	Without LTC Insurance
Adjusted Gross Income for Married Couple	50,000	50,000
Personal Exemptions	7,000	7,000
Itemized Deductions: Medical Expense	8,000	0
Charitable Contributions	2,500	0
Taxes	4,500	0
Total Itemized Standard Deduction	15,000 13,000	13,000
Total Deductions from AGI	22,000	20,000
Taxable Income	28,000	30,000
Marginal Federal Rate	15%	15%
Total Federal Taxes*	3,398	3,698

Tax savings with LTC insurance = $300

This amount is based on the Federal Tax Rate Schedule Y-1 (Married, Filing Jointly) which can be found at www.irs.gov. It is not determined by multiplying taxable income by 15%. An estimate was used for the 2008 Schedule, which was not published as of this writing.

Proposed legislation in Congress will make the age-based amounts of long-term care insurance premium an "above-the-line" tax deduction, which means your taxable income would be lowered by the premium amount allowed for your age and you wouldn't even have to itemize your tax return. The premium would no longer be subject to the 7.5 percent medical expense threshold. You can help get this important piece of legislation passed by writing your congressional representatives. Tell them we need an "above-the-line" tax deduction for long-term care insurance premium in order to make it more affordable for all Americans.

IRS-Approved Medical Expenses

It is surprising how many things count as a medical expense in the eyes of the IRS. A partial list includes: contact lenses, eyeglasses, hearing aids, false teeth, artificial limbs, wheelchairs, oxygen and oxygen equipment, prescription drugs and insulin, medical and hospital insurance premiums, cost and care of guide dogs or other animals aiding the blind, deaf, and disabled, medical fees from doctors, dentists, surgeons, specialists, and other medical practitioners, hospital fees, wages and certain taxes for nursing services for chronically ill people, transportation for needed medical care, stop-smoking programs, meals and lodging provided by a hospital during medical treatment. Contact your local Social Security office for a complete list.

▲   The allowable percentage of an LTC insurance premium is now treated like health insurance premium for the self-employed tax deduction, which provides a first-dollar tax deduction of 100%. "Self-employed" means sole proprietors, partnerships and "greater than 2% shareholders" of S-Corporations and Limited Liability Corporations.

Mary owns an S-Corporation, so she is considered self-employed by the IRS. Her health insurance premium is $1,500 per year and her long-term care insurance premium is $1,000 per year. Based on her age of 48, she is allowed to add $580 of her long-term care insurance premium to her $1,500 health insurance premium for a total premium of $2,080, of which she will receive 100 percent as a first-dollar tax deduction for tax year 2008. Therefore, her adjusted gross income for 2008 will be lowered by that amount.

▲   Employers who are defined as a C-corporation will receive a tax deduction for any portion of the long-term care insurance premiums paid for employees, regardless of ownership in the company. Self-employed business owners (see previous bullet) must count a long-term care insurance premium as part of their salary just as they do their health insurance. This makes it taxable income if they allow the premium to be paid by the business, and it is deductible only in the form of salary or compensation.

Premium paid for their employees, on the other hand, does not count as income for the employees, and the entire premium is 100 percent deductible as a business expense to the company. Even though it has to be counted as taxable income, some self-employed owners want the business to pay the premium for cash-flow purposes, and they still get the first-dollar self-employed deduction described in the preceding bullet.

▲   Premium contributions made by all types of employers are not taxable income to employees.

▲   Long-term care insurance premiums are an acceptable medical expense under Health Savings Accounts (HSA's). Here's a general description of how they work (the dollar amounts cited below for 2008 increase each January):

Individuals must purchase a high-deductible health insurance plan (HDHP) with a minimum deductible of $1,100 and families must purchase a deductible of at least $2,200. Policyholders can deposit a maximum of $2,900 ($5,800 maximum for families) into the HSA with pre-tax dollars, and unused money at the end of the year grows tax-deferred—this is not a "use it or lose it" model. Funds can be used at age 65 for any reason without penalty. Prior to age 65, a 15 percent penalty is imposed for funds withdrawn for other than an acceptable medical expense (see a partial list of IRS-approved medical expenses on p. 22) plus three types of insurance premium: COBRA premium, health insurance premium only if the applicant is receiving unemployment, and "qualified" long-term care insurance premium, which means the age-based amounts listed in this section.

In addition, individuals over 65 may use HSA dollars to pay premiums for Medicare Part A or B, Medicare HMO, premium for employer-sponsored health insurance (including retiree health insurance), but not Medicare supplement premiums. (Note: Americans who are eligible for Medicare can't set up a Health Savings Account, but if they set one up prior to becoming eligible for Medicare, they can keep it – they just can't make new contributions after becoming eligible for Medicare.)

Premiums are typically 30%–50% lower than managed care or traditional health insurance plans. HSA's are available to both individuals and through employer-sponsored health insurance plans. (Some employers pay the high-deductible health plan premium, then also make a contribution into each employee's HSA account.)

The really exciting advantage of Health Savings Accounts is that now Americans can pay their age-based long-term care insurance premium with pre-tax dollars!

▲ Qualified long-term care insurance premiums are eligible expenses in a Section 105 Medical Reimbursement Plan, which is available to small businesses and farms to deduct family health insurance premiums and medical, vision and dental expenses not covered by insurance. To be eligible, a sole proprietor must be married and be legitimately able to employ his/her spouse.

▲ The age-based LTC insurance premiums on p. 19 are an acceptable medical expense under a Health Reimbursement Arrangement, the employer-provided medical care expense plan in which reimbursements for medical care expenses made from the plan are excludable from employee gross income. (Rev. Rule. 2002-41)

▲ Unreimbursed expenses for qualified long-term care services—the cost of long-term care itself, not LTC insurance premiums—will count toward the itemized medical deduction if paid on behalf of yourself, your spouse or your dependents. (See **Claims** in the next chapter for a definition of qualified care.)

This means unreimbursed qualified care, as well as long-term care insurance premiums that you pay for a parent, will count as long as you contribute more than 50% of your parent's support. The allowable portion of long-term care insurance premiums that count is based on the parent's age, not yours. Sometimes children form a "multiple support agreement," which means collectively they provide more than 50% of a parent's support.

In this case, one child each year can take the tax deduction as long as that child individually provides at least 10 percent of the parent's support.

▲   Certain benefit provisions are required, which will be discussed in the next chapter, *Features of a Good Long-Term Care Insurance Policy.*

The Message is Loud and Clear

What is this law really saying? The message is loud and clear: Take care of your long-term care needs with private insurance, because there isn't enough money to create a new entitlement program for everyone.

Apparently many states agree. The following states have implemented state tax incentives for long-term care insurance: Alabama, Arkansas, California, Colorado, Hawaii, Idaho, Indiana, Iowa, Kansas, Kentucky, Massachusetts, Maine, Minnesota, Missouri, Montana, New Jersey, New Mexico, New York, North Dakota, Ohio, Oklahoma, Oregon, Utah, Virginia, West Virginia, Wisconsin, and the District of Columbia. Several states offer private long-term care insurance to state employees. In 2002, the strongest message of all emerged when the federal government introduced long-term care insurance to active and retired civilians, postal workers, military personnel and their qualified family members. With no employer contribution, the FLTCIP sends an especially strong message that Americans need to take personal responsibility for planning for long-term care since there isn't enough public funding to pay for it. (See **The Federal Long Term Care Insurance Program** on p. 136.)

The Balanced Budget Act of 1997 implemented several drastic changes in the Medicare skilled nursing facility and home health benefit that will result in restricted access to these benefits for many years to come. Both types of care are now paid under a prospective payment system, which simply means Medicare pays a flat amount based on the diagnosis of the patient. This gives home care and nursing home providers an incentive to hold costs down as much as possible.

Finally, The Deficit Reduction Act of 2005 signed February 8, 2006 made access to the Medicaid long-term care benefit more difficult (see Chapter 5 *The Medicaid Benefit for Long-Term Care*). As the availability of especially the Medicare home care benefit has been reduced and access to Medicaid has become more difficult, provision of care has shifted back to the family.[54] Legislation like this makes LTC insurance policies more meaningful as government shifts costs away from public programs to private LTC insurance.

The Private Sector Solution

Almost ten million Americans have turned to private long-term care insurance plans to protect their assets.[55] Over 9,200 employers offer group long-term care coverage, and the number of employer plans in force has almost doubled in five years.[56] With LTCI tax incentives expected to increase, this trend should continue to explode in the

21st century. Many buyers are in their 40's and 50's as most insurance companies target these age groups with attractively low premiums.

Long-term care insurance is the private sector's solution to what an increasing number of people are calling the **real** health care crisis in the United States. Right now, private health insurance pays less than 10% of long-term care costs, and welfare (Medicaid) is paying almost half.[57] If private long-term care insurance doesn't flip those percentages for the baby-boomer generation, the tax consequences to all of us will be unprecedented. Sweden, for example, has a government-funded long-term care program -- and a top income tax rate of 60%![58] Most importantly, long-term care insurance for many represents the best opportunity to retain a sense of dignity—in the form of purchasing power—which all too many people who thought they were affluent have lost to the merciless financial demands of long-term care.

People who are not affluent also are buying long-term care insurance. About a fourth of purchasers in 2005 had assets less than $100,000, and 29% had an income of less than $35,000.[59] These statistics are not so surprising when you look at the most frequently cited reasons for purchasing the insurance—**to maintain independence and choice** by guaranteeing affordability of care in order to avoid depending on others for care. Asset protection was the second most important reason for purchase.[60]

Based on today's current economic environment with lower investment earnings, it is strongly advisable for individuals to consider LTC insurance when their asset base ranges between $50,000 and $2 million, not counting the home and automobiles. A special section on retirement planning in the *Wall St. Journal* made this assessment:

"Failing to consider long-term care needs is the #1 mistake investors are making with their retirement savings."[61]

A prominent national group of financial planners who specialize in wealth preservation and wealth transfer extends the asset figure to $5 million for its clients. Many people in the "several million" asset range plan to self-insure their long-term care risk. If you are in this category and self-insuring is a viable option, you may want to seriously consider the single premium/life insurance or annuity LTC policies, since these types of policies will pass any money you don't use for long-term care on to the beneficiary of your choice (heirs, church, charity, your estate, etc.). However, if you do need long-term care, your dollars are maximized for long-term care coverage. (See Chapter 6, *Alternatives for Financing Long-Term Care,* for a description.)

It's difficult to box appropriate purchasers for long-term care insurance into a range of assets and income, because people buy things for different reasons. Consider this story:

David Miller, an Ohio insurance professional, sold long-term care insurance to a man who owns ten McDonald's. Mr. Miller was understandably shocked that this gentleman wished to purchase insurance and asked why. With tears in his eyes, the client pointed to an oil painting of a young man and said, "That's my reason for wanting to do this. That is our son who was killed in an automobile accident 17 years ago, and I want to make sure his children will be taken care of for college and someday buying their own homes, and I want to take care of my other kids and grandkids. I don't want one dime of my money ever going to a nursing home!" Mr. Miller understood quickly that here was a man who was determined to spend his money on his family just as much as it was in his control to do so and sold him and his wife long-term care insurance policies.

People with larger estates especially need to determine the amount of liquid assets that can be used upon demand. Otherwise a long-term care need may require the sale of investments or property at a loss. If you are "house rich and cash poor," you may want to consider a reverse mortgage, which will allow you to leverage the money from your home to pay for long-term care insurance instead of paying premiums out of the income you use for living expenses. (See **Reverse Mortgages,** p. 210.)

But think about it, affluent people don't usually spend their own money when they don't have to. Eighty percent of Americans over 65 have private health insurance in addition to Medicare, at a time when there is very little left to pay after Medicare pays. The average annual out-of-pocket expense, excluding home care and nursing home expenses, for someone with no supplemental insurance of any type to Medicare is less than $2,600.[62]

Affluent people also have homeowners' policies even when the mortgage is paid off, yet the odds of needing long-term care, at 1 out of 2, are much higher than losing a home. Just think, if you looked out of your window and saw one out of two houses burning in your neighborhood! We can't sleep at night without a homeowner's policy, yet losses for long-term care can be much greater than the cost of replacing our house. This is probably why the Employee Benefit Research Institute advises:

> *Having adequate long-term care insurance is the single most influential determinant of whether an individual will have a financially secure retirement.*[63]

People with assets greater than $50,000 who believe in Medicare supplement policies and homeowners' policies are well advised to

consider long-term care insurance. This means that the $500,000
or more they might spend on long-term care could go to a favorite
charity, church or be split among the grandchildren.

The following chart shows that a couple with $500,000 will spend
down to nothing in less than five years, with only one spouse needing
long-term care at $60,000 per year. Another consideration is that
affluent people may be interested in around-the-clock home health
care, which can triple these costs.

Year	Assets at Start of Year	Income Needs	LTC Expense	Investment Yield	Assets at End of Year
1	$500,000	$60,000	$60,000	$30,000	$410,000
2	$410,000	$62,000	$63,000	$25,000	$310,000
3	$310,000	$63,000	$66,000	$19,000	$200,000
4	$200,000	$65,000	$70,000	$12,000	$77,000
5	$77,000	$67,000	$73,000	$5,000	($59,000)

Note: "Income Needs" is the portion of household income needs that the assets had been
relied upon to provide and assumes annual inflation of 3%. "LTC Expense" is based on a
typical annual cost and is subject to 5% annual inflation. "Investment Yield" is assumed
at 6% annually after taxes.

People with lower assets are purchasing long-term care
insurance to maintain independence and receive the same
treatment as private pay patients if care is needed, or
their children are buying it for them for the same reason.

Most of us can imagine the consequences of walking into a hospital
or doctor's office with no health insurance! Harley Gordon, one of the
founding members of the National Academy of Elder Law Attorneys,
believes that planning for long-term care is a critical part of a retirement

plan. He says the price for not planning can be harder on the caregiver than the person who needs care:

Ironically it is not necessarily the afflicted who suffer most, but rather the caregiver. He or she will be taken care of by the family which struggles to provide the care necessary to keep their loved one in the community. This effort exacts a terrible price on the caregiver's health (typically a daughter) and relationships with other family members, most notably those siblings who do not share the burden.[64]

Probably the most touching story I've heard recently came from one of my own clients, Mr. C. Vernon Duckett. He and his wife Helen bought long-term care insurance policies from me back in 1990. He called earlier this year and demanded as soon as I answered the phone, "How in the world did you talk me into buying these long-term care insurance policies?" Fearing that this would be my first complaint from one of my policyholders in the almost 20 years I've been in the long-term care insurance field, I carefully answered, "Well, Mr. Duckett, your wife Helen invited me over to talk to you and then you bought – why, is there a problem?" His reply elicited a quick sigh of relief on my part, then tears as I listened while he assured me it was the best financial decision he had ever made in his life. It turned out his wife Helen was in a nursing home with Alzheimer's. He tearfully told me that his beautiful wife Helen was his most precious asset, not his money, and the fact that her long-term care insurance policy enabled him to give her the best care possible meant more to him than anything at that point. At my request, he wrote me this beautiful letter on the next page:

Parents who buy long-term care insurance are taking care of their children far into the future. As many caregivers can attest, caregiving

To: *Phyllis Shelton*
2/21/06

From: *C. Vernon Duckett*

I enjoyed talking with you the other day about how we met and how Helen and I made the decision to buy an LTC policy. So you know money was tight in those days. I want you to know that we will be __eternally__ indebted to you...This has turned out to be the best investment we ever made. This LTC policy has given me peace of mind, security, and independence. As you know, I have had two heart attacks, and it's great to be able to go to bed at night and know that my precious wife will be taken care of the rest of her life. I know that the Lord had His hand in this all along.

Thanks again,
C. Vernon Duckett

takes a phenomenal toll mentally, physically and even spiritually. Exhausted caregivers may become care recipients themselves, leading to a further, often preventable, drain on their children's resources. A researcher from the Albert Einstein College of Medicine said "Family caregivers experiencing extreme stress have been shown to age prematurely. This level of stress can take as much as 10 years off a family caregiver's life." [65] A tragic example was the early demise of Dana Reeve who passed away just short of her 45th birthday on March 6, 2006, only two years after the passing of her beloved husband, Christopher. Her death was attributed to lung cancer, although she had never smoked. Many would say the ten years of intense caregiving contributed heavily to her passing. Their 13-year-old son, Will, is left to carry the torch of his famous parents of furthering medical research to help paralytics.

In addition to accidents and other traumas that cause younger people to need long-term care, our rapidly aging population is putting insupportable demands on families in this century. Families simply can't shoulder this monumental burden alone. They have to have help.

LTC insurance means choices and options when that help is needed. For most of us, long-term care insurance may be the main key to not outliving our money—a very real fear that a number of people have as life spans continue to increase.

Chapter 2

Features of a Good Long-Term Care Insurance Policy

∿∿∿∿∿∿∿∿∿∿∿∿∿∿∿∿∿∿∿∿∿∿∿∿∿∿∿∿∿∿∿∿∿

Long-term care insurance policies today operate under legislation that was effective January 1, 1997, which required insurance companies to offer "tax-qualified" policies that contain certain standardized benefits that were recommended by the National Association of Insurance Commissioners (NAIC), the regulatory body composed of all of the state insurance commissioners. Most of these guidelines were already being followed by the insurance companies and simply provide extra protection for the consumer to ensure high value for premium dollars.

Congress ruled that long-term care insurance policies issued prior to 1/1/97 will count as qualified policies and do not have to be exchanged for a new policy. This includes employer-sponsored plans that were set up prior to 1/1/97, so that new enrollees after 1/1/97 have a "grandfathered" plan. However, if you materially change a policy that you purchased prior to 1/1/97, the policy will lose this "grandfathered" status and will no longer be considered tax-qualified by the IRS. An example of a "material change" would be adding an inflation rider, which is a benefit increase for additional premium. A partial list of changes that are not considered a material change and therefore would not affect the grandfathered status are:

▲   Premium modal changes; for example, changing an annual payment to monthly payments.

▲   A class rate increase or decrease, which means a rate increase or decrease that applies to an entire segment of policyholders.

▲   Discounts that you receive after the original issue date of your policy due to other family members purchasing a policy; for example, if your spouse purchases a policy at a later date than you do.

▲   Premium decreases due to a reduction in coverage.

▲   Provision of alternate forms of benefits that do not increase the premium for example, companies sometimes add coverage for new forms of care, like assisted living, without increasing your premium.

▲   Allowing policyholders to continue group coverage if the policyholder is no longer part of the group; for example, because he or she terminates employment with an employer who offered a group long-term care insurance plan.

(Caution: Some insurance companies are still marketing non-qualified policies. Please be aware that if you purchased a non-qualified policy in 1997 or later, there is a chance that the IRS will say that benefits received from the non-qualified policy will be taxable income to you. A quick way to see if your policy is tax-qualified is to check the first page of your policy. All tax-qualified policies issued after 1/1/97 have a sentence that says the policy is intended to satisfy the requirements for a tax-qualified policy. As you read this chapter, you also will learn how to check the benefits to ensure that you have a tax-qualified policy.)

To provide you with a measuring stick for value if you already have a long-term care insurance policy or if you are currently shopping for a policy, this section will explain each feature of a long-term care insurance policy in detail to give you an in-depth understanding of how long-term care insurance works. If you are shopping for a policy, you will find helpful recommendations for appropriate benefit selections that you can apply to your situation. An insurance professional who sells long-term care insurance can help you finalize your choices.

Level of Care

Make sure the policy pays all levels of care—skilled or non-skilled—in any setting: the home, in an assisted living facility, in an adult day care center, or in a nursing home. (Sometimes you will hear non-skilled referred to as intermediate or custodial care. "Intermediate" means some skilled care but not every day, and "custodial" means no skilled care at all. These terms are old and just refer to non-skilled care.) Benefits should not be reduced because the level of care is less than skilled. Also, the policy should not require skilled care before non-skilled benefits are paid.

Home Health Care

More than ten million Americans need some type of long-term care and only about 1.5 million are in nursing homes. This means that most people are being cared for at home or in a community setting like assisted living or adult day care and that only about 15 percent of long-term care is in a nursing home.[1] The number of nursing home patients has actually declined in recent years due to an increased availability of home health and other community services, especially assisted living facilities.[2] Understandably, coverage for home health is a popular addition to long-term care insurance policies. Here are some points to keep in mind when choosing a policy:

▲ The home health care benefit is not intended to provide benefits for 24-hour care because around-the-clock care at home is more expensive than nursing home care. The home care benefit is most helpful when you have someone to live with; i.e. a "primary caregiver," such as a spouse, son, daughter, or other family member or friend. If you qualify for benefits under the policy, a home health aide can stay with you for an eight- to ten-hour shift while your primary caregiver is at work, for example. The aide can do the heavy caregiving, such as giving you a bath (something you may not want a family member to do), washing your hair, changing your bed, preparing meals, supervising your medicine, and maybe light housework and laundry. Then perhaps your family can take care of you at night. Even if you have a primary caregiver who doesn't work, no one can provide 24-hour care, so home health care can make it possible for your primary caregiver to get adequate rest.

Here's a story that illustrates how consuming home care can become for the caregiver:

Judy Geck, Chattanooga, Tennessee, has seen both of her parents in long-term care. Her father had a major stroke late in life, which was magnified by complications from the diabetes he had suffered with since his early 40's. After almost two years of caregiving, he passed away within weeks prior to being admitted to a nursing home. Her mother had a severe stroke three months after his death which, coupled with dementia, made it necessary for her to move in with Judy and her husband, Richard. Having a solid position with the same company over fifteen years, Judy was unable to give up her job for financial reasons, especially since she had a new grandchild to buy for! In order to keep her demanding job and get adequate rest at night, it was necessary to have home health aides 16 hours a day, from 7 a.m. till 11 p.m. Judy slept in a chair four nights a week next to her mother and had an additional home health aide the other three nights.

Judy had to be home every evening, because her mother could not be left alone. In addition to the dementia, she was unable to speak and could not respond to verbal commands to move her body due to damaged motor skills from the stroke. Activities or even vacation ideas that would take Judy away from home were out of the question. This went on for four years after her mother's stroke. In the fifth year, her mother's savings began running out and the paid home care had to be cut back. The home aides had to leave at 7 p.m. Judy took over after that and slept in a chair next to her mother for seven nights as there was no money for home health aides to come at night. When her mother died after five years of care, Judy had just refinanced her home to find more money for caregiving. Judy and Richard have purchased long-term care insurance on themselves.

A common statement is "I'm not buying long-term care insurance because I'm never going to a nursing home." The irony is that a long-term care insurance policy with great home health benefits may be the only thing that keeps you out of a nursing home by providing financial and emotional support to the people who care about you so they can keep you at home. I don't believe most caregivers would have been able to maintain the exhausting schedule that Judy kept in the above story for five years. Long-term care insurance could be the only thing that makes it possible for a family to keep a patient at home in a similar situation.

If you want to design your policy to pay 24-hour home care, work with your insurance professional to determine the cost for that service in your community so you can select a daily or monthly benefit that is high enough to accomplish your goal in combination with your savings. This selection will substantially increase the premium. But understand – there are still some situations that make staying at home impossible.

At almost 250 pounds, it takes four people to lift my Aunt Jeannette who can't walk due to crumbling cartilage in both knees. At age 84, she is not a candidate for knee surgery. One or even two caregivers at home wouldn't be enough to provide adequate care for her and certainly, my uncle at 160 pounds dripping wet, couldn't lift her. She was admitted to a nursing home three months before he passed away. Now the staff at the nursing home use a Hoyer lift, a hydraulic device manufactured that will lift up to 400 pounds. She cheerfully hangs on with her arms while they swing her in and out of bed and her nurses tease her for being such a "swinger".

▲   Home health coverage is automatically included in some policies—these policies are called "comprehensive" policies—

and optional in other policies. If the coverage is optional and you have no one to live with when you need care, you might consider putting your premium dollars toward a policy that covers just assisted living and nursing home benefits. This is called a "facilities-only" policy. You can use the additional premium of 30%-40% that you would have spent on home health benefits to buy a higher daily or monthly benefit to help you afford a really nice assisted living facility or a private room if you ever need nursing home care. Or, you could use the additional premium for a longer benefit period such as five years or even a lifetime (unlimited) benefit period. Probably the best use of the premium difference would be to purchase the best inflation option if you haven't included it in your benefit selection already (see **Inflation Protection** on p. 62).

▲ There are a handful of policies that pay only for home health care with no coverage for assisted living or nursing home care. No policy can guarantee that you will never need nursing home care, so a policy that focuses 100 percent on home care may not be a wise choice. (It's doubtful that very many of the 1.5 million Americans in nursing homes today "planned" to be there!)

▲ The most valuable home health benefit pays the same level of benefit for home care as for nursing home care, or at least 75%-80%, instead of paying home care at a lower amount such as 50 percent of the nursing home benefit, as many policies offer. Why? Because an eight-hour shift of home health care costs almost the same as a semi-private day in a nursing home, and a ten-hour shift can cost more.

▲   If the policy allows family and friends to provide the care, a lower benefit can work since these people may charge less. A policy like this has a higher premium which buys you additional flexibility. The policy will pay a monthly benefit to you, and you can hire anyone you like, or use the money for other needs because you don't have to provide proof of services or file claims in any way as long as you qualify for benefits. No surprise, additional flexibility usually brings additional responsibility. There are two cautions to this type of policy, which some refer to as a "disability-based" or "cash" policy:

1) Since this is a cash benefit, the temptation can arise in a family to use the money for a purpose other than for which it was intended; so why not buy a big screen TV for the whole family or a trip to Disney World?

2) If you hire caregivers and pay them yourself, the IRS probably will view you as an employer, which normally means you are responsible for the employer's contribution for the caregiver's Social Security, Medicare and state employment taxes. The good news is these expenses are deductible medical expenses for you.[3] Your accountant can help you understand any employer responsibilities you may have in this capacity.

▲   A few policies will allow immediate family members to care for you – even your spouse – but you still have to document their services and submit bills to the insurance company. (Your spouse will enjoy finally getting paid for your care!) Check the policy carefully to understand any limits on the percentage of payment or the amount of time paid for immediate family members.

▲ Most new policies do not require that the care be provided through a home health agency. A policy like this will pay "professionals operating within the scope of their license," such as a Registered Nurse (RN) or Licensed Practical Nurse (LPN) who is freelancing his or her services. It is possible to find a policy that will pay for a family member, friend, or other person of your choice, except for an immediate family member, to obtain the necessary license or certification in your state to be paid as a freelancer. This can be helpful if you live in a rural area without a strong network of home health care agencies. (To find out more about your state's home care licensing and certification training program, call your state's Agency on Aging in *Appendix B* of this book and ask for the telephone number of your state's association for home health professionals.)

▲ To help family members who are willing to be free caregivers, most policies pay for caregiver training to teach a family member how to provide care in the most effective and safest way for both patient and caregiver. This can include skills such as lifting techniques, patient positioning to avoid pressure sores, insulin injections, changing bandages, and so forth. The benefit amount for this feature is usually five times the daily benefit.

▲ On the other end of the spectrum, some policies require care to be provided by a licensed home health care agency and do not pay for family and friends (unless the family member is a licensed health care professional and services are billed through a third party, such as a home health agency).

▲   The policy should not require a nursing home stay prior to providing coverage for home health care.

▲   The policy should pay for non-skilled care at home (bathing, dressing, helping the patient get in and out of bed, etc.) with no requirement for skilled care (care performed by nurses, physical therapists, speech therapists, etc.) Many policies also pay for companion care and homemaker services like cooking, cleaning and laundry.

Adult Day Care

If the policy covers home care, it will also cover adult day care. Aging adults who might otherwise succumb to isolation and depression if kept at home with an aide, sitter or companion can blossom in the socially more active setting provided by adult day care. Throughout the United States, more than 3,500 adult day care centers are in operation. That is well under the 8,520 that are needed, according to a report funded by The Robert Wood Johnson Foundation, but the industry is growing.[4] Dollars from long-term care insurance policies will stimulate this growth as more families have funds to pay for adult day care.

The average cost of adult day care is about $62 per day,[5] which is much less than assisted living at $695/week or home care or nursing home care, which can easily reach $1,300 a week.[6]

To locate adult day care centers, an eldercare locator can be reached at 800-677-1116 or www.eldercare.gov. Other resources are the National Adult Day Services Association (www.nadsa.org) local senior centers, Area Agency on Aging, and of course, the Yellow Pages.

Assisted Living

Sometimes people may need help with one or two Activities of Daily Living (ADL), such as bathing or dressing, but may not need total 24-hour care in a nursing home. Retirement centers and nursing homes often have special sections for people who need just slight assistance. This type of assistance is called "assisted living." This type of care also is available in some independent facilities such as personal care homes or bed and board homes. Assisted living is a popular form of long-term care because the setting is more like a home setting and costs less than nursing home care. (Compare the cost of about $88 a day for assisted living vs. $187 day for semi-private nursing home care.)[7]

Assisted living is a wonderful alternative to nursing home care and consequently may be the fastest growing form of long-term care. To further explain the difference, nursing home residents typically need help with three or more Activities of Daily Living, while assisted living residents only need help with 1-2 ADLs and are certainly not bed bound. Although many assisted living residents would not qualify for benefits under long-term care insurance policies because they don't need very much help, the National Center for Assisted Living reports that about 60 percent of assisted living residents need help with two or more Activities of Daily Living and probably would qualify. Others may qualify under the cognitive impairment benefit trigger as half of the residents have significant cognitive impairment.[8]

The real attraction is that assisted living provides a place that looks like independent living to many people who can't stay home anymore because they need extra help. Also, assisted living facilities make it possible for spouses to remain together, whereas nursing homes usually do not, at least not in the same room.

Older policies commonly provided assisted living benefits at a percentage of the nursing home benefit, but most policies today provide equal benefits. If you want the assisted living coverage and can do without home care benefits, you can save about 30%-40% in premium by considering a "facilities-only" policy that covers only assisted living facilities and nursing homes, as we discussed in the previous section.

Guaranteed Renewable

Policies today are "guaranteed renewable", which means the policy cannot be cancelled as long as premiums are paid, even if the insurance company stops selling long-term care insurance. However, if the insurance company you bought your policy from goes out of business you can still lose your coverage, so it pays to consider large, reputable companies (see **Rates vs. Ratings** on p. 75).

Beware of anyone who tells you not to worry about the stability of the insurance company because the state guaranty fund will bail you out. This is a special pool of money that assumes responsibility for claims of policyholders from failed insurance companies. Generally, you have to be "on claim", which means receiving benefits, on the date the company becomes insolvent to receive help from the guaranty fund. The guaranty fund is funded from assessments made by the insurance department on the other insurance companies in the state that sell similar insurance policies, and its liability does not extend to claims past the date of insolvency, so it doesn't pay for future claims.

In addition to meaning the policy can never be cancelled, "guaranteed renewable" also means the rates can increase only if they go up on a "class" basis, not just on your policy. A class is usually defined as a specific policy form number, perhaps in a specific geographical area. Rates won't be increased by age groups or benefit features, such as "all 75+ policyholders who purchased a five-year benefit period". Rather, a rate increase could be imposed on everyone who bought policy form #XYZ in the southeast or in a particular state, if the insurance department agrees that the rate increase is justified for that block of policies. Some policies offer rate guarantees from three to 20 years. Additional premium is normally required for rate guarantees longer than three years.

If the idea of a rate increase is particularly worrisome to you, you might want to consider a limited pay plan. This means that you pay additional premium for a specific number of years; then you never pay premium again. Your plan is subject to a rate increase during the years you are paying premium but not after your premium is paid up (see *Lowering or Eliminating Long-Term Care Insurance Premiums in Retirement* on p. 80).

Prior Hospitalization

It is illegal today to sell a policy that won't pay nursing home benefits without a prior hospital stay. Many older policies were sold with this restriction, and their premiums are lower because these policies screen out a large number of claims. With strict hospital admission guidelines set forth by private insurance and Medicare, doctors can no longer admit patients just to satisfy an insurance requirement such as this. For example, Alzheimer's patients or the frail elderly usually do not need hospitalization. Less than half of the nursing home patients in the last major survey came directly from a hospital.[9]

Daily or Monthly Benefit

Some long-term care insurance policies pay a flat amount per day or per month for nursing home care with selections ranging from $40–$500 per day, or $1,000–$15,000 per month. These are called indemnity policies. Other policies will not pay more than the actual charge, regardless of the daily benefit you select. These are called reimbursement policies. Most reimbursement policies will allow the amount of daily benefit not used to carry over, thus extending your benefit period. Knowledge of local nursing home costs is helpful in making this selection. Costs nationwide average $187 per day for semi-private nursing home care.[10] If home health care benefits are offered, the benefit ideally will equal the nursing home benefit but could be a percentage of the nursing home benefit, if it's at least 75%-80%.

A policy with a monthly benefit will pay if home care for a particular day exceeds a normal daily benefit. For example, a therapist and an aide could come on the same day, and charges for both might total $250. A $150 daily benefit would pay no more than $150 for that day, but a $4,500 monthly benefit would pay the entire $250 or whatever the daily charges are until the $4,500 is used up for that month. Some policies provide a weekly benefit instead of a monthly benefit for home care. This can be helpful because there is less risk of using up all of your home care benefit in the early part of the month. Some newer policies give you a weekly or monthly benefit if you use a care coordinator at claim time (see **Care Coordination** on p. 73).

Note: Some applicants intentionally select a benefit lower than area charges to merely supplement their assets and income. For example, someone with $2,100 in monthly income may figure that he would use $1,000 of his income to pay toward his care, which is the equivalent of $30 per day. He then might purchase a policy that will pay $150 per day, which results in a potential $180 per day available for an eight- to ten-hour shift of home health care or for semi-private nursing home care. Just be careful when you do this calculation to consider how much of your income you will need to pay your living expenses, which will be higher if you are receiving home care vs. nursing home care.

Some people prefer a private room and purchase a daily or monthly benefit to accommodate private room costs (i.e. $200+ daily benefit or $6,000+ monthly benefit).[11] The daily benefit usually applies just to room and board. Personal items such as laundry, television, hairdresser, etc. aren't covered. Care-related supplies like adult diapers or support stockings are usually not covered if they are billed separately. Selecting a benefit fairly close to the average cost in your area probably means you will still be self-insuring some of the costs. Make sure the policy will pay the percentage of costs you expect so you won't be surprised when the bills start coming in.

The advantage of an indemnity policy that pays the daily benefit regardless of charge is to provide extra money to pay for these extra charges. The advantage of a reimbursement policy that pays no more than the actual room and board charge is to hold claim payments down and avoid rate increases for as long as possible. Since benefits above $270 per day (indexed annually)[12] that exceed actual costs are taxable income, most newer policies are reimbursement; however, a new trend is to offer an option to change a reimbursement policy into an indemnity policy for additional premium, or at least the nursing home portion of the policy. A hybrid policy (indemnity nursing home benefits and reimbursement home care benefits) can make it easier for a company to keep rates the same, more so than a policy that is a total indemnity policy.

Note: A few reimbursement policies allow any difference between the daily benefit you select and the room and board charge to be used to pay miscellaneous charges that are not personal items, such as care-related supplies.

Benefit Period/Benefit Maximum

This is the amount of time (benefit period) or money (benefit maximum) the insurance company is obligated to pay benefits. This doesn't mean how long you can be covered. You might have your policy 15 years before you need to file a claim for benefits. After you file a claim, the benefit period is how long the insurance company is responsible to pay benefits. Benefit periods from one year to unlimited are on the market, although some states require benefit periods of at least two years to be offered. Common choices are three years, four years, five years, six years, or unlimited.

Most insurance companies express the maximum benefit in dollars instead of time. Benefit maximum usually means a specific number of days multiplied by the daily benefit you select. For example, a benefit maximum of 1,095 days multiplied by a $200 daily benefit would be $219,000. This type of policy is usually a reimbursement policy. (See **Daily or Monthly Benefit** in the previous section.) If the charge happens to be less than your daily benefit, the remainder stays in this "pool of money" and extends your benefits. Instead of having the equivalent of a three-year benefit period with the pool of $219,000, your benefits may last 3 ½ years or even longer. The insurance company won't stop paying benefits until all of the dollars are used. If you purchase inflation coverage, the daily or monthly benefit you purchased will grow each year. The overall benefit maximum usually grows as well. A few policies will allow it to grow without deducting any claim payments that were made that year. On the other hand, newer policies may sell you a dollar maximum, say $1 million, and allow you to access a specific percentage each month, usually 1% – 3%. Companies that do not offer an unlimited benefit period are concerned about future rate increases and want to be able to plan on a maximum payout for each policyholder.

After you have collected the maximum in benefits, the policy is over and you start paying out of your assets until you spend down to the qualifying level for Medicaid in your state (Medi-Cal in California and MassHealth in Massachusetts). A few states have a special program called The Partnership for Long-Term Care that allows you to shelter some of your assets and still qualify for Medicaid as a reward for purchasing a long-term care insurance policy (see Chapter Four, *The Partnership for Long-Term Care*).

To give you an idea of the nursing home usage, the chart in this section illustrates the length of stay information for patients in 2004 for all patients and also for those who stayed longer than three months. [13]

The average nursing home stay is 2.3 years.[14] Three-fourths of nursing home patients stayed less than three years and 44 percent of the patients stayed less than one year. However, 12 percent of the patients stayed longer than five years. However, if you subtract the short stays of less than three months which are typically for short-term recovery care such as accidents, mild strokes, broken hips and the like, the five or more year percentage becomes almost 16 percent. Since women live longer than men, the majority of patients who need longer periods of care are women.[15] Accordingly, most insurance companies will allow couples to choose different benefit periods as a way of reducing premium; i.e. a husband might choose a three-year benefit period and a wife might choose a lifetime (unlimited) benefit period.

Most caregivers are women, so men typically are taken care of at home by a wife or daughter as long as possible before entering a nursing home. [16] When a husband buys a long-term care insurance policy for himself, it may be the wife who realizes the greatest benefit from his policy because it pays for the support she needs to keep her husband at home as long as possible.

Length of Stay for All Patients	Percentage of Nursing Home Patients	Length of Stay for Patients Who Stayed Longer Than 3 Months	Percentage of Nursing Home Patients
Less than 3 months	20.0%	N/A	N/A
3-6 months	10.0%	3-6 months	11.0%
6-12 months	14.2%	6-12 months	16.3%
1-3 years	30.3%	1-3 years	39.1%
3-5 years	13.6%	3-5 years	17.8%
5+ years	12.0%	5+ years	15.8%

Source: The Lewin Group tabulations of the 2004 National Nursing Home Survey , "Nursing Home Use by 'Oldest Old' Sharply Declines", The Lewin Group, 11/21/06

Cynthia Coe, an insurance professional in Massachusetts, relates what she describes as "a career transforming experience":

I received a phone call from a local life insurance professional asking me to explain the benefits of a long-term care insurance policy his client had purchased from my insurance company when he lived in another state. He had recently suffered a debilitating stroke and moved back to our town to be closer to his children.

After setting an appointment with his wife, I arrived the next day to find one of the sweetest women I have ever met in tears, absolutely distraught and exhausted. The poor woman had lost 50 pounds and was absolutely frantic because Medicare was cutting back on home care for her completely disabled husband because his condition was "not improving." Her poor husband was confined to a wheel chair or hospital bed, could not take a step, and was unable to communicate with anyone, except in a strange, garbled speech that only his wife understood. She was adamant about caring for him at home, but it was patently clear that she needed more help. I contacted the company, which immediately sent out a really nice social worker who assessed the situation and authorized benefits on the spot. We were able to arrange increased care within the week.

Three or four weeks after all this, I was having a particularly horrible day. My company was insisting I do telephone solicitation. I would rather have walked over hot coals, been caged with hungry lions or jumped out of a plane without a parachute—and I had encountered several really nasty individuals who had sworn at me and likened me to an unethical used car salesman. In other words, despite all my belief and conviction in the importance of long-term care insurance, I HAD HAD IT! I have the heart of a social worker, not a salesperson, and my fragile little ego was quivering. But, on the way home to tell my husband that I absolutely had to find another line of work, I stopped at the bank to make a deposit, and who should be there but the wife of the client who was so disabled by the stroke. She spotted me, came rushing over, and HUGGED me with tears in her eyes and just gushed. "Thank God for you and your company, I don't know what I would have done without you." The new home care workers had given her back some semblance of a life, and she now felt she could cope with her life situation as a result of having such insurance.

Needless to say, I felt as if the Lord had given me a very strong message about the importance of the work I do. So, in spite of very regular set-backs, I still spend my days trying to spread the message about the emotional, physical, psychological and financial importance of this type of insurance—and I usually list "financial" last in this order, as the other three can eclipse everything else.

On the other hand, the wife or daughter may not have a similar caregiver and may access benefits on a long-term care insurance policy relatively soon. The more help a family has to provide home care, the easier it is to keep a family member at home who needs long-term care. The money from a long-term care insurance policy may be the only thing that makes it possible to provide extended home health care for a loved one. In fact, a recent claims study said that in the absence of their long-term care insurance benefits, half of the people receiving home care benefits would be in a facility because they wouldn't have the support to stay home.[17]

Many older policies had separate benefit periods for home care, i.e. you could have three years for nursing home care and three years for home care, for a total of six years of coverage. If either side is used up, however, you can't tap into the other side to continue the benefits in the same location. In this example, if you use up the three years of home care benefits, and you still want to stay home, your remaining benefits will only be paid if you move to a nursing home.

Because of this problem, most policies today have "integrated" benefit periods. "Integrated" means that if you buy a six-year benefit period, for example, benefits will be paid however you need them—at home, in assisted living, adult day care, or in a nursing home.

How long a benefit period should you purchase? The answer is, as long as you can afford, without being uncomfortable with the premium. A recent study said that less than 10 percent of claimants are using more than four years of benefits.[18] Who is at risk for longer periods? Four major categories:

1) People who take really good care of themselves may be the very people who need long episodes of long-term care. They are less likely to suffer a major heart attack or massive stroke, and instead, they just wear out! The healthier they are, the longer that can take—four years, six years, ten years!

2) Alzheimer's patients – the average caregiving time is eight years, but the Alzheimer's Association says it can be three to 20 years.

3) A younger person with a head or spinal cord injury (see **Inflation Protection** for an idea on how to manage this risk).

4) People with longevity in the family – is it common for relatives to live past age 90?

Here's a comforting thought for you if you are concerned about how long you could need care and want to buy a long benefit period: If you purchase a longer benefit period, such as lifetime (unlimited), and you decide later that it's too much premium, you can always reduce your premium by reducing your benefit period, and that's fine with the insurance company. If you start out with a shorter benefit period and decide later you want to increase it, the insurance company will require you to start over with new medical questions, and you will have to pay premium for the longer benefit period at your new age. It's in your best interest to start out with the maximum benefit period you think you might want, because you can always come down. Increasing benefits later is more expensive, and if you have developed a health problem, you may be ineligible for a benefit increase.

As the average purchasing age for long-term care insurance declines, insurance companies are becoming uncomfortable with the risk of younger people incurring injuries or health conditions that cause them to need many years of long-term care. Consequently, some of the newest products no longer have an unlimited benefit period option. If this is really important to you (e.g. if you have a family history of Alzheimer's), my advice is to buy a policy with an unlimited benefit period now while it's still available. Once you have it, no one can take it away from you as long as the insurance company is in business. The best premiums on the unlimited benefit period seem to be with policies that sell joint policies that price the younger spouse at a percentage of the older spouse.

Restoration of Benefits

Some policies have benefit restoration periods that depend on being able to go a certain amount of time without using the policy (i.e., a five year benefit period is reinstated if a patient is in a nursing home and goes home for six months at the end of four years and no claims are filed for the six-month period). The practicality of this feature is questionable as the policyholder must depend on someone else to provide care during the required period out of the nursing home.

Most restoration provisions, however, require that the patient be really better, which means that no care is needed for a six-month period, or at least that no expenses be incurred for six months that would be eligible under the policy for benefits. A benefit like this is good for people who have short-term problems, like mild strokes, and fully recover. Someone who needs care for an extended period of time is unlikely to get better and will not benefit from this feature.

I was enjoying a lovely dinner at the annual board meeting of the university I attended until the gentleman on my right asked me to divulge my line of work. He recoiled when he heard the words "long-term care insurance" fall from my lips. I was soon to find out why. His wife was just coming up on her fourth year in a nursing home with Alzheimer's disease. Simultaneously, the benefits of her long-term care insurance were coming to an end. The professional who sold the policy had told him a four-year benefit period would be enough, because the policy had this great restoration feature and if she used up the four years, she could get her benefits restored. Since she will never recover, this has turned out to be very bad advice.

I have, however, advised younger people to consider this provision, especially if they are buying a short benefit period such as two or three years. It doesn't cost much and a younger person could sustain a serious injury such as a fractured pelvis in an automobile accident, yet recover after a year or so, in which case the restoration of benefits provision could prove to be very meaningful.

Shared Benefit Periods

A new feature is catching on to make long-term care insurance policies more practical and affordable for married couples and even families. Four versions of this idea exist in current policy selections:

1) One version allows spouses to share a benefit period at a lower premium than two separate benefit periods would cost. (You and the insurance company are betting that both spouses won't need a lot of long-term care.) If one spouse dies without using all the benefits, the surviving spouse is entitled to the remainder of the benefit period at a reduced premium.

2) Another version has separate benefit periods, but for a little more premium it allows spouses to access each other's benefit period. For example, each spouse has a six-year benefit period. If one spouse uses only one year of benefits then passes away, the other spouse would have eleven years of benefits left.

3) A third version provides separate benefit periods of the same length for each spouse, then allows the couple to purchase an additional benefit equal to the primary benefit period to share first come, first served. For example, if the spouses each purchased a three-year benefit period, the insurance company would allow them to purchase a third three-year benefit period that both could access as needed.

4) The fourth version is a family policy. The applicant can select up to three immediate family members (parents, grandparents, siblings, children, stepchildren, grandchildren and respective spouses) to be on the same policy. This means they all share one deductible and a single benefit pool (see **Elimination Period**

[**Waiting Period**] in the next section). The unlimited benefit period is not available. If the applicant dies or no longer pays the premium, ownership of the policy can be transferred to the next named family member on the policy. In this way, parents can pass any unused benefits on to children or other family members.

Elimination Period (Waiting Period)

This is the number of days you have to pay until the insurance company pays benefits (like a deductible). Examples of choices range from 0, 20, 30, 60, 90, 100, 180, 365 or even 730 days. Some states won't allow waiting periods longer than 180 or even 100 days to be offered. Patients receiving skilled care may be able to avoid out-of-pocket costs during the elimination period because regular health insurance may pay some skilled care for people under 65, and Medicare can approve up to 100 days for skilled care for people over 65. The chances of qualifying for skilled care as long as 100 days are slim, however (see **Why Doesn't Medicare Pay More?** on p. 15).

The longer the elimination period, the greater the potential out-of-pocket costs. For example, someone with a 100-day waiting period who receives 30 days of skilled care reimbursed by private health insurance or Medicare will be responsible for the 70 days of non-skilled care before the policy begins to pay. At a $180 charge per day, the out-of-pocket cost would be $12,600.

Caution: A few policies don't count days paid by Medicare or health insurance toward your waiting period. If you have a policy like the above example, you will be responsible for the full 100 days after the 30 days paid by Medicare. Ask the insurance professional to show you the section that addresses this point in the sample policy so you will have a clear understanding of how it works.

Some policies require the satisfaction of additional elimination periods if episodes of care are separated by longer than a specified time period, usually six months. For example, a patient may have a four-month nursing home stay and need to be admitted again four years later. Both admissions would require an elimination period before benefits could be paid. Most new policies require only one elimination period in a lifetime, regardless of how long it takes for you to accumulate the days of care that equal the waiting period. However, a few policies require you to accumulate the days within a certain time frame, such as six months or two years, in order for you to never have to satisfy another waiting period.

It is wise to ask how the elimination period is calculated for home health/adult day care. Some policies count only the days actual services are provided, so if the patient does not have home health care every day, it would take longer than 100 calendar days to satisfy a 100-day elimination period. Some policies count all seven days in a week toward the waiting period even though home care was only received on one day of that week. Others start counting when the physician first certifies the need for long-term care (see **Claims** on p. 93). Policies of the latter type may not require charges to be incurred during the elimination period. In other words, family members could provide the care until the elimination period is satisfied. For additional premium, a few policies allow days of care for one spouse to count toward the waiting period for both spouses.

Beware of policies that have choices of only 0 or 100 days, with no choice in between, especially if the insurance professional is urging you to choose a 0-day waiting period, which means first day coverage and no deductible. This sounds great on the surface, but if that insurance company sells most of its policies without a deductible, it will likely be paying out claims much faster than other insurance companies. Again, this sounds good, but it means the company will be much more apt to need rate increases to stay in business than other companies.

A new trend in long-term care insurance is to waive the elimination period for home care benefits or even for all benefits if you agree to use a care coordinator provided by the insurance company (see **Care Coordination** on p. 73). Or a policy may not have an elimination period at all for home care benefits, regardless of whether a care coordinator is used or not. This is another consumer-friendly benefit that can have an adverse impact on that company's future rate stability as no deductible normally increases both the frequency and dollar payout of claims.

In addition to home care, many companies don't require the waiting period to be met prior to receiving benefits such as hospice, respite care, caregiver training, Emergency Response System, and so forth (see **Miscellaneous Benefits** on p. 70).

Mental Conditions

If you qualify for a policy, many policies will cover mental conditions only of an organic nature, such as Alzheimer's and other dementias. Look for a written statement about coverage for "cognitive impairment," which includes Alzheimer's disease. Tax-qualified policies will cover severe cognitive impairment that causes the patient to be a threat to himself or others. For example, if you have high blood pressure and you can't remember to take your medicine when you are supposed to, this could certainly make you a threat to yourself, because you could cause yourself to have a stroke. Many policies will not cover mental conditions of a non-organic nature such as schizophrenia, manic-depressive disorders, etc. Some cover all types of mental conditions. Why is this important? Sometimes at older ages, the lines can blur between dementia and depression, for example. A company that covers all types of mental disorders may be more likely to pay the claim without a problem.

Waiver of Premium

In most policies, premiums are waived after a specified time, usually expressed in days of benefit payments. For example, older policies typically waived premiums after 90 days of nursing home benefits. Some policies do not require these days to be consecutive. Newer policies also waive premiums when you receive assisted living, home care or adult day care, and most policies waive premiums on the first day of benefits. The premium only comes back in most policies, if you get truly better, which means you don't incur any eligible expenses, for six months. A new trend is the "dual waiver", which means the premium is waived for both spouses when one spouse starts receiving benefits. This can be an optional benefit that requires additional premium, or it can be built into the policy at no additional charge.

Inflation Protection

The policy should have some provision to help the benefits keep pace with inflation because home care and nursing home costs are projected to grow 5%-6% compounded each year.[19] At that rate, costs will triple in the next 20 years. Here are two common inflation options offered by insurance companies:

Future Purchase Option (also called Cost-of-Living, or CPI method)

This method allows policyholders to buy extra coverage at certain intervals (i.e. every one to three years) equal to the percent of increase due to inflation. Typically, the amount of coverage offered is determined by changes in the Consumer Price Index and is offered as long as you haven't filed a claim in a certain period of time. Some states and some policies require those offers to continue even if you have had a claim. Some policies discontinue the offers if you turn them down two or three times, or even one time.

The problems with this method of inflation protection are:

1) The amount of the offer is usually determined by the overall Consumer Price Index, which is lower than the medical component of the CPI, neither of which is keeping up with actual increases in long-term care costs. Since 1913, CPI for all items has averaged 3.5 percent, and medical CPI usually runs between 4%-5%, according to the Bureau of Labor Statistics. A few policies offer a minimum 5 percent compound annual offer.

2) One popular plan only offers 5 percent of the original daily benefit every three years, so it would take sixty years to double!!

3) The offers are priced at your attained age, which means the age you are when you accept each offer, not the age you were when you purchased the policy.

Guaranteed Annual Increases

Other policies allow the policyholder to purchase a rider that automatically increases the daily or monthly benefit by 5 percent—compounded or simple—for life. A few charge a lower premium and allow the daily benefit to compound annually just until the benefit has doubled or allow it to compound for 20 years before it stops. A few policies offer other percentages besides 5 percent, such as 3%-4%. (Remember that long-term care inflation is projected to average between 5%-6% a year.) Whichever factor is used, only the benefit increases annually,   not the premium, with one exception: a few policies have a "step-rated compound benefit increase" which means both the benefit and the premium increase at a compounded rate of 5 percent annually.

Proponents of the future purchase option method argue that since medical costs can increase faster than 5 percent per year, policyholders with the guaranteed annual increase rider may experience a shortfall at the time of a claim, which would result in increased out-of-pocket costs. However, when the cost-of-living offers are determined by the overall Consumer Price Index, these offers are even more inadequate since CPI for all items normally grows only about 3.5% each year.

People who like the 5 percent guaranteed annual increases method best say that the periodic premium increases under the cost-of-living method are unmanageable for most budgets, and the extra benefit usually can't be purchased if there is a claim. Someone who has a five-year claim has a frozen daily benefit throughout the claim. (As noted above, some states and some policies require the future purchase offers to be made during a claim, but that's rare.) The 5 percent guaranteed annual increases occur even if there is a claim and - a pleasant surprise - the premium is usually waived (see **Waiver of Premium**, p. 62).

Even if the future purchase offers are at 5 percent compounded so that the benefit will wind up in the same place as the guaranteed annual increase method, the biggest problem with the future purchase option method is that it has a lower premium when the policy is first purchased, but over the long run can cost much more. For example, let's compare both types of inflation coverage for a married 54-year-old purchasing this plan:

- $100 daily benefit for all types of care
- 20 day waiting period
- unlimited benefit period

One popular company illustrates that the annual premium for the Future Purchase Offers (FPO) method starts out at only $818 but would grow to $25,462 annual premium at age 86 if she accepted the 5 percent benefit offer every year. By comparison, she could have purchased the policy with a level premium and the 5% benefit increases are guaranteed for the rest of her life at an annual premium of $1,919. By age 86, she would only have paid $63,330 in premium vs. $203,051 with the FPO method! In both cases, the daily benefit would have grown from $100 per day to about $500 per day.

If you are considering the future purchase offer method, be sure and ask the insurance professional to show you a printout of the projected premium increases over your lifetime. The insurance companies who offer this method of inflation protection are required to include that information in the proposal. If the proposal shows significantly lower premiums at older ages than I have just illustrated in this section, check to see what the benefit has grown to under the FPO method. For example, the plan cited in #2 in the "problems with the FPO method" on the preceding page allows the daily benefit to increase by 5 percent of the original amount every three years. So a $100 daily benefit would grow $5 every three years. By age 87, the benefit would be only $155 vs. $502 with the 5 percent compound rider. Premiums at age 87 are substantially lower with this version but the obvious tradeoff is that the benefit is only 30 percent of what it would have been with the compound rider.

If you elect the 5 percent guaranteed increase rider instead of the future purchase offer method, you may be wondering if you should choose the 5 percent simple (if your state allows that option) or the 5 percent compounded rate of growth. "Simple" means the benefit grows 5 percent of the original amount and doubles in 20 years. "Compounded" increases grow faster, doubling in 15 years, because the 5 percent increase is based on the previous year. Walter Newman, a North Carolina insurance professional, tells how this benefit really paid off at claim time:

> *In 1992, a locally prominent man bought a policy from me with a $100 daily benefit. After some persuasion, he agreed to add the 5 percent compound inflation rider. He was a wealthy individual and wanted to buy a plan without inflation coverage, intending to self-insure the difference.*

> *Three years later he was diagnosed with Alzheimer's and was cared for at home for the next two years. When his family could no longer manage him, he was admitted to a skilled nursing facility. Thanks to the inflation coverage, he is currently receiving benefits of $141 per day, instead of the original benefit of $100 per day. The cost of his care is $5,500 a month, leaving a difference of $1,138. His family tells me his Social Security check just about makes up the difference, so all his other income and assets are available to his family. If he hadn't bought the inflation rider, the difference would have been almost $2,500!*

Obviously, the younger the applicant, the better sense the 5% compounded makes, since long-term care costs are projected to triple in the next 20 years.[20] Anyone 70 and younger is well advised to consider the 5 percent compounded inflation method because people are living so long today. People in their 70s may want to choose 5 percent simple to get a lower premium. The example on the next page shows that the growth for the first 10 years is very close to the 5 percent compounded rate.

Another way people age 75 or older can protect against inflation is to buy a higher benefit than the average cost of care (i.e. $250+ per day at age 78, or $400+ per day for high cost areas like New York, Massachusetts, Alaska, etc.) to build in extra benefit to accommodate future costs.

An interesting question for a 75-year-old is should she buy what the benefit will grow to in ten years or opt for a benefit that reflects current costs with a simple or compound inflation rider? The majority of purchasers in this age range don't buy the inflation riders. At age 75, the premium is about the same for a lower benefit with the 5 percent compound rider vs. a benefit that reflects what the lower benefit will grow to in ten years —say $150 with 5 percent compound inflation vs. $240 without the rider. (Simple inflation is about 10 percent less premium at age 75.) The benefits will be close between simple and compound by the 10th year of the policy. If the person lives longer than age 85, the benefit gap widens — $30 a day apart by age 87, $40 apart by age 90, and so on.

But listen carefully. What about the person who bought $240 with no inflation coverage? What happens if that person lives longer than 85 years old? The benefit is stuck at $240 and does not grow at all.

At age 79, Spencer Jones had his foot in a cast when he bought his long-term care insurance policy from me in 1989 due to a fall in the yard. I looked at the twinkle in his eye and listened as he, his daughter and son-in-law (who were also purchasing policies in their early 50s) told me how active Mr. Jones normally was. My gut-level instinct said to me, "This man is not old." I sold him the 5% compound inflation rider.

I got a call that Mr. Jones is ready to file a claim for assisted living benefits at age 92! He was walking a mile a day until a few

The following chart shows a comparison of a $100 daily benefit with a 5% simple growth vs. a 5% compounded growth.

Year	5% Simple	5% Compounded
1	$100.00	$100.00
2	105.00	105.00
3	110.00	110.00
4	115.00	116.00
5	120.00	122.00
6	125.00	128.00
7	130.00	134.00
8	135.00	141.00
9	140.00	148.00
10	145.00	155.00
11	150.00	163.00
12	155.00	171.00
13	160.00	180.00
14	165.00	189.00
15	170.00	198.00
16	175.00	208.00
17	180.00	218.00
18	185.00	229.00
19	190.00	241.00
20	195.00	253.00
21	200.00	265.00
22	205.00	279.00
23	210.00	293.00
24	215.00	307.00
25	220.00	323.00
26	225.00	339.00
27	230.00	356.00
28	235.00	373.00
29	240.00	392.00
30	245.00	412.00
31	250.00	432.00

Pay Now or Pay Later

Age:	**65, married**
Daily Benefit:	**$150**
Waiting Period:	**20 days**
Benefit Period:	**Lifetime (Unlimited)**
Home Health:	**Same benefits as nursing home**

Client #1: Daily benefit grows 5% compounded annually for life

Client #2: Either no inflation or policy has future purchase offers, but client doesn't purchase future amounts

Annual Premium:
$4,286.52 x 20 years = **$85,730**

Annual Premium:
$2,313.36 x 20 years = $46,267

ASSUMPTION: Client #2 has a long-term care need in 20 years at age 85. Daily cost in 20 years: **$450/day*** or **$165,000**

Client #2's deficit = $300 per day ($450 cost - $150 daily benefit purchased) X 365 days = <u>$109,500 shortfall first year.</u>
(Shortfall grows each year as cost continues to grow with inflation.)

Client #2 "saved" $39,463 in premium over the twenty-year period which grew to $97,511 at 8% annual return before taxes and investment fees. But applying the entire savings and investment earnings to the first year shortfall still leaves, $11,989 coming out of Client #2's pocket and the shortfall will continue to grow with inflation for years two and forward.

QUESTION: Did Client #2 Really Save!

* Annual growth rate of 5.8% according to the Centers for Medicare and Medicaid Services 2006.

months before he suffered a heart attack. My instinct had served me well. He was a young 79-year-old and didn't need his policy for 14 years. Was that compound inflation rider a wise decision for him? You decide.

It's the old "pay now or pay later" problem if you are thinking about not buying inflation coverage because it increases the premium so much. You can wind up on Medicaid with limited care choices quickly if your benefit is far below the cost of care when you have a claim and you can't make up the difference out of your pocket. Look at the example on p. 69 before making your decision.

Miscellaneous Benefits

The better policies today offer a variety of benefits in addition to those already described.

Alternate Plan of Care—If your doctor and the insurance company agree that you can be taken care of at home adequately, most policies allow money taken from your benefits to provide enhancements to your home, such as handrails, wheelchair ramps, shower stall improvements, etc., or even an emergency response system to make it easier for you to stay home. This benefit is also used to pay for new long-term care services as they are developed. This is a great feature, because without it, the insurance company would have to amend your policy to pay for new services, a process that can take a long time.

Caution: Beware of anyone who tells you the alternate plan of care benefit means it is not necessary to purchase home health coverage when you buy your policy. You may be able to get some home care assistance under the alternate plan of care provision, but it is by no means a defined benefit for home care, assisted living or adult day care. If you want home care benefits, make sure that the "home care" or "community care" block is checked on the application, and that your policy specifically states that you have benefits for home care, assisted living and adult day care. (The real intent of the alternate plan of care provision is to find ways to provide care that is less expensive than nursing home care.)

Hospice—Most long-term care insurance policies cover hospice, which is care for terminally ill people to keep them as comfortable as possible and provide respite care to family members. Most health insurance policies also cover hospice and Medicare has a virtually unlimited benefit for hospice. Tax-qualified policies are not allowed to duplicate Medicare payments, so when would the long-term care insurance policy pay? Medicare's inpatient respite care benefit for hospice is only five days per stay and the family may need a longer period of respite care. Medicare's home care benefit for hospice won't pay eight-hour shifts or longer except in a crisis situation. Long-term care insurance will pay eight-hour shifts indefinitely as long as benefit triggers are met and benefit maximums are not exhausted.

Respite Care—a specific benefit to give the primary caregiver a break. The break could be a few hours off to go shopping or a week or two for a vacation. This benefit is usually paid at home but the better policies pay also in a nursing home or assisted living facility to cover the 24-hour care that will be needed if the caregiver needs to be away several days. Benefit triggers (Activities of Daily Living or cognitive impairment) usually must be met to access the respite care benefit, but the elimination period often does not have to be satisfied.

Homemaker Services—a benefit that pays for personal caregiving services such as cooking, cleaning, laundry, shopping, telephoning and transportation when a benefit trigger is met. Some policies will pay homemaker services only when you are receiving other home care services, such as care provided by a home health aide, nurse or therapist.

Alternate Payer Designation (Third Party Notification)—The policyholder has the opportunity to designate someone else to get a copy of a lapse notice in case the policyholder doesn't pay the premium. Take advantage of this opportunity because this feature protects against policies lapsing if policyholders develop a mental or physical problem that makes them unable to pay the premium.

Impairment Reinstatement—If the policyholder allows the policy to lapse due to a cognitive or physical impairment, the insurance company will reinstate the policy with appropriate premium payment within a specific time period, such as five, six, or nine months. Without this provision in the policy, an insurance company is under no obligation to reinstate your policy if you miss the grace period by even one day. Tax-qualified policies are required to have a minimum reinstatement period of five months.

Bed Reservation—If you have to go to a hospital during a nursing home stay, this benefit will pay to hold your bed at the nursing home. Without this benefit, your family would have to pay or the nursing home could give the bed to someone else. Since nursing homes are 86 percent full nationwide,[21] many nursing homes have waiting lists. Without a bed hold payment, you would have to find another nursing home if you lost your bed to someone else and the nursing home was full. Newer policies provide the bed-reservation benefit when the patient leaves the nursing home for any reason, such as for short visits with family and friends, and policies also pay to hold your bed if you have to go to the hospital while you are in an assisted living facility.

Care Coordination—This benefit pays a third party who ideally doesn't work for the insurance company or the provider of care to manage your care and report regularly to your family, although some companies require you to use care coordinators affiliated with the insurance company and even raise or lower the benefit level by whether or not you use the recommended care coordinator. The care coordinator would perform services like helping to determine the best place for you to receive care, i.e., at home, in an assisted living facility, adult day care or a nursing home and making sure you are getting the best care possible.

A care coordinator is especially helpful when children or other family members don't live nearby, because the care coordinator can give care reports regularly to the family members. Some companies want policyholders to use this benefit so much that they don't reduce the benefit maximum whenever you use it, which makes it a free benefit. They feel this way because they know a care coordinator will help you get the most out of your long-term care insurance policy by using your benefits most effectively and efficiently. Some companies require the use of care coordinators before paying benefits at all, but you may have the option to hire a private care coordinator if for whatever reason you don't wish to use the free care coordinator provided by the insurance company. For example, a separate benefit for a private coordinator might be 25 times the daily benefit per year. This benefit payment would be subtracted from your lifetime maximum.

Survivor Benefit—Some policies will not require a surviving spouse to pay premiums after the death of a spouse if the death occurs after the policy has been held a specified period of time with no claims on either spouse, usually 10 years, but it could be less. For example, if the death occurs prior to the 10th year, the surviving spouse would not have a premium waiver. A few policies have a more liberal provision, however, and will waive the premium on the 10th policy anniversary of the surviving spouse. This feature is rarely part of the basic policy; it is typically an option which requires additional premium, and a few companies offer both types of survivorship waivers.

Worldwide Coverage—Most long-term care insurance policies will not pay outside the United States and Canada, but a few will pay worldwide, or in a list of specified countries, especially if you live in the U.S. at least six months of the year. Payment is usually made to you in U.S. currency and benefits may be reduced to compensate for the additional administration required to process claims with international complexities. If this is important to you, ask if there are any benefit reductions for worldwide coverage. If this is really important to you, you might want to consider a cash plan that gives a monthly benefit check that you can use anyway you like without proving services. That way you will have total freedom to purchase whatever services are available in the other country.

Coordination with Medicare and Other Insurance—Tax-qualified policies are not allowed to make a payment if Medicare pays or if Medicare would pay in the absence of a deductible or coinsurance. Some companies interpret this provision in its strictest sense, i.e., if Medicare makes a payment on days 21-100 for nursing home care, the long-term care insurance policy will not make a payment, even though you are responsible for a daily co-payment for those days. Most people, however, have coverage to supplement Medicare for the first 100 days—either a Medicare supplement, retiree plan or a Medicare Advantage plan. (This is further evidence that Congress intends long-term care insurance to pay for long-term conditions beyond three months, not short-term recovery conditions.)

A few policies won't duplicate benefits paid by any other health insurance, which could include another long-term care insurance policy but rarely does. Some companies police it another way: They won't sell you a daily or monthly benefit that, together with the policy you already have, would exceed the maximum daily or monthly benefit they offer.

Additional Benefits—Long-term care insurance policies commonly include payment for a medical alert/emergency response system (usually $25-$50 a month), ambulance (four trips per year) and medical equipment (30-50 times the daily benefit). Some of these expenses are picked up by Medicare and most policies will not duplicate Medicare's payment. These types of benefits are nice to have, but they shouldn't be given equal weight in the buying decision with the other benefits discussed in this chapter.

Rates vs. Ratings

Virtually all policies today lock in the rate at the time of purchase based on the age of the applicant and cannot increase premiums unless all policyholders in a certain class receive the same increase. Very few policies are "noncancellable," which means the premium can never increase. Some states will not approve a noncancellable policy because higher than anticipated demand for long-term care benefits could make it difficult for an insurance company to hold the rate. Initial pricing and the type of underwriting, liberal or conservative, play major roles in an insurance company's rate stability. "Underwriting" refers to the type of health conditions that an insurance company will accept when a person applies for coverage. Below-market rates, liberal underwriting (i.e., accepting a lot of people with major health problems), and a small asset base make future rate increases almost a certainty.

Another cause for rate increases is when an insurance company sets rates based on an assumption that a significant percentage of policies will lapse (cancel) before a claim is filed. For example, if a company assumes that 15 percent of policies will terminate and only 3 percent do, you can see that many more claims will be payable than the company originally thought. Higher than projected claims can make a rate increase necessary. This has happened to a number of companies because long-term care insurance policyholders typically hang onto their policies. Why? Because the premium is determined by age and sometimes by health status. So it's expensive to buy a new policy at an older age, and the policyholder may be charged more or declined due to health conditions. This is why some policyholders who wish they had purchased a higher benefit just buy an additional policy to go with what they already have instead of replacing their original policy with a brand-new policy at an older age. If you think you need additional coverage or if you're just not sure, ask a long-term care insurance professional to help you make the best decision for your situation.

Do not even think of shopping for the cheapest long-term care insurance policy you can find. Some companies that started out with extremely low premium (i.e., half to two-thirds of other companies' rates) have already experienced terrific rate increases, whereas most companies have not experienced a rate increase for policies issued in the past decade, if ever. If a company is having rate increases now, what will happen to it when the baby boomers begin needing long-term care? This point can't be overemphasized. There have been cases of premiums not just doubling, but increasing 800%! If the premium is significantly less than other policies, run, don't walk, away from it.

Landmark legislation in Florida passed in 2006 [SB2290/ HB1329] that is supposed to address the issue of rate increases. Just in Florida, insurance companies are no longer allowed to:

1) raise rates on existing policies higher than new policyholders are being asked to pay for the same benefits; or
2) deny a claim based on fraud unless the fraud was discovered in the first two years after the policy was purchased.

Policies will cost more in Florida to absorb these requirements, especially #2. If someone applies for long-term care insurance, knowing he or she has early signs of dementia, it can be years before the dementia is obvious enough to be detected in the underwriting process.

Legitimate Premium Savings

Some legitimate premium savings can be had by paying annual premium vs. a monthly bank draft. A few policies don't charge extra or may even reward you with a small discount for bank draft, but annual premium is the least expensive payment with most companies. Adding additional premium of 9% for monthly and 5.5% for semi-annual is a common practice. Rather than pay the additional premium, many people pay annual premium out of their investments. A common strategy to find the money to pay a long-term care premium without taking it out of monthly living expenses is to convert a low interest-bearing fund such as a CD or money market account to a deferred annuity that will earn a higher interest rate tax-deferred. Most annuities allow you to withdraw 10 percent or so annually with no penalty or surrender charge and that makes a great funding vehicle for the annual long-term care insurance premium. Check with your accountant when you are setting up the amount to ensure that the withdrawals accommodate your tax needs as well as the long-term care insurance policy premium.

Spouse/Partner Discounts

Married people get a break with spouse discounts ranging from as low as 7.5 percent to as high as 40 percent. Some companies even give a spouse discount if one spouse is declined for coverage due to a health problem or just doesn't apply for coverage in the first place. The insurance companies are betting that most married people will try to take care of each other as long as possible and not use as many claims dollars as single people without the live-in support system of a spouse. Most companies offer the spouse discount to domestic partners as well.

Some of the spouse discounts extend to live-in siblings and a few are really a household discount that could include anyone living with you in a long-term situation. There are even policies that grant a 40%-50% discount, but don't get fooled by the size of the discount. Compare with a few other policies to decide if the premium is either too low or too high.

Company Ratings

In addition to avoiding bargain basement premiums, it is not wise to consider a carrier with less than an A- rating by A. M. Best, the most well-known third-party rating service for insurance companies. Carriers with lower ratings may not have the financial strength to sustain long-term care coverage. It is also wise to ask if the carrier has assets in the billions, or if it is owned or reinsured by a company with assets that large.

"Reinsured" means that a larger company will pay claims after they reach a certain size. Some smaller companies are subsidiaries of billion-dollar companies; however, subsidiaries can be sold. A major reason some insurance companies have withdrawn from the long-term care insurance market is because they could not keep up with product design required by regulatory changes. Many smaller companies just don't have the financial flexibility to make these changes in a timely manner necessary to be competitive in the market. The chart on the next page may help you examine ratings of companies.

- A.M. Best provides a financial and operating performance rating on virtually all life and health insurance companies.

Financial Quality Ratings of Major Rating Agencies

Ranking	A.M. Best	Standard & Poor's*	Moody's**	Fitch
#1	A++, A+ Superior	AAA Extremely Strong	Aaa Exceptional	AAA Exceptionally Strong
#2	A, A- Excellent	AA Very Strong	Aa Excellent	AA Very Strong
#3	B++ Very Good B+ Good	A Strong	A Good	A Strong
#4	B, B- Fair	BBB Good	Baa Adequate	BBB Good
#5	C++, C+ Marginal	BB Marginal	Ba Questionable	BB Moderately Weak
#6	C, C- Weak	B Weak	B Poor	B Weak
#7	D Poor	CCC Very Weak	C Very Poor	CCC Very Weak
#8	E Under Regulatory Supervision	CC Extremely Weak	Ca Extremely Poor	CC Insolvency Probable
#9	F In Liquidation	R Regulatory Action	C Lowest Rated	C Insolvency Imminent
#10	NR Not Rated	NR Not Rated		DDD, DD, D Insolvent

* "pi" following a rating indicates that it is based on quantitative analysis of public financial data vs. data provided by the insurance company.

A "w" following a rating means the rating is under watch and subject to change. Ratings from "AA" to "CCC" may be modified by the addition of a plus or minus sign to show relative standing within the major rating categories.

** Ratings from "Aa" to "Caa" may be modified by the addition of a 1, 2, or 3 to show relative standing within that rating category.

- Standard & Poor's provides financial strength ratings for those insurers who request a rating. S&P also provides financial strength ratings from public information for other insurers.
- Moody's and Fitch provide ratings for those insurers who request a rating. Therefore, ratings from these two services are not available for all insurance companies. The chart on the following page outlines the rating scales used by the four primary rating services.

To get ratings on selected companies over the telephone at no cost, you can call Standard & Poor's at 212-438-7280, Moody's at 212-553-1658, and Fitch (formerly Duff & Phelps) at 800-853-4824 or 212-908-0500. The A. M. Best rating can be obtained by visiting the reference section of your local library. Ask for the most recent Best's book, because it is published annually. Ratings are updated more frequently in the monthly magazine, *Best's Review*. You can also call A.M. Best at 908-439-2200.

Lowering or Eliminating Long-Term Care
Insurance Premium in Retirement

A few policies allow you to pay two years' annual premium when you purchase the policy in exchange for a lower lifetime rate; e.g. a 10%-25% discount for the second year forward. Or, a policy may allow you to pay enough extra premium each year so that at age 65, your premium drops to half the original premium. These types of options can be meaningful for people who are trying to reduce expenses in their retirement years.

For people who don't want to pay long-term care insurance premium at all in their retirement years, there are "limited pay" policies that allow you to stop paying after 5, 10, 15 or 20 years or at age 65. A few companies even offer a single premium. States vary greatly on whether limited pay policies are allowed to be sold, as some insurance departments worry about limited pay policies having a potential adverse affect on rate stability. A long-term care insurance professional can tell you what is available in your state.

Rates (premiums) are the same for men and women, but are based on age. Policies are available for ages 18+, but most are sold in the 40-84 range. You're never too young to think about long-term care insurance—a 25-year-old can wind up in a coma after a car accident! If you haven't bought a policy by the time you are 40, pre-retirement ages (40s and 50s) are the best time to consider long-term care coverage, because premiums are lower and health is better at younger ages. Some people worry about buying at younger ages and experiencing rate increases that could make a policy unaffordable as they get older.

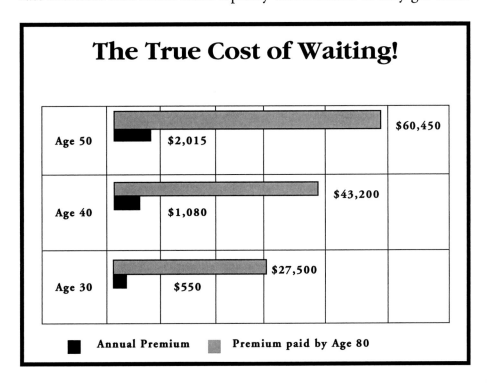

The True Cost of Waiting!

Age 50	$2,015	$60,450
Age 40	$1,080	$43,200
Age 30	$550	$27,500

■ **Annual Premium**   ▨ **Premium paid by Age 80**

A really new trend in long-term care insurance policies is to offer a limited pay option with a corresponding rate guarantee. For example, some companies offer rate guarantees from three years up to 20 years. A possibility with a policy like this is to purchase a policy that would be paid up in ten years along with a corresponding 10-year rate guarantee, a combination which provides you with a guaranteed premium.

The True Cost of Waiting

There are three solid reasons why you should ignore advice to wait until you are in your 50s or 60s to purchase a long-term care insurance policy.

1. Anything could happen to you—see examples of younger people needing long-term care in *Long-Term Care Insurance is Not "Senior Citizen Insurance,"* on p. 127.

2. Because of Point #1, you may not be insurable. No amount of money will buy you a long-term care insurance policy after you develop a serious health condition.

   Kathy Halverson's 41-year-old husband was diagnosed in 1986 with Parkinson's disease. An insurance professional in Wisconsin, he and Kathy "had it all" when it came to insurance policies—except long-term care insurance. Kathy had to learn the insurance business and take over his practice to care for him and provide for their family, especially their children's education. Her husband has since passed away, and Kathy has dedicated herself to getting the word out about how long-term care insurance can protect families. She repeatedly testifies, "We sold insurance for 31 years! We had it all . . . but not LTC . . . and after spending all our pensions, retirement, etc, to care for my husband and educate our children, we were 10 months away from seeking assistance [with Medicaid]."

3. You will pay longer, but you will pay less. The longer you wait, the more benefit you must purchase because long-term care costs are increasing so rapidly. Consider that a married 30-year-old in good health may wish to purchase a policy that will pay about 2/3 of the cost. He could consider a $120 daily benefit for a premium of $550. If that person waited until 40 to purchase, he would have to buy a $190 daily benefit for a premium of $1,080 to accomplish his goal because the cost of care in 10 years will be at least $265. At 50 years old, he is looking at a $300 daily benefit to pay 2/3 of the cost, for a premium of $2,015. Now multiply all three premium amounts to age 80 to see how much he would pay, depending on his purchase age. ($550 x 50 years = $27,500 vs. $1,080 x 40 years = $43,200 vs. $2,015 x 30 years = $60,450)

The difference is most dramatic from age 40 to age 50, but both of those ages become a moot point if he has a skiing accident at age 35 and becomes paralyzed for the rest of his life.

Consumer advocates advising you to wait until you're older to buy may change their advice when a younger sister or son is paralyzed from a car accident or rendered almost lifeless from a stroke or aneurysm.

Saving vs. LTC Insurance

Consider the following example of purchasing a long-term care insurance policy versus investing in an IRA to fund long-term care. A man or woman invests $500 in an IRA at age 40 annually until age 70 ½, which is the mandatory IRA distribution age. That consumer will have $47,500 ($500 each year compounded annually at 6 ½ percent). While that sounds like a tidy sum for a minimum investment, it will barely pay for nine months of long-term care at today's annual cost of more than $62,000, much less the projected cost of $320,000 per year in 30 years. Suppose the man or woman had decided to purchase long-term care insurance at age 40. For a little more than this $500 IRA investment, he or she can get coverage of $120 per day* for all benefits (home care, assisted living, adult day care and nursing home care) with a total benefit period of three years and a waiting period of 100 calendar days. Since this plan includes a 5% compound inflation feature, at age 84 the daily benefit will grow to $805 per day. The annual married premium is only $730 per spouse. If neither spouse has a claim until age 84, the couple will have paid about $65,850 in premiums, and the total available benefit payout for one person will have grown to a whopping $1,125,068 or about $2.25 million for both spouses. And, don't forget that the premium stops when you are using the policy!

On the other end of the age spectrum, a 70-year-old couple may decide to save $5,890 a year, instead of spending that amount to pay the premium for a rich plan with a $150 daily benefit. (The other elements are the same as the plan described above for the 40-year-old.) By age 84, the couple will have saved $181,250 at 10% before taxes and investment fees, which sounds like a lot until you realize that the cost of care at that time is projected to be at least $120,000 a year. Their savings at age 84 would pay for less than two years of care for only one person. Had the couple bought the long-term care insurance policies, the $150 daily benefit would have grown to $297 per day by age 84, and the couple would have had an available benefit of $108,405 a year for each of them, and a potential payout of $682,550 for the next three years for two people. (If you do this calculation yourself, don't

*A good plan that pays about two-thirds of the cost in most parts of the country.

forget that the daily benefit continues to grow 5% compounded each year - $297, $311, $327 and so on.)

Underwriting

Applicants for individual policies must qualify medically for long-term care coverage. Progressive conditions such as Alzheimer's, Parkinson's disease, AIDS, multiple sclerosis, muscular dystrophy, and psychiatric disorders are uninsurable. Applicants must be ambulatory to qualify for coverage, and must not need help with activities of daily living, such as bathing, dressing, toileting, transferring from bed to chair, eating or continence. Heart disease, cancer or one mild stroke can be acceptable risks after recovery periods of usually between two and five years, depending on the insurance company. Conditions such as hypertension are acceptable if controlled. Diabetes (contracted later in life, not during childhood) can be insurable if it is well under control, especially non-insulin dependent. Some companies will accept insulin as long as height and weight are reasonable and the diabetes is under control. People who take antidepressants for "situational depression" (death of a spouse, for example) usually can get a policy if their health otherwise is good.

The standard basis for underwriting is medical records from your doctor, instead of a physical exam, although some insurance companies are utilizing paramedical or "face-to-face" exams. A paramedical exam means a home health nurse visits you to check your blood pressure, height, weight, and to do a quick assessment of your overall physical and mental health. A face-to-face exam means that someone personally interviews you to be sure you are in good mental health. Most companies require this for applicants in their 70s and older. Underwriting commonly includes a telephone interview. (Tip: This is not the time to joke about losing your car keys!)

Caution: A carrier with "loose" underwriting may need future rate increases sooner than a carrier with conservative underwriting. Also, there are horror stories about carriers who do "post-claim underwriting" (i.e. medical history is thoroughly investigated **after** a claim is filed, which naturally results in a large number of denied claims.) This practice is illegal today, but be wary of a "yes/no" application with a policy issued to you in a very short period of time. It usually takes about four to six weeks for a policy to be issued, because the company is doing a good job of checking your mental and physical health to see if you qualify for coverage.

Some carriers will accept health problems if you pay a higher premium or will make alternative benefit offers. For example, you may be offered a four- or five-year benefit period instead of an unlimited benefit period, or a 90- or 100-day waiting period instead of a 20- or 60-day waiting period.

The most important thing about underwriting is that the younger you are, the better chance you have to qualify for a policy. **No amount of money will purchase long-term care insurance for you once you are uninsurable due to a significant physical or mental health problem.** Industry statistics show that the average decline rate is 19 percent but this increases significantly when people apply at older ages.[22] People are strongly encouraged to apply for long-term care insurance certainly by the time they reach their 40s and 50s (pre-retirement ages). A health care think tank found that the percentage of baby boomers with very good health drops from more than 80 percent for those under age 45, to 62 percent for those 65 and over.[23] (Of course, premiums are lower at younger ages and are locked in at the younger age unless there is a rate increase for an entire classification of policyholders.) On the other hand, don't assume you don't qualify for a policy without checking with some reputable insurance companies. You have nothing to lose and everything to gain to see if you can get a long-term care insurance policy.

Pre-Existing Conditions

An ideal policy will cover the policyholder from the effective date of the policy for all conditions disclosed on the application. Most policies have no restrictions at all for pre-existing conditions. A few policies have a 90- to 180-day waiting period for pre-existing conditions.

"Free-Look" Period

Policies issued today must contain a 30-day period after policy delivery in which the policyholder may return the policy for a full return of premium if not satisfied for any reason.

Non-Forfeiture Options

For additional premium, some policies (more commonly non-tax qualified policies) may guarantee to return a specified percentage of premium to a beneficiary if the policy was not used after being in force a specified number of years. For example, a policy may guarantee to return a scheduled percentage of the premium if the policyholder terminates the policy or dies after the policy has been held at least five years. Some policies return all of the premiums if the policy is held at least 20 or more years. This feature usually costs about 30 percent or more in premium. The odds of using the policy and getting nothing back are very high, especially if you purchased home health care benefits. However, for even more premium, a few policies will return 100 percent of the premium to you, or your estate if you are deceased, after a specified number of years even if you have used the policy.

A partial daily or monthly benefit may stay in effect if the policyholder stops paying premium after five years or so. Known as a "reduced paid-up benefit," this feature has not been popular. Because the benefit is so potentially small at claim time, the policyholder is at risk to make up large balances from the very first day of care.

The policyholder must decide if these money-back features are worth the additional premium, or if a greater return on investment can be achieved by putting the difference in premium in a mutual fund or other type of growth investment, such as annuities, individual stocks and bonds, or life insurance, which is frequently used in wealth preservation and estate tax planning strategies.

A few tax-qualified policies have a cash-back nonforfeiture benefit but any refunded premium that was used for a tax deduction creates a taxable event upon its return.

More commonly, tax-qualified policies contain an option for a nonforfeiture benefit called a "shortened benefit period." You are not required to purchase it. If you do purchase it, the value will not be cash back as described above. Instead, the tax-qualified version of nonforfeiture guarantees that if you terminate your policy after three years, in most states the insurance company must pay benefits equal to the amount of premium you have paid for any claim you have in the future, even though your policy is no longer in force.

For example, you paid $15,000 in premium and then decided to cancel your policy. If you had purchased this feature and you had a claim the day after you cancelled your policy, the insurance company would have to pay benefits at the daily benefit in force on the day you cancelled your policy up to $15,000. If your daily benefit was $100, the company would pay 150 days of benefits, or five months. If you had a claim 10 or 15 years from now, the company would still pay benefits of $100 per day up to $15,000. However, at future prices, this would probably pay for only a few weeks of care. This feature will cost you about 30 percent more in premium with most policies. Many companies will give you the shortened benefit period nonforfeiture benefit, even though you didn't pay extra for it if your premium goes up past a certain predetermined point based on the age you were when you purchased the policy. For example, if you purchased your policy at age 60, the predetermined point is 70 percent. So if you had a rate increase that took your premium to 71 percent more than your original premium, the insurance company would have to give you the shortened benefit period nonforfeiture benefit.

This is called "contingent nonforfeiture," because your receiving the benefit is contingent upon your premium being raised to the predetermined point that triggers the benefit. This means you could stop paying your premium and the insurance company would have to pay a claim for you at any point in the future equal to the premium you had paid in. Or, if you wanted to keep your policy in force without the additional rate increase, you could do so by accepting a reduced benefit offer that the insurance company is required to extend to you. Your benefit would be lowered, but you could keep the same premium and you would not have to pay the additional rate increase.

The National Association of Insurance Commissioners passed a new Long-Term Care Insurance Model Act in 2000, which requires all insurance companies to provide contingent nonforfeiture, because they believe it will act as a deterrent to unnecessary rate increases. Since companies don't want to give this benefit away without the additional premium it normally costs, this requirement serves as an incentive for the insurance companies to do everything possible to hold your premium down so it won't increase to the point that makes the company give you the shortened benefit period nonforfeiture benefit free. Each state has to pass the new NAIC model act into law, and almost two-thirds have done so:

> Arizona, California, Delaware, Florida, Iowa, Idaho, Illinois, Kansas, Kentucky, Maryland, Maine, Minnesota, Missouri, Montana, North Carolina, North Dakota, New Hampshire, New Mexico, Ohio, Oklahoma, Pennsylvania, South Dakota, Tennessee, Texas, Utah, Virginia, Wisconsin

The majority of states plan to pass it because it has additional features that are expected to create a powerful deterrent to widespread rate increases in the long-term care insurance industry. In addition to requiring contingent nonforfeiture in every policy at no additional cost, highlights of the NAIC Long-Term Care Insurance Model Act of 2000 are:

▲ The 60/40 loss ratio requirement for long-term care insurance, which means that at least 60 cents of every premium dollar must go for benefits, is eliminated. The NAIC thinks that's an incentive for rate increases - the higher the rate, the more money the other 40% generates for administrative costs.

▲ Rates must be actuarially certified that they aren't expected to increase.

▲ When a rate increase is approved by the state, 85 cents of each rate increase dollar must go to benefits and only 15 cents can go to administrative costs.

▲ The applicant must sign that he or she understands rates can increase.

▲ The insurance company has to disclose at time of sale the rate increase history on similar policies for the last ten years.

▲ If a rate increase is approved by the state then turns out to be unjustified, the insurance company has to refund the money to the policyholders.

▲ If an insurance company exhibits a pattern of inappropriate rates, the insurance commissioner can prevent the company from doing business in that state for five years.

To find out if the NAIC LTC Insurance Act of 2000 has been passed in your state, contact your state's insurance department (see *Appendix B* for contact information).

If your budget forces you to choose between nonforfeiture and inflation coverage, buy inflation coverage.

Suitability

Individuals without assets outside a home and/or car are usually not candidates for long-term care insurance as they will quickly qualify for Medicaid. The National Association of Insurance Commissioners believes you may not be a candidate for long-term care insurance if you have an income less than $20,000 and/or assets less than $30,000, not counting your house and car. The exception to this thinking occurs when a family member (such as a child for a parent) purchases a policy to provide a higher level of care than that offered by Medicaid reimbursement and to ensure an option for home health care and other community choices such as assisted living or adult day care. Or, if nursing home care is needed as a last resort, the adult son or daughter wants the parent to have a complete choice of nursing homes. Many nursing homes have waiting lists and many admit only private-pay patients or patients with long-term care insurance as both types of patients can pay higher rates than the Medicaid reimbursement level. Since a number of nursing homes no longer accept Medicaid patients, people trying to enter a nursing home as a Medicaid patient sometimes have to go to a facility several hours away from the desired location.

Because of the poor choices on Medicaid, another exception to this rule occurs when people who are "house rich and cash poor" obtain a reverse mortgage on their home and use some of that money to purchase long-term care insurance to avoid being on Medicaid.

Some people with assets of $500,000 or more consider paying for their own long-term care. Sometimes the question is: How much of your asset base is liquid? Or will a long-term care need force you to sell property and/or investments at a loss because of poor market timing? **If you have less than $2 million in assets, it is very risky to try to self-insure your long-term care expenses.** Many financial planners advise clients with less than $5 million in assets to purchase LTC insurance. (See the chart in **The Private Sector Solution** on p. 27 in Chapter One that shows how quickly $500,000 can be wiped out when faced with a long-term care need of $60,000 a year.)

Another reason people with significant assets buy long-term care insurance is to avoid confrontations with children over how much money is spent for long-term care. Others will purchase long-term care insurance to preserve privacy of financial records. Without a policy, private-pay nursing home patients usually have to show financial records to prove long-term payment capability. Finally, people with significant assets sometimes purchase long-term care insurance because they want money that would be spent on long-term care to go to other causes such as charities, church, their university alumni association or their grandchildren, like the gentleman who owned several McDonald's in **The Private Sector Solution** in Chapter One.

Claims

Prior to the tax-qualified policies that were introduced January 1, 1997, most policies required your doctor to tell the insurance company that you needed help with at least two Activities of Daily Living (ADLs) before a claim could be paid, although a few policies required help with only one ADL. These are generally dressing, eating, transferring from bed to chair, toileting and maintaining continence. Some policies included bathing in the list. These policies have the potential to pay sooner, as bathing is usually the first ADL that people need help with. Two states added a seventh ADL to the list: Texas required "mobility" and California required "ambulating"—both just a measurement of being able to move around well. Help with ADLs can be "hands on," which means direct physical contact, but better policies also allow "stand-by" or supervisory assistance from the person who is helping you.

If you can physically perform the Activities of Daily Living but have to be told when and how to do them because you have a cognitive impairment, the better policies issued prior to January 1, 1997 will still pay your claim. Cognitive impairment is usually determined by a standardized test to determine deficiencies such as short-or long-term memory loss and general orientation (knowing one's name, place of residence, current political leaders, date, time, etc.) or bizarre hygiene habits.

The new tax-qualified policies sold after January 1, 1997 changed the requirements somewhat to get a claim paid. Tax-qualified policies will pay a claim if you are expected to need help for at least 90 days with two or more of at least five Activities of Daily Living from this list:

bathing	dressing
toileting	transferring
eating	continence

This means that insurance companies can use a list of five or six ADLs, but almost all companies use the list of six. California requires insurance companies to use all six ADLs. The 90-day certification must be provided by a licensed health care practitioner (physician, registered nurse or licensed social worker). **The 90-day certification is not a waiting period.** If you have a 20-day waiting period, for example, your policy will begin paying benefits on the 21st day you need care as long as your doctor (or nurse or social worker) says that you are expected to need help with at least two ADLs for longer than 90 days.

The 90-day certification assures that long-term care insurance will be preserved to pay for truly long-term conditions. Short-term conditions like fractures and mild strokes usually require skilled care such as physical, speech or occupational therapy. The previous sections **Why Doesn't Private Insurance Pay More?** on p. 14 and **Why Doesn't Medicare Pay More?** on p. 15, explain that health insurance and Medicare pay only for skilled care and will therefore cover most short-term conditions, also called "sub-acute" or "post-acute" care.

Tax-qualified policies also pay if you can do all of the Activities of Daily Living, but you need help due to a severe cognitive impairment. This means that you are cognitively impaired to the point of being a threat to yourself or others. For example, if you can't remember how to take your medicine appropriately and you have high blood pressure, you are probably a threat to yourself since by not taking your medicine when you are supposed to could cause you to have a stroke.

Non-tax-qualified policies are still being offered by some insurance companies, even though 99 percent of individual long-term care insurance policies purchased in 2007 were tax-qualified policies.[24] Non-tax-qualified policies do not require the 90-day certification, and may require help with only one Activity of Daily Living to get a claim paid. Instead of needing help with Activities of Daily Living or being cognitively impaired, some non-tax-qualified policies will also pay a claim if your doctor says you need care that is medically necessary, which means that you need care for some type of illness or injury. Most policies like this allow only nursing home benefits to be paid if you need medically necessary care, but a few policies will allow home care to be paid as well. For example, you may be able to perform all of the Activities of Daily Living and you may not be cognitively impaired, but you can't completely take care of yourself because you have crippling arthritis in your back. If your policy pays homemaker benefits such as cooking, cleaning, laundry, etc., and pays for medically necessary care under the home health benefit, it could pay for homemaker services because your arthritis makes it medically necessary for you to have help. The medically necessary benefit trigger is not in tax-qualified policies.

Needing help with Activities of Daily Living, cognitive impairment or needing help because it's medically necessary are all called "benefit triggers," because satisfying one of these requirements is necessary to get the policy to pay benefits.

Tax-Qualified or Non-Tax Qualified

Some people say that tax-qualified policies are more restrictive than policies sold before January 1, 1997 because of the required 90-day certification and because the medically necessary benefit trigger is no longer allowed. While this is true, there is a very good reason for the tightening up of the access to benefits.

A few years before this law was passed, long-term care insurance policies began growing more liberal. Some policies would pay for any type of care at home or in a nursing home if help was needed with only one Activity of Daily Living, and the list included bathing. A growing number of policies also had the medical necessity benefit trigger. That made it easier to collect benefits, especially when it applied to home health care. A couple of policies were introduced that would pay nursing home care at the policyholder's discretion, which means you say you want to go to a nursing home and the insurance company pays your claim! Another policy that became extremely popular paid benefits if you only needed help with two "Instrumental Activities of Daily Living," such as cooking, cleaning, laundry, grocery shopping, telephoning for doctor's appointments, and the like. This brings to mind the old phrase, "If it sounds too good to be true, it usually is."

Why did this happen? The free enterprise system allows insurance companies the opportunity to sell more policies by offering policies with liberal benefit access. The combination of easy access to benefits, low premiums and liberal underwriting (which means that policies are issued commonly to people with significant health problems) means these companies could be more competitive in the marketplace and sell more policies. But these features that sound so good now mean bad news for the consumer in the long run in the form of future rate increases.

Congress saw this trend and stepped in. If the benefits are too easy to obtain, and if the policies are sold to people who have a high likelihood of using the coverage in a short period of time, the policies will pay out more than the collected premiums will support. This means that in the next 10–15 years when the claims activity is high, the long-term care insurance market could "crash" due to large rate increases that many consumers could not afford to pay. And, of course, smaller insurance companies can be hit harder and need bigger rate increases than larger, more financially solvent companies, and that's if they are even able to stay in business.

The taxation issue often is presented as the center of the controversy on whether to purchase a tax-qualified or non-tax-qualified policy, i.e., will the IRS ever rule that benefits from a non-tax-qualified policy are taxable income?

Insurance companies are required to provide Form 1099-LTC to anyone who receives benefits from any type of long-term care insurance policy, tax-qualified or non-tax-qualified. The policyholder is required to report benefits paid from any type of long-term care insurance policy to the IRS on Form 8853, Medical Savings Accounts and Long-Term Care Insurance Contracts. The IRS matches up these 1099s with individual tax filings and sends letters requesting an explanation from people who failed to report benefits received from long-term care insurance policies.

Some insurance companies that actively promote non-tax-qualified policies promise to convert your policy to a tax-qualified policy if the IRS makes such a ruling. Read the fine print, as some will not allow you to switch if you are already receiving benefits.

Beware of advisors who explain nonchalantly that it's no big deal because the cost of your care is a deductible medical expense that will offset the taxable income. Not so! IRS Form 1040: Schedule A—Itemized Deductions plainly states in the block marked "Medical and Dental Expenses": *Caution: Do not include expenses reimbursed or paid by others.* This means any amount reimbursed by a non-tax-qualified policy cannot be deducted as a medical expense.

Is the tax question the real issue or was Congress trying to use the tax liability as a velvet hammer to swing the market to tax-qualified policies with more reasonable benefit triggers?

I believe that the measures Congress took in the 1996 health care reform legislation will function as consumer protection measures to ensure that long-term care insurance is there for us when we need it by restoring long-term care insurance to its original purpose, and that is to pay for long-term conditions. For this reason, there's an excellent chance that improved tax deductions for long-term care insurance premiums will continue to apply only to tax-qualified policies.

Getting a Claim Paid

Regardless of which type of policy you buy, the better insurance companies have streamlined claims filing procedures. Most allow you to call an 800 number and notify the company that the need for long-term care has arisen. At that point the claims representative will assist you with the necessary paperwork and help you obtain the 90-day certification from the appropriate medical practitioner. Most companies will even pay for a care coordinator, which is someone to evaluate your needs on a local level to ensure that you get the appropriate level of care in the best setting for your condition, i.e., home care, adult day care, assisted living or nursing home care.

The cash plans provide a nice advantage when it comes to the claims process. The benefit qualification process is the same as any other type of policy as all tax-qualified policies require either the 2 or more ADL trigger expectation for at least 90 days or severe cognitive impairment, but once approved for benefits, the insured receives a check each month, without having to justify charges or services. The insured or responsible party signs a statement once a month that the patient still meets the benefit trigger criteria, and that's all there is to it. If you do receive benefits above the Federal threshold of $270 per day in 2008 ($8200 per month), you will have to prove that the money is being spent for IRS-approved medical expenses, but anything less than that does not have to be accounted for. Of course you will need someone whom you can trust to manage the money if you are unable to do so, and the IRS is likely to view you as an employer if you are hiring caregivers and controlling their times. See your tax advisor for further clarification on this point.

When claims are paid, the benefit checks are usually sent to you, but some insurance companies will pay the provider of care if you like, especially if the provider files the claim for you. If this is your choice, it's a good idea to get a family member or someone else you trust to audit the bills and claim payments every month to be sure you are being billed correctly for the services you receive.

Ask the insurance professional or company for references from satisfied policyholders who have been through the claims filing process. You can also ask the department of insurance in your state if any complaints have been filed about the insurance company. (See *Appendix B* for the address and telephone number of your state's insurance department.)

Policy Improvements

Policies purchased prior to 1991 may have benefit restrictions that need to be analyzed carefully to see if you need to upgrade or replace your policy with a new one. Some examples of restrictions in these older policies are:

▲ a prior hospitalization requirement before benefits for nursing home can be paid

▲ a prior nursing home requirement before benefits for home health care can be paid (if home care benefits are important to you)

▲ a requirement for skilled care before non-skilled care can be paid

▲ a lower benefit for non-skilled nursing home care than skilled care

▲ an exclusion for Alzheimer's disease and other organic mental disorders

▲ a 50 percent home health care benefit if care is required to be provided by a home health agency; home health care aides average $19 an hour when provided through a home health agency [25]

▲ no inflation coverage

Caution: Upgrading a policy that was issued before January 1, 1997 may cause you to lose the "grandfathered" status that allows it to be a tax-qualified policy. You may be better off keeping the old policy and purchasing a new one on top of it, especially if you are trying to add inflation coverage. Your insurance professional can advise you on the best thing to do. Whatever you do, never cancel an existing policy until a new one is in effect.

Your Customized Benefit Selection Process

To simplify the benefit selection process, you just need to remember that there are six major choices that impact a premium. Here is each choice and a recommendation.

1) **Daily or Monthly Benefit**—Look at the average cost in your area and buy a daily or monthly benefit as high as you can afford—even $20-$30 more than the average cost in your area if you can afford it. Inflation is strong, and you'll probably need the extra benefit at claim time. (The national average cost for semi-private room and board is $187 per day. High cost areas like Alaska and New York City can easily cost $380 per day for semi-private room and board.)[26] A private room usually costs $10-$20 more per day than a semi-private.

Some insurance professionals may be able to provide you with a local cost survey, or you can call some providers listed in the Yellow Pages: assisted living facilities, home health agencies, adult day care centers and nursing homes. Your local Agency on Aging also may have this information. You can get that number by calling your state's Agency on Aging office (see *Appendix B* for contact information). Another excellent resource for average cost information for home health care agencies, assisted living facilities and nursing homes is the Genworth Financial Cost of Care Survey at http://longtermcare.genworth.com. MetLife Mature Market Institute publishes surveys for assisted living costs as well as home health care and nursing home costs at www.maturemarketinstitute.com.

Cost surveys normally will reflect just the room and board rate for nursing home care. Most reimbursement policies will pay no more than the room and board charge and you are on your own for any miscellaneous charges like care-related supplies. An indemnity policy that pays the selected daily or monthly benefit regardless of charge makes it possible to build in extra benefit to cover the extra charges. Most policies are reimbursement, because the theory is that people will use insurance more wisely if there is some cost sharing, and a wiser use of benefits will help hold rates down in the future.

Here's an example of how to calculate a daily or monthly benefit for yourself: if you are considering a reimbursement policy and you are willing to pay about 20 percent of the long-term care cost, you could consider a daily benefit of $130, if the average cost in your area for semi-private room and board is $150.

Some people purchase lower daily benefits, however, because they decide to put some of their income toward the cost of care, especially if they do not have a spouse and do not need their income to maintain a home. For every $1,000 of income you are willing to contribute to the cost of your care, you could reduce the initial daily benefit you purchase by $30.

For an example of premium impact, the premium difference between a $140 daily benefit and a $100 daily benefit is, interestingly, about 40 percent.

2) Waiting Period (Elimination Period)—Most people will choose a waiting period (deductible) of 100 days or less. If you have over $1 million in assets (not counting your house and car), you can look at waiting periods of greater than 100 days. (Some states allow insurance companies to offer waiting periods as long as 180, 365 or even 730 days.) If you have assets less than $100,000, definitely choose a shorter waiting period like 20 or 30 days. If you have assets greater than $100,000 most companies offer waiting periods of 60 days, 90 days or 100 days. (The premium difference between 20 and 100 days with most companies is about 20 percent, so you have to contrast that with self-insuring the cost for an additional 80 days—not just at today's costs but at future costs.) Look at policies that require only one waiting period in a lifetime.

A few policies do not require formal charges during the waiting period. If you are considering that type of policy, the question becomes "How long can I wait before benefits begin vs. how long can I pay"—in other words, how long could you manage with help from informal caregivers, like family and friends before benefits start?

3) Benefit Period/Benefit Maximum—Choose at least two years and longer if you can afford it, but don't ever sacrifice inflation coverage for a longer benefit period. If you live in a "Partnership" state (Connecticut, New York, Indiana, California with many others coming on board),

Assets * *Does not include house and car	Suggested Waiting Period (in days)		
	20-30	60-90	100+
Less than $100,000	X		
$100,000 - $500,000	X	X	
More than $500,000			X

See Chapter 4, *The Partnership for Long-Term Care* for guidance. The average benefit period purchased in 2005 was five years, and 20% of the policyholders purchased the lifetime (unlimited) benefit period.[27] A recent claims study showed that less than 10% of claimants are using more than four years of benefits.[28]

Average premium differences:

> Unlimited vs. 5 years = +40%
> Unlimited vs. 3 years = +82%
> Five years vs. 3 years = +30%

4) **Inflation Protection**—The method that makes your benefit grow 5 percent compounded every year for the rest of your life is the most desirable if you are age 70 or under. If you are in your early 70s,

you can choose the method that makes your benefit grow 5 percent of the original amount, which is called "5 percent simple", for the rest of your life, if your state allows that option. (Tip: At age 75, the premium difference between compound and simple is about 8%-10%.) If your state doesn't allow a simple inflation option, purchase the 5 percent compound. If you are in the upper 70s or older, you can purchase an extra benefit—perhaps an extra $30-$50 per day—to build in immediate inflation protection. The exception? If you think you will live longer than ten years like my client, Mr. Jones, you should seriously consider either the simple or compound inflation option.

If the 5% compounded for life is out of your price range, try buying a greater benefit with either simple inflation or one of the newer inflation options like "5% compound two times", which means your benefit will double in 15 years and stop growing. Sometimes, the premiums are reasonable if you take the time to explore new options. An insurance professional can help you ensure you make the best inflation choice for your situation. Here's my formula:

1) Determine the average cost of care in your area.
2) Decide how much of the cost you want the insurance policy to pay – 50%, 2/3, 80%, full coverage?
3) Project what the cost of care will be in your area by the time you are in your 80s.
4) Construct your inflation benefit so the daily or monthly benefit will pay that percentage of the costs at that time in your life.

With this formula, if you need care at any age, you'll have a benefit that won't disappoint you.

5) **Home Health and Community Coverage**—If you have someone to live with who can be a primary caregiver, you can select this coverage if it is optional on the policy you are considering. Some policies include it and it's not an option. If you do not have a primary caregiver and home health care benefits are required, the policy may allow you to lower your premium by choosing a reduced percentage such as 50 percent. If you are younger (30s–50s) and you don't know if you will have a primary caregiver, buy it if you can afford it so you will have maximum choice when you need care.

Note: If you have no one to live with, you may be better off buying a "facilities-only" policy with "Cadillac" benefit levels – a monthly benefit high enough to get into the nicest assisted living facility in your area, 5% compound inflation, a longer benefit period, and the like. Not everyone is a candidate for home health benefits. One of my clients was a retired schoolteacher with little family. She absolutely did not want to stay home if she needed extensive help. We used her premium dollars to purchase the best assisted living/nursing home policy she could afford. She was able to reside in a beautiful assisted living facility after suffering a severe stroke. Bill Comfort, Jr., a long-term care insurance specialist in St. Louis, had a similar story:

> *After a lengthy discussion of all the wonderful long-term care insurance policy features that would allow for her to stay in her own home, a new client of mine looked at me and said, "If I ever need this kind of help, I don't want to stay in my own home."*

> *I couldn't believe it. Doesn't everyone want to stay in their own home as long as possible? No. My client is a single woman with no family in town. She knew that if she needed on-going long-term care that it would be time to move—part of life. We found a policy with the best assisted living and nursing facility benefits she could get.*

The premium difference between a comprehensive policy with home care benefits and a facilities-only policy that covers assisted living and nursing home care is 30%-40%.

6) **Non-Forfeiture**—This benefit is something you can do without. It increases your premium significantly with very little value in return. The extra 30 percent or so you would spend for this option is better spent on purchasing the 5 percent inflation rider or if you are 75 or older, at least a higher daily benefit to combat inflation or a longer benefit period if you've already taken care of inflation.

The Bare-Bones/Best Value Policy for the Premium Conscious

Summary: If premium is your main consideration, the most "bare-bones" policy with the best premium value for the dollar is a policy that pays:

▲   assisted living and nursing home only, sometimes called a "facilities-only" policy

▲   a 20- or 30-day waiting period

▲   a two- or three-year benefit period

▲   the appropriate inflation choice for your age (see **Inflation Protection** on p. 62).

You can delete the home care as long as assisted living is covered. **Do not delete the inflation coverage.** If your benefit is too small at claim time and you can't make up the difference, you could wind up on

Medicaid immediately (or whatever type of public assistance/welfare benefit is available at the time).

Some Parting Advice

Many companies are competing for your premium dollar, so don't fall prey to marketing strategies that may cause unnecessary rate increases in the future. Companies that offer very low premiums compared to most of the other companies, sell policies to people with significant health problems, and make it very easy to obtain benefits (see **Claims** on p. 93) are at a higher than average risk for rate increases—particularly if the company is small. (There are companies selling long-term care insurance with $100 million in assets and there are companies with $100 billion and more in assets.)

You can also call your insurance department to ask about rate increase activity as well as any complaints that have been filed against the insurance company. (See *Appendix B* for the contact information for your state's insurance department.)

Chapter 3

Long-Term Care Insurance: The New Employee Benefit

〜〜〜〜〜〜〜〜〜〜〜〜〜〜〜〜〜〜〜〜〜〜〜〜

*Disruptions and absenteeism due to employees' caregiving duties
cost U.S. employers up to $33.6 billion per year.*[1]
—*Caregiving in America,* The Schmieding Center
and The International Longevity Center-USA

More than 9,200 employers in the United States offered long-term care insurance to their employees in 2007.[2] This number is expected to explode in this century, as the average boomer now has more parents than children to care for,[3] and productivity losses due to caregiving are growing astronomically. If you think this isn't going to be a big deal, think again. A recent study said each year 21 percent of American households provide assistance to ill, disabled or aging persons.[4]

The fuse to encourage employers to offer long-term care insurance was lit by 1996 health care reform and fueled by the implementation of a group long-term care insurance plan for Federal employees in 2002. Benefits from policies issued January 1, 1997 and later are tax-free to employees whether the employee or the employer pays the premium. Premium contributions are now a business expense to employers and are not classified as taxable income to employees. Then in 2004, Health Savings Accounts became a reality. A growing number of employers are offering and even partially funding HSAs as a meaningful way to hold down costs in their health insurance plans with the higher deductibles and out-of-pocket thresholds made possible by Health Savings Accounts. The fortunate employee who has an HSA can pay the age-based allowable long-term care insurance premium with pre-tax dollars (see **Tax Incentives for Long-Term Care Insurance** in Chapter One).

With employer-sponsored plans having doubled in the last five years,[5] the new laws appear to be propelling the number of employers on the fence about long-term care insurance to make it available to huge numbers of Americans in the very near future.

If legislation is the fuse, employee demand is the bomb, and it is exploding.

▲ Seventy-seven percent of employees ranked LTCI as a top financial concern in a 2006 survey.[6]

▲ LTCI is the third most popular voluntary benefit with Baby Boomers but is the #1 voluntary benefit requested but not offered.[7]

▲ Nearly half of employees in The MetLife Survey of Employee Benefits Trends were concerned about providing for their own, their spouses and their parents' long-term care needs.[8]

Employers are responding to the outcry. The same MetLife survey reported that long-term care insurance "experienced the greatest rise in importance in terms of the most valued employee benefit among workers".[9]

What is driving this intense and urgent demand from employees? Quite simply, it's the caregiving needs in their personal lives that threaten to eclipse their professional lives.

Consider that 7.7 million American households are in the "sandwich generation" of caring for both children and parents,[10] and out of that is hatching caregiving demands unlike our society has ever known.

One out of four baby boomers ages 45 to 54 provided elder care in 2001 and 41 percent of Americans in this age group expect caregiving to increase in the next five years." [11]

There are approximately seven million Americans involved in long-distance caregiving for a relative or friend who lives more than an hour away.[12]

Nearly seven in ten (69 percent) respondents ages 18-79 to a 2006 John Hancock survey said that "providing care and/or assistance significantly affected their personal lives, and 62 percent said that it had a significant impact on family. Almost half (45 percent) said that caregiving significantly affected their work, and 37 percent said it significantly changed their financial situation." [13]

As baby boomers are watching the phenomenal emotional and financial price exacted on parents and grandparents who haven't planned ahead, the result is a generation that is demanding a better way. Existing health insurance and Medicare don't pay for long-term care, and the dependent care benefit that allows employees to set aside $5,000 tax-free annually for elder or child care is just a drop in a bottomless bucket with long-term care averaging $60,000 a year on up. So employees in all size companies are searching for answers through long-term care insurance. Consequently, many insurance and financial professionals are now jumping on the bandwagon, using cutting edge technology and processes to educate employers, clients, and employees about the escalating risk of long-term care.

Surprisingly, the largest growth is in small firms. In 2007, new employer-sponsored long-term care insurance plans averaged 81 participants.[14] This is probably happening for two reasons:

▲   small companies feel the productivity loss caused by caregiving needs more dramatically than large employers; and

▲   small business owners can react to a problem and make quicker decisions than large companies.

This trend will be stimulated as more people understand that long-term care insurance can be paid for with pre-tax dollars through Health Savings Accounts (see p. 18 in Chapter 1, **Tax Incentives for Long-Term Care Insurance**).

There are several kinds of long-term care insurance plans available today for employees and their families.

A growing number of insurance companies are offering their individual long-term care insurance product to small employers, all the way down to a minimum of three applications in a group. Employees have to answer only three or four health questions to be eligible. Assuming the employee is actively at work and the answer to the questions is "No," the employee is approved for a policy. Spouses and eligible family members answer all the health questions, except a new trend in 2008 is also to allow the spouse to apply with limited health questions. Finally, employees, spouses and eligible family members like parents and in-laws are entitled to a group discount of 10%–15%. This is called a multi-life product, since it is really an individual product that provides a premium discount and underwriting concessions because several people are applying at once.

"True group" long-term care insurance offered through larger employers typically allows the employee to get coverage without checking the employee's health. (A few plans treat the spouse the same way.) This "guaranteed issue" coverage for the employee normally is available only to large employers, but at least one insurance company offers it to employers as small as 15 employees as long as the employer pays the premium. Typically, however, insurance companies want 150 or more employees to provide coverage without health questions and may require the employer to contribute to the premium, at least for groups with less than 500. A couple of these group plans will even provide a small policy to employees who are declined for health reasons.[15]

Both multi-life and true group plans usually offer coverage to employees, spouses, parents, grandparents, siblings, adult children and all respective in-laws from age 18 to age 79, and some have no maximum age limit. At this point you may be rolling your eyes with wonder at why an 18-year-old would ever apply for long-term care insurance. This story explains it well.

> *My company had the honor of being heavily involved with the employee education effort for the Federal Long-Term Care Insurance Program. When it was first introduced, we conducted 2,020 employee education meetings in*

43 states and 210 cities and also produced a video and "webinar" with similar information in an attempt to reach the 20 million eligible civilian, military and postal employees, retirees, and their families. When filming the video, the studio manager shared with me that his 22-year-old son had been away in college just four months ago and had sustained an injury that paralyzed him from the shoulders down in a car accident. His son is now back at home in the care of his parents for the rest of his life. His story left such an impression on me that when we are in front of employees, we always ask if they have a "20-something" adult child for whom they would be responsible if the child became a victim of similar circumstances.

The premium for both the employee and spouse's portion of the premium is automatically deducted from the employee's paycheck via payroll deduction. Family members may be billed directly or the employer may allow the insurance company to deduct premium for family members out of the employee's paycheck as well. This particularly happens when parents buy it on their adult children. If the employee terminates employment or retires, the policy is portable and the employee may keep the coverage, usually at the same premium and the same benefits.

Some would argue that the multi-life product is more reliable because each applicant is a policy owner. With true group plans, the employer is the policy owner and changes in benefits and premium may occur if the employer switches carriers. This can happen if the new carrier doesn't want to take over the existing plans with the same benefits and premium, usually because the two insurance companies couldn't reach an agreement about transferring the money that is being reserved to pay claims.

Employees are buying long-term care insurance for two reasons: to help with the escalating need for elder care, and for their own long-term care needs. Let's address the need for elder care first.

Productivity Insurance

The National Alliance for Caregiving/AARP study referenced earlier reports that almost half of the 13 million caregivers who provide substantial assistance to the people they take care of are employed full or part-time.[16] About 13 percent of the workforce today provide care,[17] and as noted in the last section, a large number of employees are very concerned about paying for long-term care for themselves, their spouses and their parents.[18] How will productivity be affected by these staggering long-term care needs?

The National Alliance for Caregiving/AARP study portrayed the following list of sacrifices made by employed caregivers who provided help with two or more Activities of Daily Living (ADLs) for 40 or more hours a week.[19]

Of *all* caregivers, 57 percent had to make changes at work to accommodate caregiving, but 83 percent of the most intense caregivers (helping with at least two ADLs for 40+ hours per week) had to make changes to their daily work schedule, 35 percent had to give up work entirely, 12 percent took early retirement and 41 percent took a leave of absence.[20]

An Indiana University study reports that middle-aged women who become caregivers for an ill or disabled family member are more likely to leave their jobs altogether than reduce their hours.[21] This could be true because the recipient gets progressively sicker and requires more care over time, or because either the caregiver

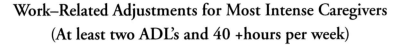

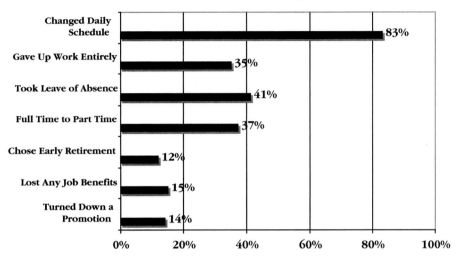

Work–Related Adjustments for Most Intense Caregivers
(At least two ADL's and 40 +hours per week)

- Changed Daily Schedule — 83%
- Gave Up Work Entirely — 35%
- Took Leave of Absence — 41%
- Full Time to Part Time — 37%
- Chose Early Retirement — 12%
- Lost Any Job Benefits — 15%
- Turned Down a Promotion — 14%

or the employer is no longer comfortable with having to make workplace accommodations. The MetLife Mature Market Institute and National Alliance for Caregiving estimates replacement costs to be 50 percent of the annual salary of the employee who quits.[22]

Born in 1919 and married at 15 to Everett Corker, Margie Evelyn Bowles Corker devoted her life to motherhood. She raised her children, Justine and Bill, with strength of character, teaching them to respect others and to aspire to high values and the reflective behavior. When Terri and Perry put in their surprise appearance 20 years after Justine, she hadn't changed—they received the same basic values training as their older brother and sister. Statistically, they beat the odds—not one black sheep out of a flock of four. Margie wondered when Terri, the younger of the twins, turned toward music, and she really worried when Terri left home to tour with a popular singer.

Her fears were groundless. Terri's straight-arrow upbringing didn't fit with life on the road where booze and drugs were the roadmap.

When lung cancer took Everett in a few short months in 1983, West Virginia didn't seem as confining, but Terri knew the music couldn't happen there. A few years after his death, she made the move to Nashville, with Margie in tow, who was already using a crutch due to the instability caused by degenerating arthritis. Her mother refused to drive in the big city, and the role reversal began.

Renting an apartment with her mother, Terri couldn't afford the footloose, hand-to-mouth existence of many Nashville musicians, nor did she want to live that way. She advanced in her day job to Operations Manager with an industrial supply firm and worked the songwriter venues nights and weekends. After several years of dues-paying, some of her original songs were recorded and things looked promising. Then Margie's health began to fail rapidly. Terri gave up a weekly songwriter night she had hosted for two years and began to pass paying music "gigs" to other musicians. Her first CD coincided with a blur of breast cancer, surgeries due to severe arthritis, pneumonia, congestive heart failure and an endless stream of multiple medications. The CD bypassed the back seat and went into the trunk of her life. Personal relationships came and went as Terri's first priority was to Margie. She wrote three new songs instead of 10 the following year. Terri saved furiously, knowing what was ahead, even though she had to pay a sitter three hours a day to help Margie with her meals. She never returned to work after a four-month leave of absence from her job in 1998 while Margie underwent extensive radiation treatments.

After Margie's death in January 2000, the eight year circus finally ended. Five months after the funeral, Terri was still looking for the identity she felt she had lost through it all. She doesn't regret the time with her mother in any way—she's just trying to assess where she is at age 42 with her career, her personal life, and what's left after the many years of caregiving that brought her to this point. Her motto "The only routine is there is none" no longer applies. Have the years of caregiving stolen her dream for a music career?

Even long-distance caregivers who don't do the most intense caregiving and live more than an hour away from their older family members devote an average of 35 hours a month, equal to nearly one work week, to providing or arranging housekeeping, meals and other services for these aging family members, says a MetLife Mature Market Institute study. Twelve percent of these long-distance caregivers report taking unpaid leave from work, and more than a third have missed work days periodically.[23]

The really astounding bird's-eye view is that among all caregivers, not just intense or long-distance, 22 percent have provided care for five to nine years, and 10 percent for 10 years or more.[24]

Caregiving Periods

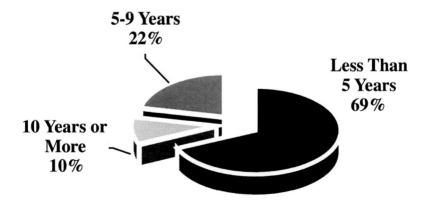

5-9 Years 22%

Less Than 5 Years 69%

10 Years or More 10%

And the chart below adds a whole new meaning to the term "multi-tasking". Seven in ten caregivers provide care to just one person, but 23 percent take care of two people, and eight percent care for three or more people![25]

Caregivers' Responsibilities

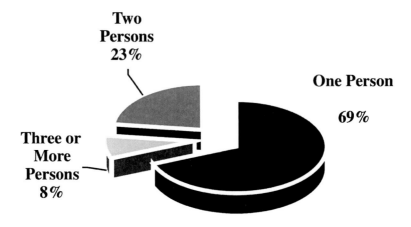

Two Persons 23%

One Person

69%

Three or More Persons 8%

Caregiving responsibilities have a number of hidden impacts on job performance and overall company expenses, including:[26]

▲ workday interruptions to handle emergencies and phone calls

▲ absenteeism

▲ increased employee stress often resulting in health-related problems

▲ increased necessity for time off and leaves from work

▲ decreased willingness to relocate or travel for work

▲ decisions to cut back to part-time or leave the work force altogether

▲ decrease in motivation and morale due to pressures outside the workplace

▲ decline in productivity

▲ replacement costs (10 percent of employees went from full-time to part-time and six percent left work entirely to manage caregiving responsibilities)[27]

The annual price tag for employers is somewhere around $33 billion,[28] although a new Alzheimer's study puts costs to employers at $88 billion for Alzheimer's alone![29] This list just adds up to one big word for the employee: Stress.

Since most people under 65 must work, long-term care insurance can provide a wonderful solution to employees with elder care needs. LTC insurance provides financial assistance, which in turn reduces stress levels by allowing the employee to keep his or her job, and by giving the employee peace of mind knowing that the parent or in-law is receiving high quality care while the employee is at work.

What if you can't afford to pay your parent's premium by yourself? You might consider entering into a multiple support agreement with your siblings under which together, all of you agree to provide funds for the parent so that the parent can be claimed as a dependent for income tax purposes. If you do it soon enough, your brothers and sisters can also join in purchasing an LTC insurance policy for the parent.

This way, the LTC insurance policy can relieve both children's and parents' anxiety by making sure that many choices for care exist when needed, i.e., alternatives to nursing home care, which is usually the only option when the patient is on Medicaid. The LTC insurance policy also acts to safeguard the children's inheritance instead of spending the parents' savings on long-term care expenses. Many attorneys recommend LTC insurance policies for this reason.

Part or all of the premium based on the parent's age is counted as a medical expense and becomes a potential tax deduction for the child paying the premium, as long as the parent is a dependent. (This just means the child or children must provide greater than 50 percent of the parent's support.) In the case of multiple support agreements as explained above, one child each year can take the tax deduction as long as that child contributed at least ten percent of the parent's support for that tax year.

The wave of the future is companies like Lancaster Labs in Lancaster, Pennsylvania, which offers on-site adult day care at a reasonable cost to employees of $45 per day, in addition to on-site child care.[30] Long-term care insurance will pay for adult day care. How many insurance policies will pay for child care?

Susan Meisinger, President and CEO of The Society for Human Resource Management, said "The increasing need for elder care is an inevitability. Employers have an opportunity to either anticipate and manage it in a way that benefits both the employer and employees, or let it smack them in the face a few years from now, dragging down productivity and increasing turnover as a result. Organizations simply can't afford to ignore the cost of this reality."

Lifestyle Insurance

Numbers like this affect all segments of society, but the fastest growing segment of corporate America—small business—has a huge stake in this problem. Many Americans look forward to getting their children at least in high school or even through college, and then experiencing

"The American Dream"—starting the business they've always dreamed of. Starting a business usually means long hours—60+ hours a week is not unusual for the entrepreneur. Suddenly, a spouse, parent, or in-law has an accident or a stroke, and caregiving becomes the #1 priority. The dream never happens.

Bev Fulkerson is 42. On the surface, her life seems to be going well. She just got a promotion to state director of a new suicide prevention grant for a crisis intervention center in Nashville, Tennessee. Without talking with her, you wouldn't know how deeply she appreciates being back in the workforce with a meaningful job. Her appreciation is tinged with sadness, however, because it means she isn't running her own private practice as an addictions /mental health counselor for adolescents, a business she tried to start six months ago.

Two years ago, her energetic 72-year-old mother, known for her pep, spunk and tremendous sense of humor, entered a Louisville, Kentucky, hospital for a routine heart bypass. Her father's similar surgery a year earlier had kept him in the hospital a mere five days. The day of the surgery, Bev accepted a new job as director of a counseling center just outside of Nashville that catered to adolescents. After 16 years in the field, she was ecstatic.

Her mother came home 12 ½ months later.

Allergic to the medications used during surgery, her recovery time stretched past two months. Just as she was being transferred to the rehabilitation wing, she couldn't shake the feeling that something was wrong, that the wound wasn't healing properly. She had a staph infection, a phrase that strikes terror to anyone in the medical profession, especially the people who handle the billing and the legal functions. Did the hospital cause it? Will the exorbitant bill be paid in full? (Mrs. Fulkerson's bill went over $2 million.)

It was five more months before the actual rehabilitation treatment could begin and another three before she was transferred to an independent skilled nursing facility in Louisville. She was there 3 ½ months before coming home, unable to walk or even turn herself in bed. She began eight months of home health care which ended in mid-April, 2000. Today her youthful looks have dissipated, she has lost 70 pounds, and her sense of humor is a dim light in the distance. In the midst of the hospital stay, Bev was successful at getting an anti-depressant prescribed for her mother only after four months of insisting and a meeting with the hospital administrator, a feat which deeply underscores the need for family advocacy even when someone is in a medical facility. Bev was lucky. Her younger brother in Louisville took a three-month family leave when the problems began and has been extremely supportive during the entire episode. Bev was able to keep her job by commuting to Louisville, two hours away, every weekend and usually at least once during the week for two years.

Last December, when it looked like Mrs. Fulkerson might actually come out of it, Bev decided to go for her big dream, which was to start her own private practice as an adolescent counselor. By January, she was ready to go. Then her father discovered a lump in his groin, and was diagnosed with lymphoma. Her mother couldn't be left alone during the weeks of extensive testing, so for Bev, the nightmare began all over again.

The good news is that the lymphoma appears to be dormant so no ongoing treatment is necessary and Bev is free to return to the workforce. The bad news is that financially she no longer has the resources to start her own practice. In her words, "The dream of having a private practice went out the back window. Anything I wanted to do or needed to do for myself is put on the back burner."

The following caregiver wasn't so fortunate.

Linda, a 48-year-old supervisor at a bank and a divorced mother of two children in college, had planned a very different life for herself.

Five years ago she was anticipating her youngest child's departure for college and looking forward to a new personal chapter in her life—a chapter that included more time for herself, a chance to study art history and perhaps even a second career. Instead, her mother, previously an independent and active widow in her early 70's, was diagnosed with Alzheimer's disease. Since then, Linda's dreams have ceased to exist. Her mother has lived with her three years, with Linda footing the bill for adult day care so she can continue working. The strain on her budget is unbelievable, especially when combined with the cost of drugs and a few other medical services not covered by Medicare.

Linda also had never imagined how difficult things would be as a result of no personal time. She misses her shopping trips, movies with her friends and is frustrated by her inability to attend parent functions at her children's colleges. But the hardest part is the isolation she feels. She doesn't want people at work to think she's down all the time.

The caregiving responsibilities Linda has undertaken will continue to increase, especially now that her mom has started wandering at all hours.

The above caregiving story is an excerpt from the National Family Caregivers Association (NFCA)/Fortis Report, members of which are primarily involved in intense caregiving situations. The NCFA web site's fact sheet about family caregivers reports that 61 percent of intense caregivers (21 hours per week and up) have suffered from depression.[31]

The most reported emotion is a sense of isolation, even among the employed, because, like Linda, they probably feel as though they have to be "up" while on the job.

Suzanne Mintz is the president and co-founder of the NCFA. Ironically, her husband was diagnosed with multiple sclerosis, and in taking care of him without regard to the toll it took on her own health, she succumbed to depression. In fighting her way back, she has become a voice for the nation's caregivers and speaks nationally on the importance of asking for help from other family members. She says that anywhere from 30 percent to 59 percent of family caregivers suffer depression.[32]

A Georgetown University study said "Caregivers often report feeling frustrated, angry, drained, guilty, or helpless a result of providing care. Caregiving can also result in feeling a loss of self identity, lower levels of self-esteem, depression, constant worry or feelings of uncertainty."[33]

The 2006 John Hancock caregiver survey reported that seven in ten respondents said that caregiving significantly affected their personal lives. Sixty-two percent said it had a significant impact on their family, almost half said it significantly affected their work, and 37 percent said caregiving significantly changed their financial situation. When asked how they paid for the care, the answer was through mostly personal sources:

- 27 percent used money set aside for immediate goals such as a new car or vacation
- 15 percent used money set aside for retirement
- 13 percent used current income/money out of pocket
- 7 percent used savings

Finally, 12 percent gave up a job to provide care, which is counterproductive to spending extra money to care for their family member or friend.[34]

If they don't give up a job, it's easy to see from these numbers that caregivers often suffer significant drops in income as a result of a caregiving situation. Genworth Financial's "The Impact of Long Term Care on Women" quantified an average total lost wealth amount of $660,000 ($566,433 lost wages, which caused an average of $25,494 in lost Social Security benefits since they couldn't work as much and earn as much, and for those eligible, losses in pension benefits averaging $67,202). The Genworth study also said there are 10.6 million woman-owned businesses and taking time off to care for a family member can put the business at risk.[35] You read in Chapter One, *Long-Term Care and Your Financial Security,* that the number of majority (51 percent or more) women-owned employer firms has grown at twice the growth rate of all employer firms in the last decade.[36] So you can see that caregiving has a tremendous effect on our entire economy, not to mention each individual employer who suffers the loss of a good employee.

What sacrifices were made in both time and money in these families? How did each individual family member suffer? How welcome would a home health aide providing at least 40 hours of care per week have been? The most frequently reported unmet needs are finding time for myself (35%), managing emotional and physical stress (29%), and balancing work and family responsibilities (29%).[37]

The typical caregiver in the National Alliance for Caregiving/ AARP study is a married woman in her mid-40s who works full or part-time and provides more than 20 hours of care each week. One out of five of these typical caregivers provided 40 or more hours of care a week.[38]

How do you function in an executive position or grow your own business with those kind of hours? Now let's throw in another dimension. The really hard part comes when caring for children and parents or grandparents happens simultaneously. At least 12 percent of caregivers are both employed and have children under age 18 at home.[39] The second annual Allstate "Retirement Reality Check" survey reported that nearly ten percent of baby boomers and 19 percent of Hispanic baby boomers expect to be sandwiched by responsibilities for both parents and children during retirement.[40] African-American women are more likely to say they are working and have children under 18 at home while they are caregivers.[41]

Because the predominant number of caregivers are women, caregiving may turn out to be the biggest threat to the women's movement in this century. Women fight so hard to achieve the professional success level they want, then overnight the dream can vanish when a spouse or parent has an accident or stroke. With intense caregiving, the caregiver can quickly reach a point at which they can't handle a job and caregiving duties at the same time.

Here is an example of what the incredible pressure from both ends looks like:

> *Jenny is an example of multigenerational caregiving. Jenny and her husband provide support for her 88-year-old mother and her husband's 89-year-old mother, and their 28-year-old daughter just moved back home with her three children ages six and under. Jenny's name was on a prayer request list.*[42]

Families can't do it alone. They have to have help, and long-term care insurance may be the main key to the help they need, in addition to lots of prayers! The National Alliance for Caregiving/AARP study says "prayer is the most common way of coping with the stresses and strains of caregiving— three in four caregivers use this method."[43] Future long-term care insurance policies may earn the name "lifestyle insurance," because the policy may be the only thing that allows an adult child to continue a career or even keep a marriage from falling apart from the strain of a caregiving need of a very long duration.

Well-known columnist Terry Savage from the *Chicago Sun-Times* wrote about buying long-term care insurance on her parents in the June/July 2000 issue of *Mirabella* magazine:

When I bought a policy for each of my parents as a holiday gift a few years ago, the reaction was predictable. My father smiled and thanked me...and then went out for a jog. My mother's reaction was a little more emotional: "After your grandmother, you promised you'd never..." The words trailed off as we both remembered. Then I smiled at her and reminded her that this policy would pay for someone to come into her home and give needed care. We'd never have to face the issue of a nursing home (I hope and pray). And if we do, I know I've ensured her the best of care. That's why I also bought a policy for myself.

Long-term care does not happen to an individual. It happens to the entire family, and this popular columnist sees this clearly.

Long-Term Care Insurance Is Not "Senior Citizen Insurance"

Long-Term Care and Your Financial Security explained there is a greater than 60 percent chance of needing either home health, assisted living or nursing home care at age 65, if you don't need it at a younger age.[44] The two-edged sword of long-term care is that it can be needed at any age. As noted on p. 9, 40 percent of Americans needing long-term care today are working age adults ages 18-64![45] Only about 12 percent of nursing home patients are under 65,[46] so most of these younger people needing long-term care are being cared for in the community, at a very large sacrifice for family members. Consider these actual cases:

▲   After earning his Doctorate in Psychology from Tennessee State University in 1994, Alan Yarbrough developed a successful private practice serving a wide range of clients including school-age children, teenagers, adults, and the geriatric population. In November 2002 at age 49, Dr. Yarbrough was diagnosed with ALS (Lou Gehrig's disease) and eventually closed his private practice in 2004 when he lost his speech to the disease. Today, he has written several books, including "Letters to My Teen" (21st Century Christian, 2007), which began as letters to his 16-year-old daughter to express his feelings, advice and concepts in a lasting way. The initial writing took three months. As he can no longer use his hands, a laser patch on his chin allows him to point at letters, which are then transferred to a laptop computer. [47]

▲ A 25-year-old Cookeville, Tennessee, man who slammed into the side of a dump truck that pulled out in front of his motorcycle was discharged from a nursing home seven months later after an extended coma, then spent the next three years relearning every skill he was born with. His wife's life stopped with his as she stayed by his side throughout.[48]

▲ A young couple in their mid-30s were joyfully looking forward to the birth of their triplets due in late July 2005. In mid-June, the doctor decided to deliver the babies the Sunday before Father's Day. The births were successful. All three babies weighed 4-5 lbs and were very healthy. Then disaster struck. In the middle of the night, the new mom had a stroke – a blood clot went straight to her brain. Her husband was spending the night with her and called the nurses. Her room was next to the surgery center – the doctors did immediate surgery and didn't think she would live through the surgery. She lived. After a coma that lasted three weeks, she woke up and was fine mentally but was paralyzed on her left side permanently. She was transferred to a nursing home for a projected four month stay, leaving her husband to manage three new babies and eventually find home care for her. Their cousin, a successful insurance broker, had sold them disability insurance and life insurance. Who would have thought they would need long-term care insurance? [49]

And consider the nursing home stories of younger people:

▲   a 50-year-old man who is in a nursing home from a May, 1999 stroke that incapacitated his left arm, the only independent functioning part of his body left from a bout with polio as a child. [50]

▲   a successful attorney who suffered a cerebral brain hemorrhage at age 41 and has been in a nursing home for the last eight years. A divorced father, he had an 11-year-old son when it happened. After six months at a well-known rehabilitation center, he was still paralyzed on one side of his body and could not take care of himself. His reasoning has returned but he has to have help with all of his basic activities of daily living except eating. [51]

▲   Here's a personal story close to my heart:

My cousin Carolyn was beautiful. She was my favorite baby sitter when I was four. She could play the piano by ear and I remember watching her with awe on our black and white television when she played "Down Yonder" on a local television station when I was five. She was in high school and went to all the dances -- she could jitter-bug like nobody's business. I loved to watch her get dressed for a dance in her pretty dance dresses of all colors with huge crinoline petticoats under them. My favorite one was the red dress. With her raven black hair and sparkling brown eyes, it made her look gorgeous. Maybe I loved her so much because every day when she combed my long hair after my nap, she made me feel pretty, too.

Carolyn suffered a massive stroke at age 61. She has been in a nursing home five years and can do nothing for herself. She is tube-fed, paralyzed on one side of her body, and can't speak.

A really sad part to this story is that her husband assured me years ago that he bought the group long-term care insurance plan offered through his employer. When Carolyn had the stroke and I rushed to the hospital to be with them and their three children, I said "Aren't you so glad you bought that long-term care insurance, Lester? Now she can be taken care of and you won't have to worry." Instead of the expression of relief that I expected, his answer astonished me. "We didn't get it," he said in a flat tone. He had just told me that several years ago to stop me from bringing it up. Carolyn is in a nursing home today as a Medicaid patient in a room with two other people, occasionally three. But when I visit her, her eyes speak volumes of love so I know my favorite cousin is still here.

A quick reminder: conventional group health insurance does not cover long-term care because it covers mainly skilled care in a nursing home or at home, and almost all long-term care does not require skilled care. People who just need help with bathing, getting in and out of bed, taking medicine, toileting, eating, etc. do not receive payment for this type of help from conventional health insurance. A perfect example of someone who needs this type of help and who is not helped by traditional health insurance is someone who is paralyzed from an accident or stroke. Once the patient settles into a chronic, maintenance state and just needs help with basic activities of daily living, payment for caregiving stops under regular health insurance.

After 50 years of marriage, my Uncle Rawleigh still prided himself on taking care of my Aunt 'Net who never learned to drive. He assured me that he did not need long-term care insurance when I approached him early in my long-term care insurance career in 1991. He was positive his General Motors retiree health insurance would take care of it. I didn't push it since I had no idea how it would affect my life 15 years later. When my Aunt 'Net became unable to walk due to severe degeneration of her knee, she had to go to a nursing home. My uncle was on oxygen by that time, due to emphysema. My aunt had been his caregiver as he was growing more frail each day. They both needed help so he had me call General Motors to ask about his benefits for home care and nursing home care. He just couldn't believe it when I confirmed what I had told him in 1991 – no coverage for either. My aunt's nursing home bill was paid by Medicare for a couple of months while she received physical therapy for the knee. As she was too old and too heavy to be a candidate for knee surgery, her condition was declared chronic, maintenance care and Medicare stopped paying. She couldn't go home because at 250 pounds, my uncle couldn't begin to lift her in and out of bed.

I had to help them through the Medicaid spend-down process, including taking most of the cash value of their life insurance policies, to get her qualified for Medicaid. He had to pay out-of-pocket for a caregiver at home for 11 hours per day. I live four hours away but talked with him almost daily and heard the heartbreak in his voice as he realized he had no insurance coverage for either of them for long-term care. He was such a planner and thought he had all his bases covered. When he died a few months later, I had to finish the spend-down process to keep her on Medicaid, including the sale of their home.

Becoming a caregiver for my aunt and uncle was not on my radar screen. They had no children but were very close to my first cousin, Elizabeth Ann. Elizabeth Ann died of lung cancer at age 54. Then my cousin Carolyn who lived a few blocks away became their main support person. After her stroke at age 61, I was next in line for the responsibility and gladly consented to be Power of Attorney for financial and medical issues, because they were always kind to me. The moral to my story is that you can't say that you will never be a caregiver. I am now one of seven million long-distance caregivers. Life has its surprises.

Many younger people think disability income insurance takes care of them. Disability income coverage just provides money with which to pay bills (mortgage, utilities, food, etc.) and does not provide an extra $3,000-$6,000 a month to pay for long-term care expenses.

The Life Insurance Market Research Association (LIMRA) reports that the average age of employees who have purchased long-term care insurance in 2005 is 46.[52] Younger people are more likely to see long-term care insurance as just another part of their plan for retirement. The money accumulated in pension plans, 401K, investments, annuities, real estate, etc., is in jeopardy if long-term care is needed. The 40-year-old today is facing long-term care expenses of almost $600,000 per year in 40 years if present trends continue with an annual growth rate of 5.8 percent.[53]

Tips for Benefit Choices in Group Long-Term Care Insurance Plans

Group long-term care insurance plans are similar to individual policies, but there are a few specific areas you should check before deciding on a plan:

Inflation Coverage—You may be offered a plan with or without inflation coverage. **BUY INFLATION COVERAGE.** There are different types of inflation coverage. For example, you may be offered a plan with low premiums now and a chance to buy additional coverage in the future. Usually, if you have a claim, these offers are withdrawn. If you are offered the opportunity to buy a plan that guarantees your daily or monthly benefit will grow automatically each year as long as you hold the policy, take it. The premium will be more than the other kind in the beginning, but you will pay much less over the long haul and your benefit has a much better chance of keeping up with the rising cost of long-term care. Also, if you have a claim, your benefit will continue to grow and in most plans, your premium will stop. Select the automatic increase option that grows compounded (not simple) each year and only the benefit should increase annually, not the premium, unless the premium stops growing at a certain age, like age 65.

Home Health Care—Many group plans offer benefits that cover long-term care outside of the nursing home, such as home health care, adult day care, foster home care, etc. as an option. You are well advised to take it because even today, nursing home care makes up only 15 percent of the long-term care picture.[54] With the baby boomers' aversion to nursing home care, it is expected research will provide more and more ways to provide future long-term care in the community.[55] If you have a choice between a home care benefit that pays less than the nursing home benefit (i.e., 50%) and one that pays equal to the nursing home benefit, choose the one that is equal (the best choice), or at least 75%-80%, since home care costs can equal or exceed nursing home costs, depending on how many hours you have.

Non-forfeiture/Return of Premium Benefits—Some group plans include a return of premium at death benefit and you have no choice but to accept it. Others offer this benefit as an option or they offer the shortened benefit period option we discussed in Chapter Two, *Features of a Good Long-Term Care Insurance Policy.* If extra premium is charged for this privilege, analyze carefully if the extra premium is a wise expenditure. The odds are great that you will use the coverage, never get any money back, and you will have paid the extra premium for nothing. You might be better off putting the extra premium in your 401K or other retirement fund or a mutual fund, etc., or use it to buy a higher level of benefit: an increased dollar amount of coverage, or better inflation or home care benefits.

Also, some group plans don't offer a lifetime (unlimited) benefit period or shorter waiting periods like 20, 30 or 60 days unless you specifically request them.

Here is a summary of why employees are buying long-term care insurance:

1) To take care of their own long-term care needs, as the need can occur at any age.

2) To help with elder care needs so they can continue working while taking care of aging family members.

3) To take advantage of underwriting concessions for themselves, in particular since the employee usually gets covered with few or no health questions, and for any available underwriting breaks for spouses who may

find it more difficult to qualify medically for individual LTCI policies.

4) To take advantage of lower group premiums for themselves and their eligible family members, such as parents, siblings, grandparents, and adult children.

5) To help the private sector fund the long-term care crisis, because the more people who wind up in nursing homes on Medicaid (welfare), the higher our taxes will be to help the government pay the bill. (Sweden has a national long-term care program and a tax rate greater than 50 percent!)[56]

You may be able to enroll in a group or association long-term care plan by mail, but you and your spouse should attend any meetings held by your employer or association so you will get a first-hand explanation of long-term care issues and the products offered. Your parents and in-laws are usually welcome at these educational meetings.

Whether you review the Federal Long-Term Care Insurance Program following this section or private group or individual long-term care insurance policies—**DON'T WAIT** to purchase a policy for yourself and anyone you even think you may wind up taking care of. **Caregivers whose family members have long-term care insurance are twice as likely to stay in the workforce as those whose family members don't have long-term care insurance.**[57] American families desperately need to prepare today for a long-term care need that could strike at any time.

The Federal Long-Term Care Insurance Program
(The Long Term Care Security Act of 2000)

The largest employer-sponsored long-term care insurance program with eligibility estimated at 20 million people, was launched in March of 2002 with limited benefits, and expanded during Open Season (July 1 – December 31, 2002) with full benefits and abbreviated underwriting for active employees and spouses. The Office of Personnel Management (OPM) selected John Hancock and MetLife to offer The Federal Long Term Care Insurance Program (FLTCIP) and those two companies formed a new company, Long Term Care Partners (LTCP). Long-Term Care Partners is exclusively dedicated to serving the long-term care insurance needs of the Federal Family.

Even though Open Season has ended, the FLTCIP is still available with full underwriting to all eligible classifications of the Federal Family. A good rule of thumb is to realize that it is offered to anyone who is eligible for the Federal Employees Health Benefits Program – they don't have to be enrolled in the FEHB, just be eligible for it, and they have to be eligible at the time they apply for FLTCIP. (This means it's not enough to just have FEHB because they could have FEHB due to a continuation of coverage provision and no longer be eligible for it.) Two exceptions: 1) Tennessee Valley Authority employees are not eligible for FEHB but **are** eligible for FLTCIP and 2) Some District of Columbia employees and retirees are eligible for FEHB, but **are not** eligible for FLTCIP.

Eligibility

<u>**Actives:**</u>

▲ Federal Civilian and Postal Employees in positions that convey eligibility for the Federal Employees Health Benefits Program, whether or not they are enrolled in the FEHB (must be in pay status).

▲ Tennessee Valley Authority employees (even though they may not be eligible for FEHB coverage)

▲ D.C. Government employees who were first employed by the D.C. Government before October 1, 1987

▲ D.C. Courts employees

▲ Navy Personnel Command (BUPERS) NAF employees Temporary employees have to complete one year of continuous current employment. Non-appropriated fund employees are not eligible to apply. (These are people who work on military bases in the PBX exchange or commissaries who are paid out of funds not appropriated from Congress.)

▲ Members of the Uniformed Services, including National Guard (must be on active duty at least 30 days)

▲ Selected Reserve but not the Individual Ready Reserve- Selected Reserve includes Drilling Reservists and Guardsmembers assigned to Reserve Component Units; Individual Mobilization Augmentees who are

Reservists assigned to Reserve component billets in Active Component units, performing duty in a pay or nonpay status; Active Guard and Reserve members who are full-time Reserve members on full-time National Guard duty or active duty in support of the National Guard or Reserves

Annuitants (Retirees)

▲ Federal Civilian and Postal annuitants, including survivor and deferred annuitants

▲ Retired Members of the Uniformed Services who are entitled to retired or retainer pay

▲ Retired "Grey" Reservists, even if they are not yet receiving their retired pay

▲ Separated employees with title to a deferred annuity, even if they are not yet receiving that annuity

▲ Tennessee Valley Authority annuitants

▲ Compensationers receiving compensation from the Department of Labor

▲ D.C. Government annuitants first employed by the D.C. Government before October 1, 1987

▲ D.C. Courts annuitants

▲ Navy Personnel Command (BUPERS) NAF annuitants

The "five-year rule" doesn't apply – this means there is no requirement to have had the coverage for a designated length of time as an employee in order to be able to carry it into retirement.

Qualified Relatives (even if employee, annuitant, member or retired member of Uniformed Services does not apply or applies and is declined)

▲ Current spouses, including surviving spouses of a member or retired member of the uniformed services as long as they are receiving a survivor annuity. Receipt of Dependency and Indemnity Compensation (DIC) from the Dept. of Veterans Affairs qualifies as a survivor annuity. (Former spouses are not eligible even if eligible for FEHB and/or receiving a survivor annuity.

▲ Parents, parents-in-law and stepparents (those of annuitants and retired members of the Uniformed Services are not eligible)

▲ Parents-in-law include parents of a deceased spouse, as long as the employee or member of the Uniformed Services has not remarried

▲ Stepparent must be currently married to the employee's parent or was married to the parent at the time of the parent's death

▲ Adult children 18 and up (includes adopted and stepchildren, but not foster children) but spouses of adult children are not eligible unless they fall into another eligible group

Applicants must be age 18 and up. There is no age maximum.

Benefits

You may want to review Chapter Two, *Features of a Good Long-Term Care Insurance Policy*, for additional information on definitions of any of the following.

Two plans are offered: Comprehensive and Facilities-Only

Daily Benefits – $50 - $300, in $25 increments

There is an option that I recommend on the Comprehensive plan to have benefits available on a weekly basis for home health care. This means that instead of a daily maximum, you can have a weekly maximum equal to seven multiplied by the Daily Benefit for an average additional premium of six percent, well worth it for the added flexibility. One hundred percent of the Daily Benefit applies to nursing home, assisted living, hospice (facility and home), bed reservations, caregiver training, respite services (facility and home). **For facility benefits (nursing home, assisted living and hospice), the plan covers drugs, incontinence supplies, dietary supplements, personal medical equipment and laundry services.**

Waiting Period – 30 or 90 days of eligible charges

The waiting period is met by actual dates of service and days do not need to be consecutive. The waiting period does not have to be met to receive benefits for hospice care, respite care and caregiving training. The waiting period can never repeat. Informal care counts toward the waiting period if received as part of an approved plan of care.

Benefit Period/Benefit Max -- Three or five years or lifetime The three or five year benefit period is a "pool of money", which means it is the daily benefit multiplied by 1095 days or 1,825 days. For any day the charge is less than the daily benefit, the difference stays in the pool and can extend the benefit longer than the three or five years. The lifetime benefit is unlimited and averages 35 percent more premium than the five year benefit period. Care coordination services continue after the benefit maximum is exhausted (see below for definition of care coordination).

Home Health/Adult Day Care– 75 percent of daily benefit (optional weekly benefit as described above)

Home health care services do not have to be provided by a home health agency. The plan will pay for licensed professionals (RNs, LPNs, professional therapists – physical, respiratory, speech or occupational) who are freelancing, as long as they are operating within the scope of their license.

Informal care: If approved by an LTC Partners care coordinator, the plan will pay for a non-licensed caregiver who did not live with the insured at time of claim; however, the person could move in after benefit eligibility is established. This benefit can include a homemaker not provided through a home health agency. Evidence of services must be submitted (caregiver name, social security number, number of hours, along with a charge for each service). For family members (parents, grandparents, siblings, adult children and respective spouses) this benefit is limited to a lifetime benefit of 365 days.

Home health care is optional. A Facilities-Only plan, which covers assisted living, hospice and nursing facilities, averages 30% lower premium than a Comprehensive plan.

Assisted Living – 100 percent of Daily Benefit

Access to Benefits – Tax-Qualified definition (includes standby assistance), as the FLTCIP is a tax-qualified plan (see p. 35 for this definition). LTC Partners also has to agree in addition to the health care practitioner, and LTC Partners has to approve a written plan of care established by a licensed health care practitioner **or** an LTC Partners' care coordinator. Benefit eligibility is reassessed at least once every 12 months but no more frequently than every 30 days. In the event of a dispute, the policyholder is entitled to an independent third-party review.

Inflation Options – Automatic Compound Inflation or Future Purchase Option

Automatic Compound Inflation Option: The Daily Benefit and the remaining lifetime maximum less any claims paid out that year will increase 5 percent, compounded annually.

Future Purchase Option: The Daily Benefit will increase based on the medical Consumer Price Index (or another index mutually agreed upon by OPM and LTC Partners) every two years on January 1st with no underwriting, unless receiving benefits or unless the insured has declined three times. (Underwriting will apply after the insured has rejected a FPO three times and wishes to resume receiving offers.) Notification will go out in the fall, and the insured has to submit a written rejection to stop it. (Coverage must have been in effect 12 months to get the first increase.) Increases due to the FPO are priced at attained age and premiums in place at that time, so with this option, premiums will increase every two years and will eventually surpass the ACI premium. With each FPO notice will come an offer to switch to the Automatic Compound Option. The premium for ACI will be at the insured's age on the date of the switch, and the switch won't be allowed if the insured is receiving benefits.

Some people who need an initial low premium due to pressing current financial obligations (e.g. college tuition for children) buy the Future Purchase Option to keep their premiums low in the first few years with the intention of switching to the Automatic Compound Inflation option as soon as possible in order to stabilize their premium. This can be a good strategy as long as they understand the risk that they won't be able to switch if they start receiving benefits.

Waiver of Premium – First day of the month following the date eligibility for benefits is established and the waiting period is met, unless that date happens to be on the first day of a month, in which case it would be the same day.

The premium waiver applies to hospice even though there is no waiting period for hospice benefits. Premium resumes on the first of the month following the month in which the insured is no longer eligible for benefits. Premium that has been paid is refunded for any time period paid after death or after the waiver of premium starts.

Pre-Existing Conditions – No exclusion for pre-existing conditions

Reimbursement/Indemnity – Reimbursement, including informal care

Coordination of Benefits – This plan will be secondary to Medicare, group medical benefits and any other employer-sponsored long-term care insurance plan.

The FLTCIP is secondary to any benefits for long-term care services received under any plans established by the Federal or a state government. It does not coordinate with individual or association long-term care insurance policies. The Coordination of Benefits provision doesn't apply to international benefits (see below). The FLTCIP will not pay for care in a government facility, including a Department of Defense or Department of Veterans Affairs facility.

Nonforfeiture – Contingent nonforfeiture is built into the policy at no extra charge.

The shortened benefit period for additional premium is not an option.

Rates – Rate increases must be approved by The Office of Personnel Management (OPM).

There is no spouse or preferred discounts as OPM spread the discounts equally in order to provide equal treatment for all. Premiums can be viewed by using the premium calculator on the LTC Partners website: www.LTCFEDS.com.

Portability – The policy is portable at no increase in premium if the policyholder is no longer a member of the Federal family.

If the group policy ends for any reason, OPM will replace it with another group policy with substantially same coverage and premium based on issue age under the old group policy. (Note: The claims reserve for this program does not belong to the insurance company or companies who administer the plan, nor is it available for any other lines of business or to creditors of the insurance company. If OPM selects another insurance company, the fund will move to the new carrier.)

Additional Benefits

Alternate plan of care: In the Facilities-Only plan, this benefit can mean an alternate facility, but nothing outside of a facility. In the Comprehensive plan, it can mean home modifications, durable medical equipment and an emergency response system. Alternate plan of care benefits are subject to the waiting period and count toward the lifetime maximum. All alternate plan of care benefits must be authorized by the LTC Partners' care coordinator.

Bed reservations: 30 days per calendar year (includes assisted living and hospice facilities)

Caregiver training: The lifetime maximum is equal to seven multiplied by the Daily Benefit. The waiting period does not apply and Caregiver Training doesn't count toward the waiting period. The Caregiver Training benefit is paid in addition to the daily or weekly maximum so it doesn't figure into the daily or weekly benefit calculation.

Respite services: 30 multiplied by the Daily Benefit per calendar year. In the Facilities-Only plan, the benefit is available in an assisted living facility, hospice facility or in a nursing home. The Comprehensive plan includes respite care by a formal or informal caregiver at home or in adult day care.

Care coordination: Free (does not reduce the lifetime maximum) and is required as the LTC Partners' care coordinator is the person who approves benefit eligibility in addition to the insured's health care practitioner. The care coordinators, all registered nurses, also develop a plan of care and assist with altering it as needs change, monitor ongoing benefit eligibility and provide access to discounts for long-term care services, when available. Care coordination is available at

$59 per year to qualified relatives (single or couple), whether or not they are enrolled in the FLTCIP. This service package is also offered to any member of the Federal Family who is declined for a policy in the underwriting process.

Exclusions – No exclusion for mental disorders. No exclusion for war, except the benefit period may be shortened if the war is determined to be a Catastrophic Event as this could undermine the financial stability of the Federal Program (unlikely as Federal Program reserves grow).

International Benefits – 80 percent of the Maximum Lifetime Benefit is available for international coverage and payment is made at 80% of the domestic benefit amount. For those who choose a lifetime benefit period, the international Maximum Lifetime Benefit is ten years (3,650 days) multiplied by 80 percent of the Daily Benefit. If the policyholder returns to the United States, the benefits return to the full amounts. This means that any difference between what was paid outside the United States and the full benefit will be payable once the insured returns to the United States.

(The rationale for the 80 percent is that the 20 percent not paid compensates for the additional cost to cover higher claims expenses with provider verification and unknown utilization in another country, both of which protect the financial stability of the plan and guard against rate increases.)

The Office of Personnel Management is committed to both premium and benefit oversight of this plan to ensure rate stability and benefit modernization. For example, robotic care could be covered if that becomes an approved form of caregiving! Additional information is available on the LTC Partners web site at www.LTCFEDS.com or by calling 1-800-582-3337 (TTY: 1-800-843-3557) during the following times for a customer service representative:

Monday through Friday from 8 a.m. EST to 8 p.m. EST
Saturday from 9 a.m. EST to 5 p.m. EST
Closed on Sunday and all Federal holidays

An automated voice response system is available 24 hours a day, seven days a week.

Hopefully this chapter has made it clear that even if they are inadequate, the hours that caregivers *do* provide are taking a toll on their careers, wallets and relationships with family members.[58] It's not unusual to hear of the caregiver passing away shortly after the care recipient's death (e.g. Dana Reeve), or even before. Do everything you can to keep this from happening in your family.

Plan ahead for long-term care while your health is good and you have options.

Chapter 4

The Partnership for Long-Term Care

∿∿∿∿∿∿∿∿∿∿∿∿∿∿∿∿∿∿∿∿∿∿∿∿∿∿∿∿∿

The Partnership for Long-Term Care is a public/private alliance between state governments and insurance companies that was originally funded with $14 million in grants from the nation's largest health care philanthropy, the Robert Wood Johnson Foundation. The program is operational in Connecticut, New York, Indiana, California and approved in Iowa. Variations of the Partnership have been approved in Illinois, Massachusetts and Washington, but the main Partnership activity continued to reside in the original four states until President Bush signed the Deficit Reduction Act of 2005 (DRA) on February 8, 2006. **This landmark legislation has made it possible for other states to participate in The Partnership for Long-Term Care,** and of this writing, the following 22 states have indicated that they will do so:[1]

Alabama, Florida, Georgia, Idaho, Illinois, Iowa, Kansas, Maine, Maryland, Minnesota, Montana, Nebraska, New

Jersey, North Carolina, North Dakota, Ohio, Pennsylvania, South Dakota, Vermont, Virginia, Washington, and Wyoming

The idea of the partnership is to provide a way for the Medicaid program to work together with private long-term care insurance to help those people who are caught in the middle: they can't afford to pay the cost of the care or even the cost of a long-term care insurance policy with unlimited benefits, yet their assets are too high to qualify for Medicaid to pay their long-term care expenses. Many middle-income workers and retirees find themselves in this position.

Participating insurance companies in the Partnership recognize the needs of these middle-income Americans by providing LTC insurance policies that have built-in consumer protection benefit standards, and participating states cooperate by allowing these policyholders to access Medicaid without spending down their assets almost to poverty level if the insurance benefits run out. Without the Partnership, people have three choices to pay for long-term care:

1) Pay for care out of assets and income, which can lead to financial devastation if long-term care costs wipe out savings.

2) Transfer assets to qualify for Medicaid either to children or other family members or to a trust—either way means losing control of the money and losing financial independence.

3) Buy a standard long-term care insurance policy which works—unless the policy runs out of benefits or the benefit isn't enough to cover the cost of care. This can happen because you bought what you could afford,

and it turns out not to be enough when you need it. (For example, you couldn't afford the premium for inflation coverage, you could only afford a one- or two-year benefit period, or you bought a daily or monthly benefit significantly lower than the cost of care in your area and you couldn't make up the difference at claim time.)

A fourth option is available with the Partnership for Long-Term Care. Now consumers can purchase a state-approved LTC insurance policy that provides asset protection after the benefits run out.

Partnership Models

Here's how it works in Connecticut, Indiana and California with a dollar-for-dollar asset protection model:

▲ You purchase a special Partnership policy from an insurance professional. For every dollar in benefits paid by the policy, you can shelter a dollar in assets. For example, let's say you buy a two-year benefit period because that's what you can afford. If this policy pays, say, $60,000 in benefits, and if the Medicaid asset eligibility in your state requires you to spend down to $2,000, in this example you would be able to qualify for Medicaid when your assets reach $62,000, not $2,000. In other words, you get to keep, or "shelter" $60,000 of your assets and still get Medicaid to start paying your long-term care expenses after your policy runs out.

New York has two types of Partnership plans.

1) *Dollar-for-Dollar* – the same concept as above except the applicant chooses one of two plans: 1.5 years of nursing

home benefits and three years of home care benefits paid at 50 percent of the nursing home daily benefit **OR** two years of nursing home benefits and two years of home care benefits paid at 100 percent of the nursing home daily benefit.

2) *Total Asset Protection* -- These Partnership plans provide that once the benefits are exhausted, the policyholder can qualify for Medicaid regardless of the amount of assets. There are two plans to choose from for this type as well: three years of nursing home benefits and six years of home care benefits paid at 50 percent of the nursing home daily benefit **OR** four years of nursing home benefits and four years of home care benefits paid at 100 percent of the nursing home benefit.

While New York offers two unlimited asset protection plans, this desirable feature only happens after you have used up the benefits of the policy. A danger is that if you purchase a daily benefit that is inadequate for your needs, you could use up your assets paying the difference between your policy's benefit and the cost of care before your benefits are used up.

For example, in 2008 New York requires new Partnership policy purchasers to purchase a minimum of $218 for the daily nursing home benefit. The New York City metropolitan area averages $380[2] for a semi-private room. If you only buy the minimum, you could easily wind up paying $170 per day or more out of your pocket, which amounts to almost $190,000 over the three-year benefit period for nursing home care. Based on the 2006 map provided by The New York State Long-Term Care Partnership, it's easy to guess that the cost of care, while lower in other parts of New York, can run as high as $300+ per day.

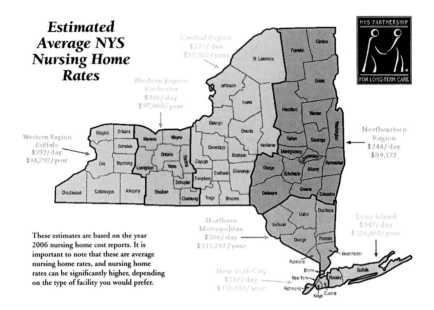

Estimated Average NYS Nursing Home Rates

Central Region
$239/day
$90,352/year

Western Region
Rochester
$266/day
$97,068/year

Western Region
Buffalo
$232/day
$84,792/year

Northeastern Region
$244/day
$89,172

Northern Metropolitan
$306/day
$111,792/year

New York City
$317/day
$115,632/year

Long Island
$347/day
$126,660/year

These estimates are based on the year 2006 nursing home cost reports. It is important to note that these are average nursing home rates, and nursing home rates can be significantly higher, depending on the type of facility you would prefer.

Indiana provides a combination of these two models. The combo plan provides the dollar-for-dollar asset protection, but if the policyholder purchases a benefit maximum that will pay about four years of benefits, the policy will provide total asset protection like the New York option. Since $228,045 represents about four years of benefits at current costs, purchasing a policy that would pay out that much in benefits would qualify you for the total asset protection feature in Indiana. (The $228,045 is the 2008 amount and will increase each year to account for inflation.) An insurance professional who is approved to sell Partnership policies can help you identify the best combination of benefits for your needs. Here are three possible scenarios to meet the 2008 requirement:

- a daily benefit of $160 with a four year benefit period, as $160 x 365 x 4 = $233,000;
- a daily benefit of $210 with a three year benefit period as $210 x 365 x 3 = $229,000; or
- a daily benefit of $320 with a two year benefit period as $320 x 365 x 2 = $233,000.

The Indiana Partnership maintains a list of professionals who have had special Partnership training. Call the Indiana Partnership telephone number or access the website listed at the end of this chapter for a directory of approved professionals.

In all states, your income goes to pay for the cost of care once you qualify for Medicaid. So the Partnership program protects assets, not income. But income is important for three reasons:

1) If your income is greater than your long-term care costs, you won't qualify for Medicaid and wouldn't benefit from a Partnership policy. People in this situation can consider a standard long-term care insurance policy—perhaps with an unlimited benefit maximum.

2) Income can guide you to a benefit selection. For example, the average cost of care in Indiana is $160 per day.[3] Indiana residents may be able to purchase a policy for $140 a day and pay the difference out of income. (In higher cost areas like New York, Connecticut or California, you would probably be purchasing policies in the $250+/day range. The average cost of care in Connecticut, for example, is $311.)[4] Just be careful—if your care costs more than the insurance policy pays in benefits, you will be responsible for paying the additional costs, and don't forget that care-related supplies are usually billed on top of the room and board charge.

Consider carefully how much you can afford to pay out of your income and insure yourself adequately. An outstanding feature of the Partnership policies is that they include an inflation benefit for appropriate ages so that inflation doesn't erode your benefit.

3) Since you are responsible for paying your premiums, your discretionary income must be sufficient to pay your long-term care insurance premiums and keep your policy in force, although there is a premium waiver if you have a claim. Individuals with income less than $30,000 or couples with incomes less than $40,000 may not have enough discretionary income to purchase long-term care insurance as premium payments may significantly impact their standard of living. If you fall into these income categories, and if you have assets less than $50,000, not counting your house and car, you probably will qualify for Medicaid in a short period of time, and LTC insurance of any type—standard or Partnership—may not be an appropriate purchase for you.

For many people, the Partnership LTC policies offer a wonderful alternative to transferring assets and relying on the government (Medicaid) to pay for their long-term care expenses. In addition to the legal pitfalls (See Chapter 5, *The Medicaid Benefit for Long-Term Care*), there are significant problems with transferring assets, such as:

▲ Children can lose the money due to divorce or lawsuits. It doesn't take bad people to do bad things. Children may be tempted to spend the money in a financial crisis by subconsciously thinking they will inherit it any way, so why not use it now when they really need it? Then when you need long-term care, the money simply isn't there anymore.

▲ We tend to judge ourselves by what we have, either consciously or unconsciously. Once we have turned our assets over to someone else, either a child or a trust, we have lost control of them. We may not enjoy the feeling of not being able to access our assets ever again.

▲   Transferring assets and using government money means using our own money as taxpayers. In New York, for example, a significant portion of each county's tax goes to the Medicaid program, in addition to state tax. County contributions are necessary to support the Medicaid program in New York which is running about $44 billion annually.[5] A really shocking equation that most New Yorkers don't realize is that one-third of Medicaid beneficiaries are receiving three-fourths of Medicaid benefits. The recipients spending most of the money are spending it largely for long-term care. Two-thirds of the remaining Medicaid recipients who are left with one-fourth of Medicaid benefits paid out in New York State are children.[6]

Let's take this picture national: One-third of the Medicaid budget in the United States is being spent on long-term care.[7] Two-thirds of nursing home patients are on Medicaid.[8] The impact of people who have transferred assets to qualify for Medicaid is hurting all of us as taxpayers.

Transferring assets has been a safety net in the past to prevent losing a lifetime of hard-earned savings, but it hasn't been a *dignified* safety net, due to losing control of assets and thereby losing financial independence. Long-term care insurance provides the dignified safety net, and particularly the Partnership policies that now make that possible for middle-income Americans.

A few points you may be wondering about with the Partnership policies:

Benefit Choices—Benefit choices are the same as for non-Partnership policies, in that there is a daily or monthly benefit, an elimination (waiting) period, a home health care/adult day care benefit level, an inflation feature, and a benefit period/lifetime maximum. You may be surprised to learn that many California and Connecticut Partnership policyholders purchase a lifetime (unlimited) benefit period. They do this because they really don't intend to access Medicaid, but if for any reason their assets are lowered for reasons beyond their control; i.e. a stock market plunge, they have asset protection provided by their Partnership policy. This is true because at any time benefits paid out equal your assets plus the amount Medicaid (MediCal in California) allows the healthy spouse to keep, policyholders are allowed to access Medicaid and shelter their assets.

For example, if a policy had paid out $250,000, the person receiving care could apply for Medicaid when the couple's assets are spent down to $356,400, which is equal to the $250,000 in benefits plus $104,400, the 2008 asset maximum for the healthy spouse plus the $2,000* allowable for the spouse who is applying for Medicaid. (Indiana and New York have total asset protection after benefits paid equal $228,045 for Indiana and after the three or four year benefit period for the New York Total Asset Protection plan is exhausted.)

Portability—If you move to another state, the Partnership policy will pay, and the benefits will accumulate toward your asset protection threshold. However, to qualify for Medicaid and take advantage of the asset protection offered by the Partnership policies when your benefits run out, you must move back to the state in which you bought

*1,600 in Connecticut; $1,500 in Indiana; $4,150 in New York

your Partnership policy and re-establish residence. Future legislation may make it possible for Partnership states to reciprocate the asset protection feature with each other, and Indiana and Connecticut have established reciprocity.

Underwriting—You still must qualify for the Partnership policy medically just as you would for a standard long-term care insurance policy. The younger you are, the better the chance to qualify for a policy, and the lower the premiums. Pre-retirement ages (40s and 50s) are strongly encouraged to apply. In fact, almost 80 percent of all Connecticut Partnership policy purchasers as of September 30, 2007 were under age 65 at time of purchase, the average age of new applicants is 58, and the age range of current policyholders is 20-88!"[9]

Arbitration—In some states, the Partnership policies have stronger mechanisms for claims appeals than standard long-term care insurance policies. In those states, a rigorous consumer protection appeal process is in place for any Partnership policyholder who disagrees with a benefit determination.

Policy Continuance—If for any reason the Partnership program is discontinued either nationally or in its particular state, all policies will be honored and appropriate benefits paid by the insurance company that issued the policy.

And now for the great news. The beginning of this chapter announced that the 2006 budget bill has cleared the way for other states to participate in the Partnership for Long-Term Care. Why couldn't they before? The original Partnership states were grandfathered, but the 1993 budget bill said that new states could offer asset protection only during the policyholder's lifetime. At death, the state was required to seek estate recovery for Medicaid's payment. This happened because of concern that the Partnership would cause Medicaid utilization to increase, when in fact, the opposite is true. Since the Partnership for Long-Term Care was implemented in the early 90s, less than 250 policyholders out of the approximately 255,000 policyholders in the first four Partnership states have had to turn to Medicaid for help.[10]

After the 1993 budget bill, Illinois and Washington tried to push ahead by allowing certain transfers during a person's lifetime as a reward for purchasing a Partnership policy. These programs met with little success without the full strength of the original Partnership concept and are no longer in existence. Massachusetts tried a different tactic. Medicaid guidelines have to be met as usual so there is no up-front asset protection, but the house is not subject to estate recovery if the policyholder enters a nursing home with a long-term care insurance policy with a minimum daily benefit of $130, a minimum two-year benefit period and a waiting period of no longer than 365 days. Nice, but not as good as the original Partnership concept.

As of this writing, a number of states are moving ahead to implement The Partnership for Long-Term Care. This movement will have a national impact in two significant ways:

▲   by saving taxpayer dollars by enabling policyholders to access long-term care insurance benefits first and Medicaid dollars as a last resort.

▲   by giving families choice when care is needed….as a Medicaid patient, someone else will make decisions for you.

Partnership policies offered by new states are required to:

- be tax-qualified (see **Tax Incentives for Long-Term Care Insurance** in Chapter One, *Long-Term Care and Your Financial Security).*

- provide the inflation benefit as follows:

  - compound inflation is required under age 61

  - some type of inflation benefit must be offered between ages 61 – 75

  - inflation may be offered for age 76 and on but is not required

▲   provide asset protection according to the dollar-for-dollar model, not the total asset protection model (see explanation at the beginning of this chapter). This means that you may still be subject to estate recovery (see **Estate Recovery** in Chapter Five, *The Medicaid Benefit for Long-Term Care*) but only for assets that exceed the amount of benefits you received from your Partnership long-term care insurance policy. However if you need to apply for Medicaid before your policy benefits are exhausted, you will be able to. (This could happen if for whatever reason you are not able to make up the difference between what your policy pays per day or month and what the actual charge has grown to be at the time you need care.)

▲   adhere to the long-term care insurance requirements set forth by the National Association of Insurance Commissioners (See *Appendix C:* **The Partnership for Long-Term Care – Document List.**)

Industry experts expect that many states will practice reciprocity which means that they will allow Partnership policyholders dollar-for-dollar asset protection at time of application for Medicaid, even if the policy was purchased while the policyholder was a resident in another state.

A really good part of the Deficit Reduction Act is that within the next year, states will start requiring that insurance salespeople be required to complete formal training on long-term care insurance in order to sell Partnership policies. In December, 2006 the National Association of Insurance Commissioners expanded that feature to include a training requirement for producers who sell any type of long-term care insurance, not just Partnership policies.

Should you wait to purchase long-term care insurance until a Partnership policy is available in your state?

No – unequivocally **NO** – for three good reasons:

1) You could develop a significant health problem or have a serious accident – either of which could render you uninsurable for long-term care insurance overnight.
2) The insurance companies are expected to work out a way for policyholders to exchange non-Partnership policies for Partnership policies.
3) States may not impose any requirement affecting the terms or benefits of a Partnership policy unless it imposes the same requirements on all long-term care insurance policies.

Reason #1 is the most important reason not to wait. Don't lose out on long-term care insurance by waiting for a Partnership policy to become available in your state. There's an excellent chance that you will be given the opportunity to exchange your policy for a Partnership policy as soon as one becomes available. If you want to be extra sure, ask the company you are considering buying from if that company plans to participate in the Partnership in your state.

What is the Timetable on the New Partnership Plans?

First, your state has to take the necessary step to allow the insurance companies to submit Partnership policies to the state insurance department for approval. While a few states will have to pass a new state law to do this, most will be able to submit an amendment to the state Medicaid rules to the Centers for Medicare and Medicaid Services (CMS), which is the government entity that oversees Medicaid and Medicare.   CMS has issued suggested language to make it as easy as possible for states to open their doors for these new Partnership policies.   (See *Appendix C* : **The Partnership for Long-Term Care – Document List.**)

Interested in finding out about your state's position on the Partnership program? Contact your state's insurance department – see *Appendix B*: **State Directory of State Insurance Departments, Medicaid and Aging Agencies.** Even if your state isn't participating in the program at this time, your phone call as an interested person can stimulate your state's legislators to become a participant.

For more information on the original state partnership policies, visit the following web sites or call these numbers:

State Partnership Offices

California (916) 552-8990 www.dhs.ca.gov/cpltc	Iowa 515-281-5705 www.iid.state.ia.us
Connecticut (860) 418-6318 www.CTPartnership.org	New York 518-474-0662 www.nyspltc.org
Indiana (800) 452-4800 (317) 233-1470 www.longtermcareinsurance.IN.gov	Other States: National Clearinghouse For Long-Term Care Information www.longtermcare.gov

Chapter 5

The Medicaid Benefit for Long-Term Care

~~~~~~

Medicaid is the public welfare program for the indigent jointly funded by federal, state and, in some states, local governments. Medicaid's huge growth in recent years is for "aged and disabled" recipients. These people make up just over a fourth of the people entitled to Medicaid benefits, but they consume more than two-thirds of the benefit dollars.[1] A third of Medicaid's spending for benefits went toward long-term care in 2006.[2]

The Problem

The aging population combined with the escalating cost of long-term care and loopholes in Medicaid eligibility laws have encouraged a growing number of older Americans to transfer assets to capture public funding for long-term care expenses. However, shrinking tax dollars caused by the severe decline in the ratio of workers to Social

Security beneficiaries, due to the aging population, have caused dire financial straits for the Medicaid program just as it has for Medicare. (A June 2006 survey for the American Health Care Association reports that 40 states were anticipating shortfalls in 2007.)[3]   There have been several attempts to actually criminalize asset transfers either for the person who is seeking Medicaid benefits or for the advisor who paved the way. These attempts to date have been unsuccessful, but many legislators believe the issue is too important to let it drop. The purpose of legislation of this nature is to restore Medicaid's original purpose— to help poor people.

Medicaid long-term care benefits are intended for people with low income and very low assets. This means that an applicant has to meet both income and asset criteria to qualify for Medicaid benefits, in addition to medical criteria. Since the majority of Medicaid's long-term care benefits are for nursing home patients, this chapter will explain the eligibility qualification process for nursing home benefits.[4]

Income Eligibility Criteria

States are able to choose one of two methods to determine income eligibility:

1) The most drastic method allows the state to cap income for the nursing home spouse to have income up to three times the Supplemental Security Income (SSI) amount, or $1,911 for 2008. Because that amount is so low compared to the cost of nursing home care ($3,500-$5,500 a month nationwide), the 1993 budget bill made a way to help people with low assets and income that exceeds this low monthly allowance but is not enough to pay privately.

These people can assign their income to a "Miller trust," also called a "qualified income trust," which is a special irrevocable trust designed just for the purpose of helping someone in a cap state whose assets qualify for Medicaid, but income is greater than the cap but not enough to pay privately. Here's how it works:

The individual is allowed to keep a personal-needs allowance, usually $30 a month, but it can be as high as $93.45 a month, as in Arizona. All of the remaining income can be assigned to the trust or just the amount that exceeds the cap plus a little extra just to be safe.

For example, if someone has $2,000 a month in income, which exceeds the $1,911 cap by $89, it would be wise to put at least $150 into the Miller trust in case of income fluctuations due to interest rates, etc. The individual's income still goes to the nursing home every month, but it will be a combination of the income retained by the individual and a monthly payment from the Miller trust, unless the individual assigned all of his or her income to the trust. In that case, the trust will make a single payment to the nursing home each month. Medicaid then makes up the difference between the individual's income and the Medicaid rate for the nursing home, which varies by facility.

The state is entitled to any excess income that has accumulated in the trust at the death of the applicant to pay Medicaid back for nursing home expenses Medicaid paid while the person was alive.

The 20 states that work this way are called "income cap" states and they are: Alabama, Alaska, Arizona, Arkansas, Colorado, Delaware, Florida, Idaho, Iowa, Louisiana, Mississippi, Nevada, New Mexico, Oklahoma, Oregon, South Carolina, South Dakota, Tennessee, Texas, and WY.

2) The remaining states allow the applicant to have income up to the cost of care, usually the Medicaid rate for the nursing home. This amount—about $3,300-$5,500 for most states, but can run as low as $2,000 a month in Oklahoma and as high as $10,555 a month in 2008 for high cost areas like Long Island, New York. This amount varies by facility but there is a maximum for each state. The Medicaid rate is lower than the private pay rate in most states, but a few states allow applicants to have income up to the private pay cost of nursing home care. Check with your Medicaid department for your specific state information. (See *Appendix B* for contact information.)

How is income determined? First, "the name on the check" rule applies. Social Security or pension income is easily attributable. Trust or investment income that is directed jointly to a married couple is divided 50/50. Starting with the gross monthly income for the Medicaid applicant, all individuals are allowed to keep the personal needs allowance. In non-cap states, there are a few allowable deductions to get the income down to the Medicaid qualifying level:

▲ health insurance premium, such as a Medicare supplement or retiree health insurance premium

▲ any medical expense not reimbursed by Medicaid or any other source (for example, a particular prescription that Medicaid doesn't cover

▲   income needed for the spouse at home, subject to a
range established by Medicaid ($1,750* minimum—
$2,610 maximum per month in 2008)

For example, Mr. Jones has $2,000 a month of his own income. After subtracting $30 for the personal needs allowance, $100 for a Medicare supplement premium, and $50 for his monthly prescriptions that aren't paid by any other source, he is left with $1,820. Mrs. Jones has $800 a month of her own Social Security income and a small pension. This means that Mr. Jones can transfer $950 of his income to her to bring her up to $1,750,* the minimum monthly Medicaid allowance for the spouse at home. This gets his income down to $870, which easily qualifies him for Medicaid to pay his nursing home bill.

His income of $870 then goes to the nursing home. Let's say that the Medicaid rate for that nursing home is $140 per day, or $4,250 a month. Medicaid will then make up the difference between his income and the Medicaid rate and will pay the nursing home $3,380 a month on his behalf ($4,250-$870).

You're wondering how the spouse at home can receive more than the minimum monthly income allowance. Some states just use the maximum and allow the spouse at home to keep that much income if the couple has that much income between them. The states that allow the maximum income allowance for the spouse at home are Alaska, California, Georgia, Hawaii, Illinois, Iowa, Louisiana, Mississippi, Nebraska, New York, North Dakota, Oklahoma, South Carolina, Texas, and Wyoming as well as the District of Columbia. Wisconsin allows $2,282.

* This amount changes each July

The other states require the spouse at home to justify the need for more income than the minimum of $1,750 per month. The justification process is based on whether or not there are shelter costs such as rent, a mortgage payment, homeowner's insurance, property taxes, a condominium maintenance fee, utilities, etc. If these shelter costs exceed a monthly amount called the Excess Shelter Allowance ($525 for 2008*), the spouse at home can keep additional income.

Here's how it works:

The difference between the total shelter costs ($900 a month, for example) and the Excess Shelter Allowance ($525) is added to the $1,750 and $2,125 becomes the monthly allowance for the spouse in this example:

$ 900	Total monthly "shelter" costs
- 525	Excess Shelter Allowance
$ 375	Additional spousal income allowable
	Minimum monthly spousal
+ 1,750	income allowance
$ 2,125	Total monthly spousal income allowance

The Deficit Reduction Act of 2005 which was enacted on February 8, 2006 established a uniform method of calculating the spousal income allocation. Prior to the DRA, some states were allowing couples to retain more resources to generate the above allowable monthly income. This is called the "asset first" or "resource first" rule. This means a

* This amount changes each July

couple could retain enough assets to generate the community spouse's income shortfall by the investment income for the retained assets. The DRA requires all states to practice the income first rule, which means the state won't allow a couple to retain resources to generate income for the spouse until the nursing home spouse has shifted all possible income to the spouse at home.[5] Then if the spouse's income is still below the minimum, the state will allow additional income from retained resources. The income first rule keeps the amount of resources retained for this purpose as small as possible. The DRA thus overruled a 2002 Supreme Court decision that states could choose whether to use the income first rule or the resource first rule.[6]

Asset Eligibility Criteria

Applicants for Medicaid also have to meet stringent asset criteria as well as income criteria. Generally, people with countable assets of about $2,000 ($3,000-$4,000 if both spouses need nursing home care) can qualify. (This amount varies slightly by state – see *Appendix D* – **What Your State Lets You Keep.**) Countable assets do not include the house if you have a spouse or a blind or disabled child under 21 still living in the house. Single applicants are not allowed to have home equity that exceeds $500,000 and the state has the right to increase the limit up to $750,000. (These amounts will increase based on the Consumer Price Index for all items, beginning in 2011.)[7] The single applicant will have to pull excess equity out of the home and spend it for acceptable reasons, such as the cost of care, in order to qualify for Medicaid's long-term care benefit.

Countable assets include anything that is available as a resource to you. In other words, anything that you can take money out of, even if you have to pay surrender charges (for example, an annuity that is only a couple of years old) or sell at a loss (for example, stock or property outside your primary residence). Here's a partial list of assets that count:

▲ cash (checking and savings accounts)

▲ certificates of deposit (CDs)

▲ money market accounts

▲ mutual funds

▲ stocks

▲ bonds

▲ deferred annuities

▲ property outside the home*

▲ cash value in life insurance for policies with a face value of $1,500 or more *(varies by state but generally a very low amount)*

▲ revocable trust (a living trust, for example)

▲ burial trusts beyond a minimum amount, unless they are irrevocable**

▲ retirement accounts like 401(k), Keoghs, SEPS, IRA plans, etc.

The rule of thumb is, if you can access the principal, it counts as an asset for Medicaid purposes.

If you are married, you can't just put everything in your spouse's name. When you apply for Medicaid to pay nursing home expenses,

---

*Some states won't count property outside the home as an asset if rented, but those states usually count the rental income toward the income eligibility requirements. Also, income-producing property outside the home, such as a business location or a working ranch or farm, usually is not counted.
**Varies by state.

all countable assets (see list above) are considered, regardless of whose name the assets are in—husband's or wife's—and includes a spouse's retirement account with rare exception. This is true even if you and your spouse have a prenuptial agreement. Some states will not honor a divorce agreement if the state believes the purpose of the divorce is solely to establish Medicaid eligibility for long-term care.

The minimum asset amount for the spouse at home is $20,880 for 2008, which means if one-half of the assets is less than the minimum, the spouse at home is allowed to keep the minimum.

Total assets are divided equally between you and your spouse. The spouse applying for Medicaid spends his or her half down to the state's asset requirement (usually $2,000) and the spouse at home can keep a maximum of $104,400 for 2008. In most states, the only way the spouse at home receives the maximum is if one-half of the assets is equal to or exceeds the maximum. Otherwise, the spouse at home receives 50 percent of the assets.

<u>**Here's how it works:**</u>

Example #1: $250,000 in countable assets: One-half is $125,000, which exceeds the maximum. The spouse at home keeps $104,400.

Example #2: $80,000 in countable assets: One-half is $40,000, which does not equal or exceed the maximum. The spouse at home keeps $40,000.

Example #3: $30,000 in countable assets. One-half is $15,000, which is less than the minimum. The spouse at home keeps $20,880.

Some states are more liberal and allow the spouse at home to keep the maximum of $104,400 as long as the couple has that much in assets. Those states are Alaska, California, Colorado, Florida, Georgia, Hawaii, Illinois, Louisiana, Maine, Mississippi, North Dakota, Vermont, Wyoming, and the District of Columbia. A few other states have minimums in between:

Alabama	$25,000	New York	$74,820
Delaware	$25,000	Oklahoma	$25,000
Idaho	$20,000	South Carolina	$66,480
Iowa	$24,000	South Dakota	$20,000
Kentucky	$22,000	Washington	$41,493
Minnesota	$28,001	Wisconsin	$50,000
New Mexico	$31,290		

With all of the states, the difference between the spousal asset allocation and the asset amount the nursing home spouse is allowed to keep must be spent down before the nursing home spouse qualifies for the Medicaid nursing home benefit.

Assets and Income Retained by the Healthy Spouse

A surprising note is that while spousal assets are not protected above the maximum spousal asset share as explained in the preceding section, spousal income IS protected. This means that a spouse can have an income much higher than the spousal income maximum of $2,610 for 2008 and not be required to contribute to the cost of care for the nursing home spouse. A few states like New York, will ask the spouse to contribute at least a portion of his or her income, but the spouse can simply refuse to do so. (Estate recovery applies.)

Therefore some couples have simply transferred assets into an immediate annuity in the spouse's name. An annuity turns assets into income for the rest of the annuitant's life, then there can be a beneficiary such as an adult child for any portion of the principal that isn't returned via the income stream during the spouse's lifetime. You will see in the following section that the DRA has made that plan unattractive.

Transferring Assets—The Myth

Surely the simple solution to all this is to just give assets to children or place them in a trust—perhaps for a favorite charity. That way the nursing home doesn't get your hard-earned assets, and you get something back for all those years of paying taxes. The really important thing is to get the house out of your name, so Medicaid and/or the nursing home can't get it.

It's clear from the tightened eligibility guidelines for the Medicaid long-term care benefit implemented by the Deficit Reduction Act that Congress thinks these are very bad ideas. Here's why:

When someone in a nursing home applies for Medicaid to pay nursing home expenses, Medicaid "looks back" 60 months to see if a transfer has occurred for less than fair market value, for example, to children.* If a transfer has occurred during that time, the applicant is ineligible for Medicaid benefits for the number of months equal to the amount of the transfer divided by the state's average monthly cost of nursing home care. (See *Appendix D*, **What Your State Lets You Keep**, for your

---

*If the application is made before being admitted to a nursing home, the look-back period is counted back from the date of nursing home admission, not from the date of application. Pre-DRA, this look-back period was 60 months only for transfers to irrevocable trusts and 36 months for all other transfers.

state's amount.) This means that the period of ineligibility, also called a penalty period, for Medicaid benefits depends on the amount of the transfer. (Note: California uses a 30 month penalty period, regardless of how much was transferred.) For example, a $300,000 transfer divided by a $5,000 average monthly cost for nursing home care equals 60 months (five years) of ineligibility. "Rounding down", the process by which partial months are ignored, is no longer allowed, thanks to the Deficit Reduction Act.

Transfers can be outright gifts or done in more subtle ways:

▲ Transferring $12,000 per year ($24,000 if you are married) to your children and grandchildren to stay within the federal gift-tax exclusion.

▲ Setting up a joint checking account with a son or daughter, then removing the parent's name from the account.

▲ Putting a home in the name of a son or daughter or other family member or friend.

▲ Purchasing a "life estate" in an adult child's home by paying off the adult child's mortgage. The DRA has made a life estate countable as an asset unless the purchaser lives in the house at least one year after the date of purchase.

▲ Transferring assets into an immediate annuity, which changes the assets into income. Medicaid compares the amount of the annuity with your life expectancy. Any projected payout that exceeds life expectancy is treated as a transfer and will trigger a period of ineligibility. Pre-DRA, some people got around that by purchasing a "balloon annuity" that has a small payout each year and then pays the remaining money in a lump sum in the last year of life expectancy. (Since the life expectancy tables have nothing to do with the health of the annuitant, the idea is that he or she will probably be deceased by the time the last payment is made.) Keeping the payout small until then preserves principal to maximize the lump-sum payout to the beneficiary. The DRA outlawed balloon annuities.[8]

▲   Transferring assets into an immediate annuity and producing a monthly income for the spouse at home, also known as the community spouse. Since spousal income is protected as I told you in the above section *Assets and Income Retained by the Healthy Spouse,* this worked pre-DRA as the amount of principal transferred into the immediate annuity for the spouse would no longer count as an asset for Medicaid eligibility purposes. However, the DRA says that for annuities issued or changed on or after February 8, 2006 on either spouse, the state must be named as remainder beneficiary or remainder beneficiary in the second position if a spouse or minor or disabled child is in first position.[9]

Further, the Tax Relief and Health Care Act of 2006, H.R. 6111, enacted December 20, 2006, made it clear that the state as the beneficiary intends to collect up to the amount that Medicaid paid out on the nursing home spouse.[10] Sounds like Greek, right? It just means that the government intends to stop people from turning assets into income for the community spouse and therefore not having to spend them down in order to qualify for Medicaid. If the state has to be the beneficiary on these spousal annuities, there's not much point in setting them up as the money isn't preserved for the spouse.

▲ Transferring assets into a trust to fund a college education for a grandchild.

▲ Setting up a trust that will benefit a charity after your death, so you can receive the income while you are alive.

▲ Setting up a trust that will benefit a charity with regular income before your death, then the principal will go to a family member when you die.

▲ Donating to a "pooled-income fund"—similar to a mutual fund operated by a charity for smaller investors to reap the tax benefits of charitable giving without having to invest large amounts.

All of these methods can count as a transfer of assets and trigger a penalty period, which means a period of ineligibility for Medicaid benefits. The motive of the transfer has no bearing on this process.

One of the most significant changes in the DRA is that the penalty period now begins on the date of application for Medicaid. Pre-DRA, the penalty period began on the date of the transfer, so it was simple to transfer half of your assets and keep half of your assets to pay privately during the look-back period. The idea was that the person wouldn't apply for Medicaid until the penalty period had expired and be eligible immediately. This was referred to as the "half-a-loaf" method. Now the penalty period is real – it is assessed whenever one would otherwise be eligible for Medicaid.

Note: Setting up a special trust for a disabled dependent can be accomplished in certain instances if you designate that the principal will revert to the state at the death of the disabled dependent. This is called a special needs trust. You should seek advice from an elder law attorney for help with this and any type of trust. Visit the National Academy of Elder Law Attorneys at www.naela.org for a list of elder law attorneys in your area.

Estate Recovery

People who qualify for Medicaid face yet another huge hurdle. The 1993 budget bill (OBRA '93) required states to recover from the estate of anyone who receives Medicaid benefits at the death of the second spouse. The Centers for Medicare and Medicaid, the government organization that oversees the Medicaid program, says that recovery efforts can be for Medicaid home and community care benefits as well as nursing home benefits and for hospital and prescription drug services while the patient was receiving Medicaid benefits for any of those care locations.[11] Some states have extended this recovery effort to include assets that are passed to others outside of probate; for example, assets passed to a spouse or adult child through joint tenancy, tenancy in common, survivorship, life estate, living trust, or other arrangement. A state survey conducted for the AARP Public Policy Institute reports these states in 2004 as:

> Arkansas, California, Hawaii, Illinois, Indiana, Iowa, Kansas, Minnesota, Nevada, North Dakota, Ohio, Oregon, Rhode Island, South Dakota, Washington, Wisconsin[12]

A North Dakota case said all assets in which the Medicaid recipient once held an interest are subject to estate recovery, even if those assets had not been formally conveyed.[13]

Why Transferring Assets Can Be A Bad Idea

Divorce	Half your assets go to buy your favorite son-in-law or daughter-in-law a red BMW!
Financial Difficulties	Every family has financial down times. Your daughter is thinking "I'm going to inherit the money anyway . . ."
Mis-Use of Funds	It looked like the best stock pick of the century.
Lawsuit	Your son is sued and your assets— now his assets as far as the court is concerned—are attached.
College Financial Aid	Your grandson no longer qualifies for financial aid because you shifted your assets to his father.
Cost-Basis	You paid $10 a share for the stock you just gave your daughter. It is now worth $100 a share. She sells the stock and owes tax on the gain of $90 per share . . . the tax bill may be more than a lifetime of long-term care insurance premium for you!
Early Death of Adult Child	The unthinkable happens—your son or daughter predeceases you. Your assets are now in the hands of the in-laws.
Adverse Tax Consequences	Interest earned on the transferred assets is taxable income to your children and amounts above $12,000 in 2008 transferred in any one calendar year use up part of your lifetime estate and gift tax exemptions. Some states have separate gift taxes from federal gift taxes.

A good long-term care insurance policy can mean you don't have to worry about these problems!

The recovery process also includes in most states the right to place a lien on your home in the amount of Medicaid payments made on your behalf for your care. When the property is sold or title is transferred, the lien must be paid. In the case of joint ownership, the title is subject to the lien, even though the title transfers to the joint owner(s) immediately upon the Medicaid recipient's death. The state will refuse to release the lien until the joint owner has satisfied the Medicaid liability. States have the right to place a lien on even a life estate, which is simply a legal interest you keep in your home after you have transferred the deed to someone else. And if you give your house away outright, you lose the capital gains exclusion.

Your children (or whomever you give your house to) could take advantage of the capital gains exclusion, but only if they live in the house at least two of the last five years before the house is sold. Giving your house to your kids and continuing to live in it can mean your children wind up paying a steep capital gains tax when the house is sold if they don't adhere to the capital gains exclusion rules of living in the house the appropriate time before its sale.

As of 2004, the following states were using liens as part of their estate recovery process:

Alabama, Alaska, California, Connecticut, Delaware, Hawaii, Idaho, Illinois, Indiana, Maryland, Massachusetts, Minnesota, Montana, New Hampshire, New York, Oklahoma, South Dakota, Wisconsin and Wyoming.[14]

The lien is not enforceable, however, until the death of the second spouse, even if he or she does not live in the house, and Medicaid must notify your family in advance that a lien is being placed. Nevada places liens on the homes of the surviving spouses of deceased Medicaid beneficiaries. While the lien isn't enforced until the surviving spouse dies, he or she can't sell the home and use the money for other purposes without paying off the lien first.[15]

Liens also cannot be enforced if:

▲ There is a child under age 21, or who is blind or disabled, whether or not the child lives in the house.

▲ There is a brother or sister with a joint ownership for the year immediately prior to the nursing home admission, but only if he or she lived in the house continuously since that date.

▲ There is a non-disabled adult child who had lived in the house two or more years prior to the parent's admission to a nursing home, and who had provided care that delayed admission, but the child must have lived in the house continuously since then.

Just because a state doesn't use liens as part of the estate recovery process, don't assume you're out of the woods. Some states like Tennessee will not allow the estate of a Medicaid patient to be probated until the family obtains a letter from the estate that says no money is owed to the Medicaid division.[16]

As the states are dealing with an aging population and the prospect of paying for the baby boomers' long-term care needs, estate recovery efforts are growing in intensity. As of this writing, all states except Michigan have implemented an estate recovery program. At least a dozen states either wholly or partially utilize private contractors to conduct estate recovery.[17]

An excellent publication, entitled *Questions and Answers on Medicaid Estate Recovery for Long-Term Care Under OBRA '93,* is available free from AARP by writing the Public Policy Institute, 601 "E" Street, NW, Washington, DC 20049, or you can access it online at http://research. aarp.org, along with a copy of the 2004 state survey mentioned in this section. You also will find useful information in the Medicaid section of the government website, Centers for Medicare and Medicaid, www. cms.hhs.gov/MedicaidEligibility/08_Estate_Recovery.asp.

The Bigger Problem—The Criminal Side Revisited

A variety of legislative attempts to criminalize asset transfers for the sole purpose of qualifying for Medicaid has put a huge chill on the practice of "Medicaid planning," the process of impoverishing oneself on paper to qualify for Medicaid's nursing home benefit. Michael Leavitt, the government official who oversees the Medicaid program, had this to say:

> *Medicaid must not become an inheritance protection plan. Right now, many older Americans take advantage of Medicaid loopholes to become eligible for Medicaid by giving away assets to their children. There is a whole industry that actually helps people shift costs to the taxpayer.*[18]

Why does such a strong interest exist to close the loopholes for Medicaid planning?

Because there aren't enough tax dollars to pay for a national long-term care plan, and that's the direction this program is taking when you consider that Medicaid pays 44 percent of nursing home costs and two-thirds of all nursing home patients are Medicaid recipients.[19,20]

Fifty-three cents of every Federal income tax dollar in the U.S. goes to pay for entitlements (mainly, Social Security, Medicare and Medicaid), and this is only a prelude *before* the baby boomers start applying for Medicaid long-term care benefits![21] In view of these facts, it is reasonable to expect that legislative activity to curtail Medicaid planning will continue.

The Biggest Problem

All of the above are problems, but the biggest problem is that by giving your assets away, you lose access to them. That's why you gave the assets away to start with—to keep from losing them to a nursing home—and now for one or more of the above reasons, you've lost them anyway. Most importantly, you lose the one thing that matters most—**your independence and control.**

Here's what it means to be a Medicaid patient in most states:

▲   You can't get into strictly private-pay facilities that don't accept Medicaid patients.

▲   Medicaid does not pay for extensive home health care; i.e. daily eight- to ten-hour shifts, so being on Medicaid in most states means being in a nursing home when that much home care is needed. The DRA gave states permission to use Medicaid dollars for home care and even provided some additional funding for 12 months after a nursing home patient is transitioned back into the community. However, a Georgetown University study said states are permitted to cap enrollment, maintain waiting lists, and offer the home care option without providing services statewide.[22] The demand for the home and community-based services has exceeded what is available and has resulted in waiting lists in most states.[23] The reality is that priority must be given to the people who require nursing home care, and this makes dollars for home care scarce.

▲ Medicaid pays less than private-pay rates in most states, so the waiting lists are long for Medicaid patients in many states. The average shortfall was projected at $13.10 per Medicaid patient day for 2006.[24]

▲ You have to go wherever there is a bed, which could be hours away from your family.

▲ If the facility doesn't accept Medicaid and you run out of your own money, you can be required to move to a facility that accepts Medicaid, and that's a hard situation for families to deal with.*

▲ Nursing homes that operate with predominantly Medicaid patients don't have as much funding as private-pay facilities to upgrade services, furnishings, etc.

▲ You simply don't have as many choices as a private-pay patient—a private room, for example, is not allowed—because as a Medicaid patient, you aren't paying the bill.

In her May 2006 article that explains the tightened Medicaid rules from the Deficit Reduction Act, Mary Beth Franklin with *Kiplinger's Personal Finance Magazine* says, "If you don't own a long-term-care insurance policy -- or if you rejected the idea before -- you should seriously consider getting one now . . . Having long-term-care insurance has always been preferable to relying on Medicaid because it gives you more options..."[25]

Long-Term Care Insurance—A Better Way

The message sent by the federal government is clear: Medicaid is a program for poor people and is not to be used by middle- and upper-income Americans. Many well-known authors such as Suze Orman, Terry Savage and Jane Bryant Quinn encourage people to buy long-term care insurance instead of relying on Medicaid. A *Wall St. Journal* article had a very strong opinion:

> *Long-term care accounts for about one-third of federal and state expenditures on Medicaid, to the tune of $100 billion this year. It is the biggest driver of skyrocketing Medicaid costs that are bankrupting many states and localities. Medicaid was created 40 years ago to care for the needy. The rest of us have an obligation to pay for our own care -- or to protect our wealth with private insurance.*[26]

Ultimately, transferring assets may prove to be ineffective if there are no Medicaid beds available when you need one. Even today, some communities have year-long waiting lists for Medicaid beds!

The primary reason people are purchasing long-term care insurance policies is to maintain choice, and consequently, **independence**.[27] (See Chapter One: *Long-Term Care and Your Financial Security.*)

If you are the type of person who enjoys being in control, a long-term care insurance policy may be the only thing that makes it possible for

---

*On March 25, 1999, President Clinton signed into law the Nursing Home Resident Protection Act of 1999 which means that nursing homes that voluntarily drop out of Medicaid can refuse to admit new Medicaid patients, but they can't force Medicaid patients already in residence to leave. This does not, however, prevent nursing homes from dropping out of Medicaid altogether and being totally private-pay facilities. To prevent surprises, this law requires private-pay facilities to notify patients upon admission that they will have to leave if they run out of their own money and need to apply for Medicaid.

you to stay in control by guaranteeing that you will have purchasing power—and consequently decision-making power—when you need long-term care, which means choices other than a nursing home with a comprehensive long-term care insurance policy, you can easily choose—home health care, adult day care, and the beautiful private-pay assisted living facilities that represent the fastest growing form of long-term care.

If a nursing home patient thinks he or she will qualify for Medicaid eventually, it is recommended that an application be made to Medicaid upon admission to the nursing home so a financial assessment can be made at that time. Applicants who wait until assets are spent down to the qualifying level of $2,000 must furnish financial information back to the admission date, and that is not always easy to do.

If you are interested in applying for Medicaid to pay your nursing home expenses, contact your local Medicaid office, which is usually listed in the state government section in the blue pages of your telephone book or see *Appendix B,* **Directory of State Insurance Departments, Medicaid and Aging Agencies** for state Medicaid offices.

Since the Medicaid qualification process can be complex, some people ask an elder law attorney to help them with the Medicaid application. Contact the National Academy of Elder Law Attorneys for an elder law attorney in your area who specializes in Medicaid (www.naela.org).

Chapter 6

Alternatives for Financing Long-Term Care

〜〜〜〜〜〜〜〜〜〜〜〜〜〜〜〜〜〜〜〜〜〜〜

Other ways people consider financing long-term care are through accelerated death riders to life insurance policies, viatical or life settlements, life/long-term care insurance policies, annuity/long-term care insurance policies, reverse mortgages and critical illness policies. An overview of each of these six options is presented as additional information for the long-term care planning process.

Accelerated Death Benefits

An alternative to purchasing a long-term care insurance policy is to purchase a life insurance policy that will provide cash advances against all or a portion of the death benefit to pay for long-term care expenses while the insured is still living. Because the death benefit can be paid out early, this form of long-term care payment as a part of a life insurance policy is commonly referred to as an accelerated death benefit, but you also may hear it referred to as a "living needs" benefit.

Early versions only paid if the policyholder suffered from a terminal illness. Most policies today make the benefit available for chronically ill people as well. Some pay only for permanent confinement in a nursing home, but some pay also for home and community-based care, like assisted living.

The accelerated death benefit is an alternative to traditional LTC insurance policies for some people because this provision can be added to a life insurance policy for little or no cost. It also can help someone who cannot qualify for a traditional LTC policy at an older age if the benefit was included in the policyholder's life insurance at time of purchase, as is the case with many younger purchasers of life insurance today. And, a few life insurance policies will even allow you to add an accelerated death feature after you become sick.

Typically, monthly benefits for long-term care will equal two percent of the face value. For example, if the face value of the policy is $150,000, the benefit would be $3,000 a month.

Newer policies tend to be reimbursement policies, which means they will pay actual charges up to the available benefit equal to two percent of the face value. Older policies were commonly indemnity plans, which paid out the two percent amount, regardless of the charge. The Health Insurance Portability and Accountability Act of 1996 (HIPAA) is primarily responsible for this change (See **Tax Incentives for Long-Term Care Insurance** in Chapter One for a list of provisions.) Benefit payments in excess of $270 per day in 2008 (or the monthly equivalent) that exceed the actual cost of care will be taxed as income, so most long-term care insurance policies of all types stick with paying the actual charges to help the policyholder avoid a precarious tax situation.

The pitfalls? At two percent of the face value, the monthly benefit payments are likely to be lower and durations of coverage shorter than under freestanding LTC insurance products, because many people do not have life insurance policies with large face amounts. So if the life insurance policy has a face value of $100,000, the monthly benefit would be $2,000. In metropolitan areas, that benefit amount would only pick up about a third of the cost of either a nursing home or daily eight-hour shifts of home health care. If the policy advanced the entire face amount, in this example, the benefit duration would be only about four years.

Other pitfalls are that some policies still pay a lower benefit for home health care, typically 50 percent. An especially serious problem is that inflation may not be addressed. Also, if the primary need is for life insurance, utilizing the death benefit for long-term care expenses defeats the purpose of the insurance by leaving the survivors with little or no death benefit after the insured is deceased. Newer policies have a residual death benefit, however, which means that a percentage of the original death benefit is paid at death even if the entire death benefit had been accelerated for long-term care. A residual death benefit of ten percent is common.

The Health Insurance Portability and Accountability Act of 1996 provided much needed clarification that accelerated death benefits will be treated as if they were the proceeds payable on account of death— that is, income-tax free—if the benefits meet the criteria of HIPAA. Non-qualified versions are being sold, however, so check carefully to see if the sales brochures, sample policies, etc., have notification on the front that the policy is tax-qualified. Policies that are intended to be tax-qualified are supposed to be clearly marked.

Since the cost to add an accelerated death benefit option to a life insurance policy is minimal with most policies, younger people may consider the rider a very good purchasing decision, similar to purchasing the right to buy a discounted freestanding LTC insurance policy at older ages when purchasing a disability income policy. Many employers have an accelerated death benefit provision in their group life insurance plans.

Traditional Viatical Settlements

Taking its name from "viaticum"— the supplies needed to perform last rites that were routinely sent into battle with Roman soldiers (who commonly weren't expected to return)—a traditional viatical settlement allows a terminally ill individual to sell a life insurance policy to a third party. The core idea is that the proceeds from the sale of the policy would provide "financial supplies" for the final journey of death. The reality is that the third party (the viatical company) pays the terminally ill person a percentage of the death benefit and becomes the owner and beneficiary of the life insurance policy and takes over the premium payments. The terminally ill person gets funds to live on during the very costly time before death, and the third party receives the full death benefit after the person dies.

The definition of terminally ill for a viatical company can be anyone with a life expectancy of five years or less, but typically is two to three years.

The amount paid for the policy is based on the life expectancy of the insured and is influenced by other factors such as:

▲ **The Capitalization of the Viatical Company**—Most viatical companies do not bear the risk of the viatical arrangement of paying out a discounted death benefit and waiting until the person dies to collect the entire death amount. Rather, most viaticals are brokers who bring together investors and terminally ill people.

▲ **Case Diversification of the Viatical Company**—The viatical business started with AIDS patients. Viatical companies that have continued to purchase mainly the life insurance policies of AIDS patients are not doing well because technology has dramatically extended the lives of AIDS patients. A successful viatical company has a good mix of terminal conditions, like cancer and heart-related conditions, as well as late-stage conditions, such as Alzheimer's.

▲ **Rating of the Insurance Company**—Viatical companies make a lower payment if the insurance company has a rating of B+ or lower according to the A.M. Best company, the largest third-party rating service for insurance companies. Why? Because if the lower-rated company goes out of business, the viatical company gets stuck with a policy on which it probably can't collect.

▲ **Waiver of Premium Status**—If the premium of the policy is waived due to a provision that waives the premium because the policyholder is disabled, the viatical company will have more money available since it won't have to assume premium payments.

▲ **Investor Mix**—Investors who are short-term, high-return speculative investors demand a higher interest rate for their investment dollars which will lower the amount available to pay out in discounted death benefits.

Viatical companies buy all kinds of life insurance policies: term life, whole life, universal life, and group life. A viatical settlement can be a knight in shining armor for an employee who is too sick to work and must convert the group life policy to an individual policy in order to keep it. The premium for a converted policy can be steep, and many employees aren't prepared to pay a high premium. A viatical company can purchase the policy and pick up the premium.

The Viatical Settlement Process

The terminally ill person submits an application. The viatical company confirms the insurance policy with the insurance company and obtains medical records to determine the life expectancy of the applicant. There is no application fee.

If the viatical company decides to purchase the policy, the minimum payment to the insured based on life expectancy may follow this table which represents guidelines suggested by the National Association of Insurance Commissioners:[1]

Life Expectancy of Insured	% of Net Death Benefit* Paid
1–6 months	80%
6–12 months	70%
12–18 months	65%
18–24 months	60%
24 +	50%

* Payment is based on net death benefit, not face value of the policy. Net death benefit means the actual benefit payable at death, which may have been reduced by policy loans or withdrawals.

These percentages can be five percent lower than these guidelines if the insurance company is rated B+ or lower.[2] In 1999, a "reasonableness standard" was added as an alternative to the table of minimum payments. In recent years, viatical settlement providers have found it difficult to adhere to the above table. Your insurance department can explain further as payment criteria is jointly developed using data supplied annually by viatical settlement providers and reasonableness criteria provided by the National Association of Insurance Commissioners. Policies of all sizes are viaticated.

There is a rescission period, which means the applicant can change his or her mind for any reason and resume ownership of the policy within 30 days after executing the contract to sell the policy or within 15 days after receiving the cash settlement. If the applicant dies within this rescission period and the cash settlement is returned to the viatical service provider within 60 days after death along with any other fees expended by the provider, the death benefit can be paid to the original beneficiary.[3]

Most states have adopted viatical settlement legislation, so most of the population in the United States is covered by consumer protection regulation for viatical settlements. The National Association of Insurance Commissioners has published both a model act and a model regulation for viatical settlements for states to adopt that contain stringent consumer disclosure requirements, so that viators (people who sell their life insurance policies) understand all of the ramifications of the viatical settlement.

The Health Insurance Portability and Accountability Act of 1996 (HIPAA) enables viatical settlements to be tax-free for terminal individuals with a two-year or less life expectancy or for chronically ill individuals. Note: It is the health care practitioner (physician, nurse or social worker) who determines the tax status. The viatical company may think life expectancy is three years, but if the health care practitioner thinks two, then the discounted death benefit paid out will be tax-free because the IRS goes by the health care practitioner's certification. Also, the IRS doesn't look back. If the individual exceeds life expectancy, the IRS won't challenge the tax-free benefit status.

To receive the settlement tax-free, however, the viator must do business with a viatical company that is licensed in the states that require licensing or adheres to the NAIC guidelines for viatical settlements in those states that do not require licensing. Several states, such as California and New York, have also made viatical funds free of state income taxes.

Viatical Settlements vs. Accelerated Death Benefits

▲   With an ADB, you most likely will not accelerate all of the death benefit, which means when you die, your beneficiary will still receive something. With a viatical settlement, you receive a percentage of the death benefit, then relinquish the policy to the viatical settlement provider that takes over premium payments and receives the full death benefit when you die, and your beneficiary receives nothing.

▲   Even though the health care reform legislation of 1996 allows the terminally ill requirement for an ADB to be up to 24 months, many ADB policies are six to 12 months, much shorter than a viatical settlement which can run up to 36 months or even longer.

▲ An ADB policy can lapse if premiums are not paid. The viatical settlement is a one-time procedure and all the money due the applicant is paid out all at one time. The terminally or chronically ill person no longer has to worry about paying premium and keeping a policy in force.

Viatical Settlements vs. Long-Term Care Insurance

▲ For people without long-term care insurance, a viatical settlement can provide a solution to immediate cash needs. A small portion of the settlement could also be used to purchase a long-term care insurance policy for the surviving partner.

▲ Viatical settlements represent a great alternative to Medicaid planning for the person who is unable to qualify for long-term care insurance due to problems with health or affordability.

▲ LTC insurance stretches the money out vs. paying the full cost of long-term care services with a lump-sum viatical settlement, which can disappear quickly, especially with the temptation to spend it on things other than the cost of care.

▲ Long-term care insurance can preserve the death benefit of the life insurance policy for family members.

▲ A long-term care insurance policy with an unlimited benefit period can pay benefits tax-free for an unlimited time period vs. a lump-sum viatical settlement that will run out.

Life Settlements

In addition to traditional viatical settlements as outlined above to help people who are chronically or terminally ill, a broad expansion of this idea, entitled a "life settlement," is available **for older people who are not ill.** These are just people who no longer need a death benefit because the original reason they bought life insurance doesn't exist anymore (for example, college tuition, change in estate size, sale of a business or divorce) or perhaps they can't afford the premium after retirement, a classic problem with term life insurance.

Today older Americans who have life insurance (group, individual, term, whole life, universal life) can sell their policies to a life settlement company for their present value, an opportunity that can be a significant estate planning tool. Policies of almost any size can be sold, from $250,000-$100 million, for example, but the most common range is $250,000 to $10 million. The most common age range is 75 and up. Policies purchased include those held in irrevocable life insurance trusts, buy-sell agreements, and "key-person" policies. The proceeds from the policy sale are unrestricted, and high net worth individuals have the ability to use the funds for such options as:

▲   making cash gifts to family members
▲   purchasing a minority interest in a closely held business to reduce estate taxes
▲   facilitate the transfer of a business to the next generation
▲   funding the purchase of permanent life insurance that will insure a spouse to cover estate taxes
▲   paying long-term care expenses for someone who is uninsurable
▲   funding the purchase of long-term care insurance for a spouse

▲ making charitable gifts and funding planned giving techniques
▲ purchasing a business
▲ paying down debt
▲ investing the proceeds

As you can see, disposition of the funds is up to the imagination and simply represents a way to use life insurance while living. A common use of a life settlement transaction is to use the proceeds to purchase a new insurance product. Life insurance has gone down as life expectancies have crept up, so it's not unusual to be able to buy the same or more death benefit for lower premium even though the policyholder is older.

Although the normal age range is 75 and up, a few life settlement companies will even purchase a life insurance policy from someone as young as 60 if the life expectancy is in the 12 year range, which may be the case with certain health conditions.

Here is an example of using proceeds from a life settlement for long-term care:

An 80-year old gentleman, with some health concerns, had a $400,000 universal life insurance policy that had very little cash value. Making the premium payments was becoming a financial burden, and he and his wife were concerned about long-term care for each of them. Unfortunately, he did not qualify for long-term care insurance because of his health problems. A life settlement gave him $175,000. The sale of this policy not only relieved this couple of the monthly premium payments but the life settlement funds enabled the client to purchase a long-term care insurance policy for his wife, a second-to-die policy on the two of them with a $200,000 death benefit, and also provided funds for his own long-term care needs.[4]

Another example involves a business owner who was able to fund a secure retirement through a life settlement:

> *One 73-year-old business owner wanted to sell his company, but was unable to solicit an offer that he considered sufficient for his retirement needs. Working with his financial advisor, he realized he could sell his business-owned policy on the secondary market.*
>
> *The term policy, which had a face amount of $5 million, had no cash value. The life settlement transaction, however, yielded him $1.1 million – enabling him to take the proceeds and fund a comfortable retirement.* [5]

This gentleman could easily buy a long-term care insurance policy to protect his retirement fund with less than one percent of his newly-generated asset base.

Concerning taxation issues, the IRS hasn't released an official position on life settlements yet, but the industry thinking is that life settlement payments incur tax liability to the original policyholder in two ways. First, the difference between the settlement payment and the cash surrender value is taxed as a capital gain. The difference between the total premiums paid (the tax basis) and the cash surrender value is taxed as ordinary income. Anything below your cost basis; i.e. the money you've put into the policy, has no tax implication.

You should discuss your individual tax situation with a professional tax advisor.

Note that a lump sum received from any source could and probably would affect your ability to qualify for Medicaid as it would be counted as an asset.

The National Association of Insurance Commissioners passed a ruling in December 2006 that prohibits a life settlement within five years of the effective date of the policy without a good reason such as chronic or terminal illness, death or divorce of a spouse, retirement, and so forth. This new ruling also prohibits a person or entity loaning the money to an older American to buy a life insurance policy just for the purpose of selling it in a couple of years.[6]

Single Premium Life/Long-Term Care Insurance Policies

A growing number of consumers have expressed interest in a long-term care funding method in which a single premium is paid and that premium is guaranteed not to change. In standard LTC insurance policies, there are a growing number of companies that have a limited payment option, such as 10-pay or 20-pay or "paid up at age 65", but there are few companies with a one-time premium guaranteed not to change. When you purchase a "lifetime pay" traditional policy, you are required to pay premiums the rest of your life, just like health insurance, until you have a claim and then generally the premium is waived. The premium can be increased in the future only if it is increased on an entire classification of policyholders. (A class rate increase can occur during the limited pay period on a limited pay plan but not after the premium stops at the end of the limited pay period – see *Lowering or Eliminating Long-Term Care Insurance Premium in Retirement* in Chapter 2, *Features of a Good Long-Term Care Insurance Policy.*)

Increasingly, the consumer interested in the lump sum, paid-up approach says, "I want to pay one time, and if I don't use the policy, I want my money to be passed on to my [children, grandchildren, church, charity, etc]." The policy is then considered paid-up and no future deposits are required. Typically, this type of consumer may be thinking self-insurance is the best option vs. gambling that many years of insurance premiums may not pay off if care is never needed.

If this is the way you are feeling, you'll be glad to know this "almost too good to be true" type of funding method is actually available in a specially-designed whole life insurance policy to help pay for long-term care expenses. Here's how it works:

Issue ages for single individuals generally begin about 40, and joint policies for two people (e.g., mother and daughter, as well as spouses) can be purchased, if the average age of the two people falls within certain parameters. Age 80 is typically the maximum issue age, although there is no age limit for the benefit payments once a policy is issued. The single premium deposit can be made with cash, CDs, money market accounts, non-qualified and qualified annuities, or IRAs and Keogh plans. You may also be able to move the cash value from another life insurance policy into this one with no adverse tax consequences. Issue ages can vary based on the source of the premium (i.e., older issue ages of 59½ may be required for transfers from qualified annuities, IRAs and Keoghs).

The idea of this policy is that whatever amount you deposit purchases a death benefit like any other life insurance policy. What's new and different is that almost double the amount of your deposit becomes immediately available to you for long-term care. At the time you purchase the policy, you choose how you want the death benefit to be paid out in the event you need long-term care. The policy could pay as much as four years of benefits for you at 2 percent per month of the long-term care amount, three years of benefits at 3 percent per month or two years at 4 percent per month. While minimum deposits can be in the $10,000–$20,000 range, a meaningful benefit based on today's costs requires somewhere in the $100,000 range for a 60-year-old couple. A $100,000 deposit provides a monthly benefit for about four years of approximately $5,000 each, a meaningful amount if both spouses need long-term care. Smaller deposits, such as $50,000 or less, can be made if you are willing to self-insure a significant part of your long-term care expense.

On the other end of the spectrum, the 60-year-old couple could pay an additional $40,000 in premium one-time or $1,650 annually which would extend the benefit indefinitely, and the monthly benefit that is available after they exhausted the $250,000 death benefit would grow at 5 percent compound the rest of their lives. Again, the premium is guaranteed to never change, even if you elected the $1,650 annual premium in this example. Some people really like that security. If you do the benefit extension, I recommend that you select the 4 percent factor to accelerate the initial death benefit as quickly as possible; i.e. 24 months, so that you hit the extended benefit period quickly and tap into the monthly benefit that has been growing at 5 percent compound each year.

As with other life insurance policies, you can take out a certain amount of accumulated interest with no surrender charge. But if you need to access more, the amount you take out will generate a surrender penalty. On this product, surrender penalties are graded downward each year until they disappear in ten years. Of course, you don't want to enter into this type of policy with the intention of making withdrawals, because that would lower both the death benefit and the amount available for long-term care.

There are other single-premium life insurance/long-term care policies based on universal life insurance. This product also accelerates the death benefit at claim time tax-free but is funded by taxable withdrawals from the cash value for the long-term care insurance portion. This means the policyholder receives a 1099 each year for that amount. (However, the taxation section below explains that these withdrawals will be tax-free for tax years 2010 forward for all policies of this type purchased after

December 31, 1996, thanks to the Pension Protection Act of 2006.[7]) The surrender penalties can stretch as long as 20 years. A return of premium rider is allowed if you wish to avoid surrender charges.

Inflation coverage can be tricky on these universal life insurance/long-term care insurance plans as well. It's not uncommon for the base portion of this policy to have a lower inflation benefit option than the extended benefit portion. For example, the monthly benefit under the base portion might grow at 2 percent and the monthly benefit under the benefit extension might grow at 5 percent. The reasoning is that the base plan grows through the dividends.

However, dividend growth can be small and at claim time, one must exhaust the base benefit before being able to access the extended benefit that has grown at 5 percent compounded annually since the date the policy was purchased. Just like in the whole life version explained earlier, a good way to handle this problem is to choose the highest acceleration option, usually 4%, for the base benefit. A newer policy allows you to buy a 5% compound inflation rider that starts immediately on the entire benefit and never stops growing as long as you have the policy.

Premium for these optional riders may be included in the lump-sum deposit, or paid separately and ongoing even if you made a lump-sum deposit, depending on the insurance company offering the product. If the premium for the rider is ongoing, the good news with most of these life/LTC insurance plans is that the premium is guaranteed not to ever go up, so it is a budgetable expense. The other good news is that if you never need long-term care, your family receives the death benefit. As we mentioned in the **Accelerated Death Benefits** section, some policies will still pay a residual death benefit of perhaps 10% to your beneficiary, even if you needed long-term care and used the entire death benefit.

Your insurance professional can work with you to make the benefits meet your expectations at claim time.

Effect of the 1996 Health Insurance Portability and Accountability Act (HIPAA) and The Pension Protection Act of 2006

HIPAA allows benefit payments to be totally tax-free from any type of tax-qualified long-term care insurance plan – standard or combination - as long as benefits do not exceed the greater of $270 per day in 2008 or actual costs of care. Since the combo plans are usually reimbursement policies, which means they pay no more than the actual cost, that's not a worry. On the other hand, the separate premium for the options that extend the benefit period and/or increase the inflation coverage may be taken from the cash value of the policy and if it is, a portion may be taxable income to you. (If you are under age 59½, that amount is normally also subject to a 10 percent federal penalty.) Also, the premium for the options is the only part of the premium that will be treated as a medical expense and eligible for a tax deduction if medical expenses exceed 7.5 percent of your adjusted gross income (see **Tax Incentives for Long-Term Care Insurance** in Chapter One, *Long-Term Care Insurance and Your Financial Security).*

The taxation possibility is getting ready to change, however. The Pension Protection Act of 2006 will allow the distributions from cash value that are used to pay for long-term care insurance premium in these life/LTC policies to be tax-free at any age, beginning January 1, 2010, for all policies of this type issued after December 31, 1996. Further, the Pension Protection Act will allow exchanges of one life insurance or annuity contract for a single premium long-term care insurance policy tax-free after December 31, 2009. [Public Law 109-280, Sec. 6050U (g)(1) and (2)]

With the main portion of the policy prior to January 1, 2010, however, you get the best of both worlds—tax-deferred growth and tax-free benefits—which many people think far outweigh having just the premium for the extra inflation/benefit period extension rider as a potential tax deduction or as taxable income. People who are thinking about self-insuring especially like this policy because if long-term care is never needed, the money goes tax-free to your beneficiary as it is paid out in the form of a death benefit. Or, if for any reason you decide to cancel the policy, you can purchase the policy so that the guaranteed surrender value is never less than the single premium you paid, less any long-term care benefit payments, of course. If you need long-term care, however, there is a multiplier that makes the money available to pay long-term care benefits worth much more than the face value of the policy.

If you don't want to make a lump-sum payment, newer versions of this product are available with annual and 10-pay premiums as well.

In summary, the combination life insurance/LTC product is good for these types of people:

- People who plan to self-insure because they don't want to pay insurance premium for care they may never need
- People who can make up the difference if there is a significant shortfall between the monthly benefit and the actual cost of care
- People who have a standard long-term care insurance policy but want more coverage – this plan can be a good wraparound for the benefits they already own
- People who aren't concerned about leaving a significant death benefit to a beneficiary in the event they need long-term care and drain the policy, since the residual death benefit in those policies that have one is small.

Long-Term Care Insurance and Estate Planning

Here is a suggestion to help you with estate planning: make your adult child owner and beneficiary of a 10-pay policy with you as the insured. Give the child the premium each year through the $12,000 annual gift tax exclusion. Your accomplishments are four-fold:

▲   you accomplish the $12,000 annual gift to decrease the size of your taxable estate;

▲   the policy is not includable in your estate because you are neither the owner nor the beneficiary;

▲   your long-term care needs are taken care of if you fund the policy adequately; and

▲   your child will receive a significant death benefit if you never need long-term care.

Moreover, many estate planners recommend aggressive gifting, but many people are just not comfortable with gifting assets without a source to pay long-term care costs. Therefore, long-term care insurance, particularly the "nothing to lose, everything to gain" policy described in this section, can play a vital role in constructing and preserving a carefully crafted estate plan that requires aggressive gifting.

For example, those of you who have large estate tax problems could make the benefits of this policy payable to an irrevocable trust with your children as beneficiary, and just pay the long-term care costs yourself, which will further reduce your taxable estate. However, the benefits of the policy going into the irrevocable trust execute a large, tax-free gift to your children.

An article in an estate planning magazine several years ago summarized the advantages of the single-premium life insurance policy, which the authors referred to as "deposit-based long-term care insurance."[8] These advantages still are true today, so I'm sharing them with you. The article said by moving emergency funds that would otherwise be invaded for a long-term care need into a deposit-based long-term care insurance policy, you would:

1) preserve your principal;
2) have immediate access to the funds;
3) earn a modest return;
4) create a death benefit; and
5) most importantly, in the event of a long-term care need, multiply the value of these emergency funds by 200 percent or more, depending on your age when you are issued a policy.

Your tax advisor can tell you if any of these ideas are helpful for your situation.

Long-Term Care Annuities

A long-term care **deferred** annuity can play a huge role in helping people who cannot qualify for long-term care insurance due to age or health problems. This annuity is available to age 85 and there are very broad health questions so the medical qualification process is not as stringent as it is for standard long-term care insurance products. The questions deal with major conditions like dementia, Parkinson's disease, multiple sclerosis, Lou Gehrig's disease, and whether or not you are dependent on a walker or wheelchair or are bedridden. Being in a nursing home in the past two years would disqualify you, but having a couple of weeks of home health care in that same time frame would not.

This concept uses an annuity with two funds. One fund, which is for long-term care expenses, grows at a higher interest rate with a five-year rate guarantee, then current interest thereafter. (The interest rate as of January 2007 is 5.25 percent, which is equal to 7.5 percent in a taxable fund for someone in a combined 30 percent tax bracket.) The other fund, which is just the regular cash fund in an annuity, grows at a guaranteed rate of three percent. The five-year jumpstart on the long-term care fund ensures a higher amount available for long-term care. At the end of the fifth year, you decide if you want the strategy of growing the LTC fund at a higher rate to continue, or if you want to equalize the growth rate between the two funds. (The funds are automatically equalized around your 90th birthday.)

The purpose of the separate LTC fund is to allow you immediate access to the money for services from a licensed home health care agency, adult day care center, assisted living facility or nursing home care without a surrender charge. Otherwise, early withdrawals from an annuity mean limitations on the amount you can withdraw without a penalty, which is usually ten percent.

Benefits begin after only a seven-day waiting period when your doctor verifies that you either need help with at least two of six Activities of Daily Living (bathing, continence, dressing, eating, toileting and transferring) or you are cognitively impaired. The benefit is reimbursement, not indemnity, which means it will pay no more than actual expenses up to the monthly limit for a minimum of 36 months (18 months if a joint policy and both annuitants are receiving care at the same time). You can pay additional premium to extend your benefits for another 36 months or you can even purchase an unlimited benefit period. This extra premium is guaranteed to never increase and can be paid with a one-time, single premium or paid annually.

Here's an example of how LTC withdrawals will be calculated:

$200,000	(LTC fund balance at time of claim)
÷ 34.5	(factor to ensure a minimum of 36 months of coverage)
$ 5,797	per month available benefit for actual expenses

Money withdrawn from the LTC fund reduces the cash fund proportionally. For example, a $3,000 withdrawal from the LTC fund means a $1,500 withdrawal from the cash fund. Conversely, a $1,500 withdrawal from the cash fund means a $3,000 withdrawal from the LTC fund.

If you do not use up all of the money on long-term care, the amount remaining in the cash fund will be passed to your beneficiary outside of probate at your death, or the surviving annuitant (second-to-die) if it is a joint contract.

This product is a deferred annuity, which many people prefer over low-interest bearing accounts like CDs and money market funds because of the tax-deferred earnings. Having this product in place with money that you keep for an emergency anyway could give you the flexibility to have a longer waiting period on a traditional LTC policy. Some companies offer longer waiting periods in those states that allow it of 180 days, 365 days, 730 days or even three or five years.

Since it is a deferred annuity, you are taxed on the gain as withdrawals are made. This will change, beginning with tax years 2010 and on, thanks to the Pension Protection Act of 2006, which says that cash-value withdrawals from non-qualified annuities used to pay for qualified long-term care expenses or for tax-qualified long-term care insurance will no longer be considered taxable income, regardless of cost basis.

This product was introduced as a non-tax-qualified long-term care insurance policy. That means you are at risk of being taxed on the money that is dispersed from the LTC fund if the IRS rules against non-qualified policies. Beware of anyone telling you that you can deduct all of your LTC expenses as medical expenses at tax time so it really doesn't matter. **This is a reimbursement policy,** which means it will only make a payment from the LTC fund when a claim for an actual service or charge is presented, so it is directly reimbursing long-term care expenses. There's a very good chance the IRS would disqualify your deduction for medical expenses, because IRS Form 1040, Schedule A—Itemized Deductions plainly says *"Caution: Do not include expenses reimbursed or paid by others."* The good news, however, is that this long-term care annuity will be issued in 2007 forward as tax-qualified, and an amendment will be offered to existing policyholders which will make their policy tax-qualified beginning January 1, 2010.

This book in no way intends to give tax advice, so please see your personal tax advisor for an opinion on how this policy would apply to you or any other long-term care annuities that are not tax-qualified.

There are a number of long-term care annuities available today but some allow withdrawals only for nursing home expenses after an extended stay such as six months, or they pay a lower benefit for home care or adult day care or they may have a waiting period of several years before you can access the long-term care benefit. The PPA of 2006 will allow tax-free withdrawals after December 31, 2009 for qualified long-term care expenses if you want to consider exchanging an older annuity for a new annuity/long-term care insurance contract.

An especially nice feature of long-term care annuities is the flexibility to withdraw up to ten percent each year which gives you money to use for associated costs with long-term care that are not covered as an eligible long-term care expense, such as prescription drugs and care-related supplies.

A final caution on this product, as with the life insurance products discussed in this section, is to make sure you put enough money into it to accommodate inflation needs. Project the average cost for care in your area at a 5.8 percent compounded annual growth rate for the time frame in which you think you may need to access the LTC fund, which will be largely determined by your age (10, 15, 20 years, etc.), then decide how much of that cost you are willing to self-insure. Work with an insurance professional to be sure that you fund the annuity adequately to have the monthly benefit you think you will need at claim time.

A long-term care **immediate** annuity is available even to people already receiving long-term care, for example, a nursing home patient. This concept involves making a single premium which is converted into a monthly income guaranteed for the life of the policyholder. You can even select an annual rate for the payment to increase anywhere from one to ten percent to provide for inflation.

Why would anyone want to do this and what makes this type of annuity different than a regular immediate annuity? Here's the main reason: a regular immediate annuity is not medically underwritten and the same life expectancy tables are applied to everyone, regardless of medical condition. So an 82-year-old male desiring a monthly income of $3,000 would normally have to pay about $250,000 in a single premium. However, if he had dementia, this special long-term care immediate annuity would require only $155,000 to obtain the same $3,000 monthly benefit. Another example would be an 87-year-old female with Alzheimer's disease. A $5,500 monthly benefit could be obtained for a deposit of $238,000 instead of $411,000 in a regular immediate annuity. You can even structure the annuity so that your beneficiary will receive all or a portion of the money if you die earlier than the insurance company thought you would, particularly if you die within the first six months of purchase. Of course, you should seek advice from a professional tax advisor about the tax consequences before pursuing an option of this nature.

Reverse Mortgages

Since the majority of older Americans own their homes and have paid off their mortgages, many people find themselves "cash poor and house rich." Because of these characteristics, a certain amount of activity is occurring in the marketplace to help people tap the value of the home without giving it up as long as they live in it. Converting the equity of the home into cash can be accomplished either through sale plans or loan plans. The sale plans, which involve selling the home then leasing it back as long as the seller is able to live in it, are not popular for tax reasons. It's possible that the IRS will not view the plan as a bona fide sale if the house is not sold at fair market price, or if the buyer is receiving favorable treatment, or if the buyer does not assume full ownership until the death of the seller. If the IRS does not view the plan as a bona fide sale, the one-time capital gains exclusion is not available to the seller. In other words, people sometimes try to give their kids a bargain, and the IRS doesn't look favorably at special deals for children or any other buyers.

Home equity conversion loans in the form of reverse mortgages, are available, in which no repayment of the loan is ever required until the borrower dies, sells the home, or permanently leaves the residence for 12 months or more. Started by the federal government in 1988 to help older Americans on fixed incomes, the program allows homeowners age 62 and over to convert part of the equity in their homes into tax-free income without having to sell the home, give up the title, or take on a new monthly mortgage payment. You must be a homeowner, which can include a single family residence, condominium, townhouse, duplex, triplex, or four-plex, as long as the development meets FHA guidelines. Others who are not on a fixed income also see the benefits of "cashing in" on the equity in their home for additional investments. There are no income qualifications and limited credit qualifications, because unlike an equity loan from a bank, a reverse mortgage requires no monthly payments.

The funds available to the homeowner are tax free and don't count as income for Social Security eligibility purposes. The balance due grows as funds are disbursed to the homeowner. The funds can be disbursed in several ways. The available cash can be taken in a lump sum, monthly payments over a period of years, a lifetime, or as a line of credit you can draw down as needed over a number of years. You can even receive a combination of regular monthly payments and a line of credit. You still own the home. It can be sold at any time (for example, if you decide to move) and when sold, any balance due on the reverse mortgage is paid and the remaining equity goes to you or in the case of your death, to your estate. The amount of equity remaining depends on how long you remain in the home and the value of the home at the time of sale.

The reverse mortgage market is poised to grow substantially as the baby boomers move into their retirement years. As of this writing, there are six products available but that will increase to meet various demands of clients. Presently the most widely used product is FHA's Home Equity Conversion Mortgage (HECM). The Federal National Mortgage Association, known as Fannie Mae, offers a product called the Home Keeper. Fannie Mae doesn't make direct loans. It buys loans from lenders, packages them and resells them to investors. Financial Freedom, headquartered in Irvine, California, offers the Financial Freedom Cash Advantage loan, a private reverse mortgage product.

The older you are and the more valuable your home, the more you can borrow. Each program has a lending limit. The amount available to the client depends on the youngest homeowner's age, but all have to be over 62. It also depends on the value of the home, the amount of built-up home equity, and the interest rates at the time. Generally, a borrower in his or her early 60s could get about 38 percent of the home's equity, a 75-year-old could get about 58 percent, and someone in his or her 80s could get about 60 percent of the home's value.

Generally there is no cash out-of-pocket when you get a reverse mortgage. The proceeds of the reverse mortgage will be used to pay off an outstanding first mortgage or any other debt on the home. The associated fees such as the origination fee, the mortgage insurance fee, an appraisal fee and other standard closing costs may be financed as part of the reverse mortgage. You are responsible only for keeping up payments for your homeowner's insurance and property taxes, and to maintain the condition of your home.

Fannie Mae is utilized more frequently by older, single people than by married people, and the Financial Freedom Cash Advantage product is geared to higher valued homes.

If you take the money in monthly payments but live so long that the payments exceed the home's value, you or your heirs do not have to pay back any amount larger than the worth of your home. All reverse mortgages offered today have built-in consumer protection features that prevent you or your heirs from owing more than the value of your home at the time the loan comes due -- even if your home declines in value. This risk is assumed by the lender. After you die, your children (or other heirs) can keep the home if they like—they just have to pay the balance in full. They can pay off the reverse mortgage using their own money, or they can sell your house. If they sell your house for more than is owed, they can keep the difference. Some people (or their children) purchase a life insurance policy on the homeowner when they get the reverse mortgage so the children can use the death benefit to pay off the mortgage and keep the house.

Most interest rates on reverse mortgages are adjustable. Interest adds to the balance that will be owed when the property is sold. FHA offers either an annual or monthly adjustable interest rate and Fannie Mae has only a monthly adjustable. FHA's rate is the weekly average of the one-year Treasury Bill plus a margin of 1.5% for the monthly adjustable or 2.1% for the annual. For example, on January 9, 2007 the one-year T-Bill was 4.94%, so the annual rate was 8.08% and the monthly rate was 6.48%. Fannie Mae's rate is the weekly average of the one-month CD rate plus a margin of 3.4%. The one-month CD rate on January 9, 2007 was 5.10%, so the rate for a Fannie Mae reverse mortgage was 8.75%. Monthly adjustments to this interest rate will not affect monthly payments, unless you have chosen to take your money as a line of credit. Otherwise, fluctuating interest rates will only affect how much money is owed when you die, move out of your home, or sell your home.

Most of the cash from the various plans has been used for home modifications, home repairs, to weatherize homes, to make homes accessible for the handicapped, for supplemental retirement income, and some of the money is being used to fund long-term care services.

Rather than pay for long-term care services directly, much more mileage can be obtained from the money by purchasing long-term care insurance if you are insurable. You can purchase a long-term care insurance policy outright by paying a quarterly, semi-annual or annual premium. Some borrowers take the reverse mortgage as a line of credit, then use the interest growth each year to pay their long-term care insurance premiums. Or, a lump-sum obtained from a reverse mortgage can be used to purchase a single-pay long-term care insurance plan that is available in some states or an annuity, which can then be set up to pay the LTC insurance premiums for the rest of the insured's life. Or, the lump sum can be used to purchase a life insurance or annuity long-term care insurance policy as described in the preceding section that pays LTC expenses with a guaranteed premium.

For a list of lenders that offer reverse mortgages in your state, call the National Reverse Mortgage Lenders Association at 866-264-4466 or visit the website at www.reversemortgage.org and click on "Find a Lender".

To make sure families understand the program, FHA requires a free individual information meeting with a HUD-approved housing agency separate from the lender so you can learn about the program objectively and decide if it's right for you. You can get the name of a local counseling agency or qualified telephone counselor from a reverse mortgage lender or by calling AARP (888-687-2277), Fannie Mae's Homepath service (800-732-6643) or HUD's Housing Counseling Clearinghouse (800-569-4287).

Your State Agency on Aging also has information on organizations to contact if you are interested in obtaining a reverse mortgage. An AARP bulletin contained a warning from Andrew Cuomo, while he was secretary of the Department of Housing and Urban Development (HUD). Mr. Cuomo cautioned against salespeople contacting you to do a reverse mortgage and charging hefty fees for information and forms that HUD offers free. HUD counseling is a free service, and no one should ever pay a fee for the counseling, which can be done in person or over the phone, except in Massachusetts and North Carolina, where it must be done in person. If you suspect a scam, you can check out the organization that contacted you by calling HUD directly toll-free at 1-800-569-4287 and HUD will investigate at no charge to you.

Critical Illness Insurance

Critical illness policies were introduced in the United States in the mid-1990s and pay a lump-sum upon diagnosis of one of a dozen or so conditions including Alzheimer's (for people who need help with three or more activities of daily living and require permanent daily supervision as diagnosed by a board-certified neurologist), multiple sclerosis, heart attack, stroke when effects of the neurological injury last for at least 30 days, life threatening cancer (malignant and growing uncontrollably outside its original location), major organ transplant, paralysis, kidney failure requiring dialysis, blindness, deafness, and perhaps severe burns. Some policies even pay if you need help with three or more activities of daily living for at least 90 days, even if you don't have Alzheimer's. Some policies have a return of premium benefit, which means the premium will be returned to a beneficiary less any benefits paid out if the policyholder dies without receiving all of the benefits.

A partial benefit, perhaps 25 percent, is paid for conditions such as malignant cancer in one location, heart angioplasty and heart bypass surgery.

You may be charged a higher premium if one or more of your immediate family members (parents and siblings) have had any of these conditions.

Common issue ages are 20-64 but you can keep the policy as long as you live. However, benefits usually reduce to 50 percent at age 65 or five years after the effective date if you were older than 60 when you purchased the policy.

The lump-sum benefit can be anywhere from $25,000 to $1 million, depending on how much you purchase when you buy the policy. One company recommends three to five times annual salary for employed people plus any outstanding mortgage balance.

Critical illness policies can be standalone, or some are sold as an optional benefit with a life insurance policy or annuity. If sold in the workplace, there may be only a few medical questions in order to qualify.

The lump-sum benefit of a critical illness policy can be used to cover the miscellaneous expenses connected to a major illness such as:

▲   insurance deductibles and co-pays
▲   travel expenses such as meals, lodging and airfare to
     seek additional medical treatment
▲   experimental treatment and/or drugs
▲   treatment outside of a managed care network
▲   child care or elder care
▲   salary replacement for time away from work
▲   household help like cooking, cleaning and laundry
▲   home modifications
▲   mortgage payments and other debts

The point is, the lump-sum benefit of a critical illness policy is a cash benefit that can be used for anything.

Critical Illness Insurance vs. Long-Term Care Insurance

Can critical illness coverage be an alternative payment option for long-term care? Possibly, especially if you are not able to qualify for long-term care insurance and you are able to get a critical illness policy through your employer with simplified underwriting, which means just a few medical questions.

What are the pitfalls?

1) Access to benefits is tougher as even Alzheimer's patients would have to need help with at least three activities of daily living. Long-term care insurance policies require help with only two ADL's and there is no ADL requirement for an Alzheimer's patient. Rather, the Alzheimer's patient can collect benefits when he is considered a threat to himself or someone else.

2) The critical illness benefit is a lump-sum cash benefit which can bring a strong temptation to spend it for things other than long-term care services.

3) A lump-sum cash benefit may be difficult to budget so that it lasts throughout a long-term condition – you might remember from Chapter One that the average lifespan of an Alzheimer's patient is eight years but can be three to 20.[9]

4) Benefits reduce at age 65, and a long-term care insurance policy is sometimes most needed at older ages.

5) A $1 million benefit is projected to pay about three years of care in 30 years,[10] and that may not be enough long-term care coverage for someone purchasing a critical illness policy at age 50 or younger.

On the positive side, critical illness insurance can be relatively inexpensive at younger ages, especially if it is a rider on a life insurance policy, and the benefit would be invaluable if long-term care is needed at a young age. At any age, critical illness makes a good supplement to long-term care insurance as the money can be used for any need.

In summary, one funding method for long-term care does not fit all. Since this is America, it's safe to say that we will continue to see much product innovation as our country struggles to find a way to pay for long-term care with private funding as much as possible and prevent unprecedented taxation—the inevitable result if the baby boomers wind up on any kind of public assistance for long-term care.

People Who Do Not Qualify for LTC Insurance

People with significant health issues may not be able to qualify for a long-term care insurance policy. Here are some suggestions:

▲   Apply with another insurance company. Seek a company that doesn't just say "yes" or "no." There are companies that will sell you a policy for extra premium or will issue you a policy with an alternative benefit offer—perhaps a three-year or five-year benefit period instead of lifetime, or a 100-day waiting period instead of 20 or 60 days. The majority of long-term care claims are less than three years, so a policy with a shorter benefit period may work out fine for you.[11] However long your policy will pay is that much time for you to be a private-pay patient, which will increase your choices and independence.

▲   If long-term care insurance is offered through your employer, be sure to apply when it is first offered, because there usually is a one-time opportunity to apply with few or no health questions.

▲   The new long-term care annuities discussed in this section may be an especially good option for you since some of them ask only a few medical questions, and one will provide benefits even if you already need long-term care.

▲   A viatical or life settlement as discussed in this section may be an option for you if you have any type of life insurance.

▲   A reverse mortgage as discussed in this section may be an option if you have your home paid off or almost paid off.

▲   You may be able to get a critical illness policy that asks only a few medical questions, especially if it is offered through your employer.

▲   There are annuities on the market that have no surrender charges if the withdrawal is used for nursing home expenses.

▲   Seek the advice of a good elder-law attorney and your State Agency on Aging. Contact the National Academy of Elder Law Attorneys, 1604 North Country Club Road, Tucson, Arizona 85716 or go to www.naela.org for a national registry of elder-law attorneys.

Where Do I Go From Here?

To choose the best long-term care insurance policy, call an insurance professional you can trust. Call as soon as you can to take advantage of rates based on your current age and your good health. Health is our most precious asset. Once health problems occur, it can be impossible to get a long-term care insurance policy.

For decades, most of us have lived in denial regarding the physical, emotional and financial trauma that often characterizes LTC. We refuse to talk openly about the possibility of someday needing protracted medical care. Instead, we say, "I'll never have a stroke or develop Alzheimer's disease. Even if I do, the Veteran's Administration or Medicare or my Elk's Lodge or my children will take care of me. After all, we reason, I'm sure that after working and paying taxes for 40 years, I'm at least entitled to some kind of care."

Tragically, the ultimate consequence of that denial is often both traumatic and unnecessary to the individual, their [sic] spouse and family, and their [sic] community. *

---

* "Jousting with Dragons: A Manifesto" by Martin K. Bayne, "Mr. Long-Term Care"

So, go to the telephone and call for help today. Do it now, for yourself, but mostly for your family.

Appendix A:
Senior Benefits

Medicare Benefits

~~~~~~

Medicare, a federal program, is the cornerstone of the older American's health care benefits and is available to all Americans at age 65. Some people think Medicare is sufficient to handle their health care financing needs, but as this chapter will show, the program has some very big gaps—gaps that can leave you with huge bills if you are not prepared. The largest gap is long-term care, according to America's Health Insurance Plans, the world's largest trade association for the health care industry.[1]

Enrolling for Medicare

Most Americans are automatically enrolled for Medicare when they reach age 65. Your Medicare card shows you the effective date of your coverage. The program is administered by the Centers for Medicare and Medicaid Services (CMS) of the U.S. Department of Health and Human Services. The Social Security Administration provides information about the program and handles enrollment. You should contact your local Social Security office for information at least three months before you turn 65. You can also call the Social Security toll-free number 1-800-772-1213 any business day from 7 a.m. to 7 p.m. EST (toll-free TTY number, 1-800-325-0778), if you have questions about Medicare eligibility or need enrollment information.

Four Parts of Medicare

The Medicare program is made up of four parts, A-D:

1) Part A – Hospital Benefits
2) Part B – Medical Benefits
3) Part C – Medicare Advantage
4) Part D– Medicare Prescription Drug Program

Appendix A of **Long-Term Care: Your Financial Planning Guide** will explain each one.

The Original Medicare Program – Parts A and B

The original Medicare program is called a "fee-for-service" program, which means it reimburses your health care providers for each specific service they provide to you. It has two parts. **Part A** covers inpatient-type care—inpatient hospitalization, skilled nursing facility stays, psychiatric hospitalization, as well as hospice care and home health care. **Part B** covers medical services—physician services, related medical services and supplies, outpatient hospital treatment, X-rays and laboratory tests, ambulance services, physical, occupational and speech therapy, mental health services and certain preventive services.

Part A is financed through part of the Social Security (FICA) tax paid by all workers and their employers. You do not have to pay a monthly premium for Medicare Part A if you or your spouse are entitled to benefits under either the Social Security or Railroad Retirement systems, or have worked a sufficient period of time in federal, state or local government employment to be insured. If you do not meet the qualifications for premium-free Part A benefits, you may purchase the coverage if you are at least age 65 and meet certain requirements. The Part A premium for 2008 is $423 per month if you have less than 30 quarters of Social Security coverage. It is $233 per month for 30–39 quarters.

Part B is optional but is offered to all beneficiaries when they become entitled to premium-free Part A. It may also be purchased by most people age 65 or over who do not qualify for premium-free Part A coverage. (Note: If you purchase Part A, you must purchase Part B as well.) The Part B premium is deducted from your Social Security or Railroad Retirement check and for the first time, it is based on income starting January 1, 2007. Most people will pay the lowest amount of $96.40 per month in 2008, but higher-income individuals and couples will pay more according to this schedule:

If Your Yearly Income Is:		You Pay
Individual Tax Return	Joint Tax Return	
$80,000 or less	$160,000 or less	$96.40
$80,000 - $100,000	$160,001-$200,000	$122.20
$100,001 - $150,000	$200,001 - $300,000	$160.90
$150,001 - $200,000	$300,001 - $400,000	$199.70
Above $200,000	Above $400,000	$238.40

You are automatically enrolled in Part B when you become entitled to Part A unless you state that you don't want it. Although you do not have to purchase Part B, it is an excellent buy because the federal government pays 75% of the program costs.[2] Your Medicare card will show the coverage you have—Hospital Insurance (Part A), Medical Insurance (Part B) or both—and the date your coverage started. If you have only one part of Medicare, you can get information about getting the other part from your local Social Security office.

If you are still covered under an employer's health insurance plan after you are 65 or because you or your spouse is still working, you should accept Part A Medicare but elect to postpone enrolling for Part B until you are no longer covered through the group. You will save the monthly Part B premium by delaying your Part B enrollment. Once you retire or your group insurance terminates (whichever comes first), you have eight months to enroll in Part B without a penalty. Contact your Social Security office as soon as you know your group coverage is going to end to obtain the necessary forms: 1) for the employer to certify that you have had group coverage and 2) for you to complete indicating that you now want Part B. If you are not covered by an employer's health plan, you should enroll in Part B during your initial enrollment period, which is the seven-month period beginning three months before you are first able to get Medicare. For most people, this means three months before their 65th birthday. If you don't accept Part B during that seven-month period, you will have to wait until the next general enrollment period to enroll (January 1 through March 31 of each year). Your premium will be 10% higher for each year you wait, and the coverage won't begin until the following July.

The Centers for Medicare and Medicaid Services, U.S. Department of Health and Human Services provide free publications on specific topics. An excellent publication that explains the Medicare enrollment process in more detail is *Enrolling in Medicare.* For more detailed information about how Medicare works with other benefits such as group plans, VA benefits, TRICARE (formerly CHAMPUS), or any other plan, you may want a copy of *Medicare and Other Health Benefits: Who Pays First?*

Individuals younger than 65 can get Medicare solely on the basis of permanent kidney failure or after two years of receiving Social Security Disability benefits. This program is explained in *Medicare Coverage of Kidney Dialysis and Kidney Transplant Services.* If you have questions about specific Medicare requirements or benefit features, be sure to consult *Medicare and You.* For a free copy of any of these booklets, you can:

- write to Medicare Publications, Centers for Medicare & Medicaid Services, 7500 Security Blvd., Baltimore, MD 21244-1850; or
- pick them up from your local Social Security Administration office; or
- order them by calling 1-800-MEDICARE (800-633-4227); or
- for the quickest access to this information, you can visit the official Medicare website at www.medicare.gov and print them.

The Medicare Gaps

When Medicare was created, Congress determined that the patient should share in paying for the cost of the care he or she received. The underlying concept is simple: If the patient shares in the cost of care, he or she will be more likely to use the benefits wisely. So, the program was designed with deductible and coinsurance amounts the patient must pay.

In the first years of the Medicare program, these deductible and coinsurance charges were moderate amounts. But after more than three decades of annual increases, these charges can add up. For example:

▲ You must pay the first $1,024 of your bill when you are hospitalized.

▲ You must pay $128 each day for days 21 through 100 in a skilled nursing facility.

▲ You must pay the first $135 of the Medicare-approved amounts for doctor services, medical supplies and equipment, outpatient services and ambulance.

▲ You must pay 20% of the cost of your bills for doctor services, medical supplies and equipment, outpatient services and ambulance.

▲ You must pay charges above the Medicare-approved amount billed by doctors who do not accept Medicare assignment (up to a 115% cap—see below).

▲ In addition to your 20% co-payment, you must pay all costs for physical or occupational therapy provided by independent therapists (outside a nursing home or hospital) in excess of Medicare's maximum annual allowance. The annual allowance for 2008 is $1,810 for physical and speech therapy. A separate maximum of $1,810 applies to occupational therapy.

These expenses can add up quickly, and this is only a representative sample of some of the most common Medicare gaps. In addition to financial gaps caused by the deductible and coinsurance amounts, there are also gaps caused by coverage limitations and administrative considerations.

Medicare-Approved Charges

One of the most misunderstood aspects of Medicare is the way doctor charges are determined.

All of your doctor's charges may not be considered eligible for the 80% Medicare Part B reimbursement. Medicare payment is based on the Medicare-approved amounts, not the actual charges billed by the physician or medical supplier. The Medicare-approved amount is based on a national fee schedule. This schedule assigns a value to each physician service based on the specific service performed, his or her medical practice costs, malpractice insurance costs and a geographical factor. Each time you go to the physician, the amount Medicare will recognize for that service will be taken from the national fee schedule. Medicare will generally pay 80% of that amount. (Example: The doctor charges $100. Medicare may approve $70 and pay 80%, which means that Medicare would actually pay $56.)

Doctors who take assignment on a Medicare claim agree to accept the Medicare-approved amount as payment in full. They are paid directly by Medicare, and you pay them any deductible or coinsurance amount due. Ask your doctor if he or she accepts Medicare assignment.

Many physicians and suppliers accept assignment on a case-by-case basis. If your physician or supplier does not accept assignment, you are responsible for the bill, and Medicare will reimburse you. However, physicians who do not accept assignment of a Medicare claim are reimbursed at a lower level and are limited by law as to the amount they can charge you for covered services. The most a non-participating physician can charge you for services covered by Medicare is 115% of the fee schedule amount. (Some states also have special laws that limit how much physicians can charge—Connecticut, Massachusetts, Minnesota, New York, Ohio, Pennsylvania, Rhode Island and Vermont. Check with your state's insurance department or Office on Aging for more information. See *Appendix B* for contact information.)

Regardless of whether physicians accept assignment, they are required to file your Medicare claims for you. If they accept assignment, Medicare pays the physician and sends you a notice, called a Medicare Summary Notice (MSN), to let you know how much was paid. If the doctor does not accept assignment, Medicare pays you and you pay the doctor the amount Medicare paid plus all permissible charges, which may include your $135 calendar year deductible for Part B, your 20% co-payment, and any charge above the Medicare-approved amount up to the 115% cap. Only Medicare-approved amounts count toward the $135 Part B deductible, not the actual charges billed by the physician or medical supplier.

You may contact the insurance company that administers the Medicare Part B program in your area for a list of the doctors in your area who take assignment, or you can access a list at www.medicare. gov. However, it's still a good idea to check with the doctor when you make an appointment because the doctor may have stopped taking assignment since the list was updated.

Medicare Preventive Services

The original Medicare program typically pays for treatment once you have a health problem. In the last few years however, several "wellness" or "preventive" benefits have been added. The most notable is coverage for a "Welcome to Medicare" physical exam within the first six months of Part B coverage for those who enroll in Part B on or after January 1, 2005. Others are listed in the chart of 2008 Medicare Benefits at the end of this chapter.

Be Informed

As shown above, Medicare does not pay the entire cost for all services covered by the program. You or your Medicare supplemental insurance must pay certain deductible and coinsurance amounts and charges in excess of Medicare's approved amount. When you are enrolled in Medicare and any coverage that supplements Medicare, you will receive complete details on the limitations and exclusions of Medicare. Be sure to read that information carefully. As with any insurance plan, understanding your benefit provisions up front helps you avoid many financial and administrative problems when you file claims. **So, carefully read your Medicare and Medicare supplemental coverage literature.**

Appeals

If you don't agree with how Medicare handles a claim or if you think more should have been paid, you have the right to appeal the claim. Best results are obtained if you send a letter from your doctor with your appeal. Just ask the doctor to write a letter that further justifies the services performed. Many times an appeal results in an additional payment. Send the appeal to the Medicare carrier listed on your Medicare Summary Notice.

Get Personalized Medicare Information

If you are an Internet user, you may register at My.Medicare.gov to track your health care claims, including your preventive services, and see all of your Medicare information in one place. Explore www.medicare.gov for the wealth of information and services available at that site, including quality of care surveys on home health agencies, nursing homes, hospitals, doctors and dialysis facilities. You also can see lists of doctors who accept the Medicare-approved amount as full payment.

2008 Medicare Benefits

Medicare Part A

HEALTH CARE FACILITY SERVICES	Medicare pays:
Inpatient Hospital Services, Semi-Private Room and Board, Miscellaneous Hospital Services and Supplies, Drugs, X-Rays, Lab Tests	All but $1,024 during 1st 60 days of a benefit period*
	All but $256 a day for 61st through 90th day of a benefit period*
	All but $512 a day for 91st day through 150th day of a benefit period* (while using the 60-day Medicare lifetime reserve)
Post-Hospital **Skilled Nursing Facility Care** for a Medicare-Approved Stay in a Medicare- Approved Facility	All costs for first 20 days of a benefit period.*
	All but $128 a day for 21st through 100th day of a benefit period.*
	*BENEFIT PERIOD: A new benefit period begins after you have been out of a hospital or skilled nursing facility for 60 days in a row.
Blood	All but the first three pints during a calendar year, unless blood is replaced.

Home Health Care

When you first qualify for benefits, skilled nursing care can be provided on fewer than seven days each week or less than eight hours each day over a period of 21 days or less. Thereafter, skilled nursing or home health aide services must combine to total less than 8 hours per day and 28 or fewer hours each week. These guidelines are now subject to a prospective payment system, effective 10/1/00, for home health agencies, which allow a set amount of money for each 60 days care is needed. This 60-day period is called an "episode of care." The payment is based on what kind of health care an average person in a similar medical situation would need.

Visits are paid for a nurse or home health aide as long as skilled care is needed at least once every 60 days. (Drawing blood is no longer considered a skilled service.) Also pays for part-time services for physical therapy, speech therapy, nutritional counseling, and respiratory therapy. Patient must be homebound. (Homebound rules were relaxed in 2002 to allow special occasions such as graduations, family reunions and funerals.)

Medical equipment such as wheelchairs, hospital beds, oxygen and walkers paid at 80%.

Hospice
(Available to patients
certified as terminally ill.)

Unlimited benefits. No deductible for physician services, nursing care, medical appliances and supplies, counseling, and home health aide and homemaker services. Pays all but 5% of cost of outpatient drugs or $5 per prescription, whichever is lower. Inpatient respite care is limited to five days per stay, and hospice does not pay for ongoing eight-hour shifts of non-skilled home care.

Medicare Part B

PHYSICIANS' CHARGES	Medicare pays:
Services of a **Physician, Nurse Practitioner and Physician Assistant**	80% of reasonable charges* after $135 annual deductible, except 50% for mental health visits
	*Reasonable charges are determined by Medicare.
Outpatient Services and Medical Supplies (Other Than Blood and Immunosuppressive Therapy Drugs), Ambulance	Sometimes they are called Medicare-approved charges or Medicare-eligible expenses.
Blood	80% of Medicare-approved amount after $135 deductible after the 1st three pints unless replaced.
Home Health Care	Covers home health care if the patient does not have Part A. These services are still subject to the "episode of care" payment method set forth by the prospective payment system effective for home health providers 10/1/00 as explained in the Home Health Care section of Part A.

Preventive Services
(20% co-payment* and
Part B deductible apply,
except no deductible
for mammograms, pap
smears, pelvic exams. No
co-payment or deductible
for PSA test.

Women: Covers annual mammograms after age 40 and pap smears, pelvic exams once every two years. **Men:** Prostate cancer screening every year. **All:** Covers bone mass measurements every two years; colorectal cancer screening every year to every four years; cardiovascular screening every five years to check cholesterol and other blood fat levels; diabetes services and supplies, including glucose monitors, testing strips, and lancets including self-management tests, and smoking cessation programs.

* 25% for flexible
sigmoidoscopies or
colonoscopies done in a
hospital outpatient setting

MISCELLANEOUS:
Immunosuppressive
Drugs (Drugs after Organ
Transplant) and Some
Oral Cancer Drugs

80% of reasonable charges after $135 deductible

Medicare pays only for services it determines to be medically necessary and only the amount it determines to be reasonable.

Since 1983, reimbursement to hospitals is based on a pre-established amount based on the diagnosis of the patient's condition, which is called a prospective payment system (PPS). If you are discharged earlier than expected, the hospital makes money. If you stay longer than the standard, the hospital loses money. For this reason, doctors are under tremendous pressure to get the patient out of the hospital as soon as possible. Nursing homes and home health agencies also are paid under a similar prospective payment system. The PPS started for home health agencies October 1, 2000 and was phased in for nursing homes by 2002.

Reimbursement to physicians is based on a national fee schedule. Doctors who "accept assignment" do not bill patients for amounts above the fee schedule. Doctors who do not accept assignment can bill patients for no more than 15% above the amount on the national fee schedule for each procedure.

Expenses Not Covered By Medicare

Medicare does not provide benefits for:

▲ acupuncture

▲ care received outside the U.S., except under certain conditions in Canada (the United States means the 50 states, the District of Columbia, Puerto Rico, the Virgin Islands, Guam, the Northern Mariana Islands, and American Samoa)

▲ chiropractic services except for manipulation of the spine

▲ cosmetic surgery

▲ custodial care (non-skilled care) at home or in a nursing home; e.g. help with bathing, dressing, using the bathroom, transferring, and eating

▲ dental care or dentures, checkups except the initial physical exam, preventive services as named on the preceding page, most routine immunizations (except flu shots, pneumonia vaccines and Hepatitis B shots are covered), homemaker services, routine foot care, examinations for and the cost of eyeglasses or hearing aids

▲ most outpatient drugs*

▲ physician charges above Medicare's approved amount

▲ private-duty nursing at home or in the hospital

▲ private room in a hospital unless it's medically necessary

▲ skilled nursing home costs beyond 100 days unless you stop receiving skilled care 60 days in a row

*Ninety percent of Medicare beneficiaries had some type of drug coverage as of January 2008 - either through the new Medicare Part D program, retiree plans through an employer, through the VA or through the assistance for the low income "dual-eligible" population who are eligible for Medicaid and Medicare.[3]

Medicare Supplement Policies

M edicare supplement policies, sometimes referred to as "Medigap" coverage, are individual policies from private insurance companies that are designed to pay the coinsurance amounts, deductibles and other gaps **after Medicare benefits have been provided.** And that's the caution—Medicare supplements are designed to pay only after Medicare has made a payment. With a few exceptions, they typically do not pay for services not covered by Medicare. Medicare supplemental insurance policies can be valuable, however, as Medicare alone will not pay all of a patient's medical expenses.

Do You Need a Medicare Supplement?

Medicare supplements are purchased by a fourth of Medicare beneficiaries to fill gaps in benefits under the original Medicare program,[4] but there are four types of people who do not need a Medicare supplement:

▲ Individuals *who are enrolled in a Medicare managed care plan* (see **Medicare Advantage Plans** in the next section). Medicare Advantage plans provide all of the services provided by Medicare Part A and B without the deductibles and co-payments you learned about in the last section, so you don't need a Medicare supplement.

▲ *Low-income individuals* who can get the Medicare Part A and Part B deductibles and coinsurance payments and the Part B premium paid by their state Medicaid program. Low-income means your annual income is below the national poverty level and your assets, not counting your home or vehicle, are less than $4,000 ($6,000 for couples).

The 2008 federal income guidelines for this program are $887 a month for individuals and $1,187 a month for couples. These amounts are higher for Alaska and Hawaii. Note: These amounts include an additional $20, which is called "a monthly Supplemental Security Income disregard," which means these are the true amounts of income you can have to qualify for this program.

Call your local Medicaid office if you think you might qualify, and to obtain current income amounts which are announced each February. Ask for information about the Medicare Savings Program, formerly called the Qualified Medicare Beneficiary (QMB) program. (See *Appendix B* for contact information.)

Note: if your income is too much to qualify for the QMB program, you may still be able to qualify for the Specified Low-Income Medicare Beneficiary (SLMB) program, which will pay your Part B premium of $96.40 per month in 2008. Your assets still have to be low, but your 2008 income could be as much as $1,060 for an individual and $1,460 for a couple. (Rates for Alaska and Hawaii are slightly higher.)

▲   *Individuals who are allowed by their employers to continue group health insurance after retiring* usually do not need a separate Medicare supplement policy. Retiree group insurance usually has better benefits (i.e. prescription drugs, hearing aids, vision aids, etc.) than an individual Medicare supplement.

▲   *Individuals or spouses who work past age 65* can be covered by an employer's group health plan if the employer has 20 or more employees and should elect to do so as group plans are normally better than individual Medicare supplement policies. Upon retirement, the individual can purchase a Medicare supplement policy if the employer does not provide group coverage to retirees.

People who either don't meet the low income requirements of the Medicare Savings Program (formerly Qualified Medicare Beneficiary program) or who are not covered by an employer or former employer or who are not enrolled in a Medicare Advantage plan may consider purchasing a good individual Medicare supplement policy, unless they decide to self-insure balances to Medicare.

Can You Self-Insure Balances to Medicare?

Individuals with significant assets who wish to self-insure balances to Medicare can do so as today, balances after Medicare's payments are small. Some people elect to do this because they feel the money they have been using for Medicare supplemental insurance is better spent to pay long-term care insurance premium, because long-term care is a much bigger risk than balances to Medicare. A recent report showed that the average amount spent by people with Medicare supplement policies in 2003 was about $3,500, much higher than the average out-of-pocket expense of only $1,905 for people with no supplemental coverage to Medicare.[5]   (The $3,500 includes the average Medicare supplement premium of $1,899 for in force policies and $1,525 for new policies.)[6]

Disabled Individuals Under Age 65

The states in the list below require insurance companies to offer at least one type of Medicare supplement policy to disabled individuals who qualify for Medicare under age 65.[7] If you don't live in one of these states, there still may be insurance companies in your state that offer Medicare supplement coverage to disabled Medicare beneficiaries under age 65. There is information at the end of the Medicare Supplement section to help you find out the types of plans that are available in your state. (See **Open Enrollment** on p. 248 for legislation effective January 1, 1995 to help disabled people get better plans at age 65.

- California
- Colorado
- Connecticut
- Hawaii
- Kansas
- Louisiana
- Maine
- Maryland
- Massachusetts
- Michigan
- Minnesota
- Mississippi
- Missouri
- New Hampshire
- New Jersey
- New York
- North Carolina
- Oklahoma
- Oregon
- Pennsylvania
- South Dakota
- Texas
- Vermont
- Washington
- Wisconsin

Federal Guidelines for Medicare Supplements

The insurance industry developed very good Medicare supplement policies throughout the history of the Medicare program. But there has been abuse of this sensitive market. For this reason, the federal government implemented guidelines in 1992 that require insurance companies to simplify the Medicare supplement enrollment process. The federal guidelines say insurance companies can now sell only ten standard policies. Massachusetts, Minnesota and Wisconsin standardized their Medicare supplement plans earlier and didn't have to conform to the national standardized plans. An excellent publication to see the benefit choices available in those states is *Choosing a Medigap Policy: A Guide to Health Insurance for People with Medicare* from the Centers for Medicare and Medicaid Services. It's easy to find at www.medicare.gov, the Medicare web site or by calling 1-800-MEDICARE (1-800-633-4227) to request a copy. TTY users should call 1-877-486-2048.

The ten original standardized policies are designated A-J. Since then, two additional plans have been added, K and L. All insurance companies that sell Medicare supplement insurance have to offer Plan A, also called the basic policy. The other plans are optional. The basic policy (Plan A) covers the following core benefits:

▲ Coverage for the Part A coinsurance amount ($256 per day in 2008) for the 61st through the 90th day of hospitalization in each benefit period.

▲ Coverage for the Part A coinsurance amount ($512 per day in 2008) for each of Medicare's 60 non-renewable lifetime hospital inpatient reserve days used.

▲ After all Medicare hospital benefits are exhausted, coverage for 100 percent of the Medicare Part A eligible hospital expenses. Coverage is limited to a maximum of 365 days of additional inpatient hospital care during the policyholder's lifetime. The benefit is paid either at the rate Medicare pays hospitals under the Prospective Payment System or another appropriate standard of payment.

▲ Coverage under Medicare Parts A and B for the reasonable cost of the first three pints of blood or equivalent quantities of packed red blood cells per calendar year unless replaced in accordance with federal regulations.

▲ Coverage for the 20 percent coinsurance amount for Part B services after the $135 annual deductible is met.

The chart on the next page summarizes the standard Medicare supplement plans.

Summary of Standard Medicare Supplement Plans

A	B	C	D	E	F*	G	H	I	J*
Basic Benefits	Basic Benefits	Basic Benefits	Basic Benefits	Basic Benefits	Basic Benefits	Basic Benefits	Basic Benefits	Basic Benefits	Basic Benefits
		Skilled Nursing Coinsurance	Skilled Nursing Coinsurance	Skilled Nursing Coinsurance	Skilled Nursing Coinsurance	Skilled Nursing Coinsurance	Skilled Nursing Coinsurance	Skilled Nursing Coinsurance	Skilled Nursing Coinsurance
	Part A Deductible	Part A Deductible	Part A Deductible	Part A Deductible	Part A Deductible	Part A Deductible	Part A Deductible	Part A Deductible	Part A Deductible
		Part B Deductible			Part B Deductible				Part B Deductible
					Part B Excess (100%)	Part B Excess ((80%)		Part B Excess (100%)	Part B Excess (100%)
		Foreign Travel Emergency	Foreign Travel Emergency	Foreign Travel Emergency	Foreign Travel Emergency	Foreign Travel Emergency	Foreign Travel Emergency	Foreign Travel Emergency	Foreign Travel Emergency
			At-Home Recovery			At-Home Recovery		At-Home Recovery	At-Home Recovery
				Preventive Care					Preventive Care

* $1,900 high deductible option for Plans F and J

Features of a Good Medicare Supplement Policy

∿∿∿∿∿∿∿∿∿∿∿∿∿∿∿∿∿∿∿∿∿∿∿∿∿∿∿∿∿∿

With standardized policies, it is much easier to select a good Medicare supplement insurance policy. Nevertheless, the following features are still important considerations when evaluating which Medicare supplement policy you should purchase.

If you already have Medicare and a Medicare supplement policy, this chapter can help you evaluate your current policy. The federal Medicare supplement guidelines below only apply to policies sold after the guidelines were implemented in 1992.

Guaranteed Renewable—this means the policy can never be cancelled as long as you pay the premiums and as long as you answered all the questions in the application truthfully. It can't be cancelled even if you have a lot of claims. If you have a policy issued before 1992, it could be conditionally renewable and the insurance company could drop you. If that happens, you will have 63 days to buy a Medicare supplement plan A, B, C or F without health questions.[8]

Rating of the Insurance Company—Even if a policy is guaranteed renewable, if the insurance company goes broke, your policy might not stay in force. Buy policies from insurance companies with an A. M. Best rating of B+ or higher. Lower ratings put you at risk of losing your policy if the company experiences financial difficulties. See **Rates and Ratings** in Chapter 2 for information on how to check an insurance company's ratings and assets.

Pre-existing Conditions—If you replace your old Medicare supplement policy with a new one, the new policy has to cover you immediately for health problems you already have unless the replacement occurs in the first six months after purchasing your first Medicare supplement policy. This means no waiting period for pre-existing conditions for most replacements. If you are just becoming 65 and buying your first Medicare policy, the longest you have to wait for coverage for pre-existing conditions is six months. The government publication *Choosing a Medigap Policy* says, "the insurance company can only use this kind of waiting period if your health problem was **diagnosed** or **treated** during the six months before your Medicare supplement coverage starts. This means the insurance company can't make you wait for coverage of your condition just because it thinks you should have known to see a doctor." [9] However, if your new Medicare supplement has a benefit that wasn't in the old one, the new insurance company can make you wait up to six months before covering you for that benefit, regardless of how long you had your old Medicare supplement policy.[10] It's not common, but it could happen, so ask the insurance professional who is selling you the new policy if you have a pre-existing waiting period for any benefits.

Underwriting—Unless it is your first policy, Medicare supplement policies you apply for can decline you or charge you more if you have health problems. To get a replacement Medicare supplement policy, you must answer questions about your health. Some companies need time to review your answers and many companies get more information from your doctor. Other companies give your insurance professional the authority to issue you a policy immediately if you can answer "no" to the health questions on the application. In these cases, your professional will leave the policy with you as soon as you complete and sign the application and pay your premium.

Open Enrollment—Federal guidelines guarantee that for six months following enrollment in Part B of Medicare, persons age 65 or older can't be declined or charged more for a Medicare supplement because of health problems. Insurance companies cannot impose a waiting period for pre-existing conditions during the initial open enrollment period if you have had at least six months of health insurance coverage before you apply for the Medicare supplement policy. If you've had less than six months, you get credit for the amount of time you have had health insurance coverage.

Open enrollment for disabled people under age 65: On January 1, 1995, federal law extended open enrollment for six months at age 65 to those persons who were first enrolled in Part B of Medicare prior to age 65 by reason of disability or end stage renal disease. If you purchase a Medicare supplement policy as a disabled person prior to age 65, you probably will be able to get Plan A or B. This law means you can get a better policy (Plans C–L) at age 65 with no health questions and possibly for a lower premium, depending on your state. Some states require insurance companies to offer the best price for under age 65 applicants and some states allow companies to charge more for them. If you have had Medicare at least six months before your open enrollment period at age 65, you won't have a waiting period for pre-existing conditions, because Medicare counts as health insurance to satisfy the requirement mentioned above in **Open Enrollment.**

Open enrollment for people who work past age 65: If you or your spouse continue to work past age 65 so that you are covered under an employer's group plan, you can delay enrollment in Part B of Medicare until you are no longer covered under the group plan. When you know your group coverage is ending, you can apply for Part B of Medicare with no penalty, and you will have the six-month open enrollment period to obtain an individual Medicare supplement policy regardless of any health problems you have. You will not have a pre-existing waiting period under your new Medicare supplement policy because you will have had health insurance for at least six months prior to the effective date of the Medicare supplement.

Right to Suspend a Medicare Supplement Policy If You Go Back to Work – Thanks to the Ticket to Work and Work Incentives Improvement Act of 1999, if you have a Medicare supplement then go to work for a company that offers a group health plan, you can ask the Medicare supplement carrier to suspend your policy until you notify the insurance company of the date that you are no longer covered under the group health plan. Your premium and your coverage will be reinstated on that date without medical questions.

Premiums—Many insurance companies allow you to save money if you pay once a year (annually) or twice a year (semi-annually) versus paying monthly or quarterly. If you decide to cancel the policy for any reason, the insurance company does not have to, but may refund the balance of the premiums not used. The three most common methods for premium calculation for Medicare supplement policies are 1) community rating— all policyholders pay the same rate regardless of age, 2) issue age rating—

premium is based on the age you apply for the policy and 3) attained age rating—age 65 premium is usually lower than Methods 1 and 2 but increases either annually or in age bands such as every five years as you get older. With Methods 1 and 2, premiums go up only to reflect inflation in the cost of benefits, which means as Medicare deductibles and co-payments increase, the policy has to pay out more in benefits so you may see a slight increase from year to year. Method 3 has rate increases as you get older because premiums are actually rising with your age, in addition to medical inflation.

The following states require community rating: Arkansas, Connecticut, Massachusetts, Nebraska, New York, Vermont and Washington, whereas these states require issue age rating: Arizona, Florida, Georgia, Idaho and Missouri.[11]

Ways to save money on Medicare supplement premium – Since the ten standardized plans were introduced, two cost-saving opportunities have been introduced:

1) a high deductible version of Plans F and J – no benefits are paid until you have paid $1,900 in out-of-pocket costs in 2008. This deductible can increase each year. Also, the $250 deductible for foreign travel emergency still applies.

2) two new lower-cost plans have been introduced, K and L.

These two new plans pay a percentage of key gaps in Medicare, which is why premiums can be lower. This chart will give you an idea:

2008 Out-of-Pocket Amounts	Plan K Pays:	Plan L Pays:
Part A Hospital Deductible ($1,024)	50% ($512)	75% ($768)
Part B Deductible ($135)	Not covered	Not covered
Skilled Nursing Facility Co-payment ($128/day for days 21-100)	50% ($62/day)	75% ($93/day)
20% co-payment for physician services and supplies	50% (you will pay 10% of Medicare-approved amounts)*	75% (you will pay 5% of Medicare-approved amounts)*
Blood	50% of first three pints per calendar year	75% of first three pints per calendar year
Hospice – Medicare pays most of the costs for hospice services	50% of what's left	75% of what's left

*Plans K and L will pay 100% of the co-payment for Medicare preventive services and will pay 100% of the other co-payments including the hospital deductible after you have paid $4,000 out-of-pocket for Plan K and $2,000 out-of-pocket for Plan L in a calendar year.

A word about the hospital deductible – Many people make the mistake of thinking the hospital deductible occurs once a year like the Part B deductible for physician services and supplies. Not so. The hospital deductible is payable per benefit period, which means each time you have a hospital stay separated by more than 60 days, a new hospital deductible is required. If you were extremely unlucky and were admitted to the hospital every 61 days for a one night stay, you could have five hospital deductibles in a 12-month period! That's not going to happen, of course, but it helps you understand how it works, doesn't it?

Free-Look Period—You have 30 days after you receive your policy to send it back and get your money back. You can either return it to the insurance professional who sold it to you or send it back to the insurance company with a letter saying you do not accept the policy and you wish to have your money returned. Call your state's Department of Insurance if you have any problems getting your money back. (See *Appendix B* for contact information.)

Multiple Policies—You don't need more than one Medicare supplement policy. The reason some people have purchased more than one is because they think they can get all of their bills paid if they have more than one policy. This is an unwise use of your money. There are excellent policies on the market today that will take care of most of your expenses with just one policy. Also, federal guidelines don't allow an insurance company to sell you a Medicare supplement policy in addition to one you already have. This means if you buy a new Medicare supplement policy, you agree to cancel the one(s) you already have.

Benefits—An ideal policy will pay both the Part A deductible ($1,024 per hospital stay in each 60-day benefit period) and the Part B deductible ($135 per calendar year). It will also pay all the coinsurance for skilled nursing facility days.

Excess Physician Charges—If your doctor does not accept Medicare assignment, you owe the difference between the actual charge and the amount Medicare approves, unless your state doesn't allow the doctor to charge more (see **Medicare-Approved Charges** on p. 228). In states that do allow it, the doctor can charge no more than 115 percent of the Medicare-approved amount. Medicare supplement policies are available that will pay these balances. Again, you don't need multiple policies to get these excess charges paid. Plans F, I and J of the standardized plans pay 100 percent of the excess charges and Plan G pays 80 percent of them.

Miscellaneous Benefits—Some policies pay extra benefits in addition to Medicare deductibles and coinsurance and excess physician charges. Plans C–J of the standardized plans include at least one of the following extra benefits and Plan J includes all of them.

> *Foreign Travel Emergency* —If you become injured or get sick unexpectedly during the first 60 days of a trip outside the United States, the standardized plans C–J will pay 80 percent of hospital, physician and medical care, subject to a $250 annual deductible and a lifetime maximum of $50,000, if the care would have been covered by Medicare had it been provided in the United States.

> *Preventive Care*—Standardized Plans E and J pay up to $120 per year for such things as an annual physical examination, cholesterol screening, hearing test, diabetes screening and thyroid function test. This benefit can also cover mammograms, Pap smears, and/or flu shots if Medicare stops paying for them. Remember, Medicare covers one routine physical during the six months after you first become eligible for Medicare Part B (see **Medicare Preventive Services** on p. 229).

At Home Recovery—Standardized Plans D, G, I and J pay up to $40 per visit up to $1,600 per year for short-term, at-home assistance with activities of daily living (bathing, dressing, going to the bathroom, taking medicine, eating, etc.) The number of at-home recovery visits can't exceed the number of Medicare-covered home health visits and can't last longer than eight weeks after the last Medicare-covered home health visit.

Prior to January 1, 2006, Plans H, I and J contained a drug benefit:

Basic Drugs—Standardized Plans H and I paid 50 percent of the cost of outpatient prescription drugs up to a maximum annual benefit of $1,250 after a $250 annual deductible.

Extended Drugs—Standardized Plan J paid the same as the Basic Drugs benefit except the annual maximum was $3,000.

If you bought one of those plans, you received a letter from your Medicare supplement insurance company telling you how the drug coverage in your Medicare supplement policy compares to the new Part D Medicare prescription drug plan. Usually the Medicare drug program has better drug coverage, so you had until May 15, 2006 to enroll in a Part D Medicare prescription drug plan and switch to a Medicare supplement policy with your same company without prescription drug coverage. (Call your Medicare supplement company if you don't remember receiving that letter.) If you haven't switched, here are two reasons to consider doing so:

1) If your Medicare supplement drug benefits aren't as good as Medicare Part D, when you do switch, your Medicare Part D premium will cost at least one percent per month more for every month you waited to join after May 15, 2006.

2) Since Medicare supplement plans H, I and J aren't allowed to include drug coverage on any new policies after January 1, 2006, it's very likely that rates for those who still have them will increase faster since new policyholders aren't entering the risk pool for that set of benefits. Therefore, even if your Medicare supplement drug benefits happened to be better than Medicare Part D (which means you can wait to enroll in Part D without a penalty), you might still want to switch your drug coverage to Part D for this reason alone.

If you didn't switch to Part D, your Medicare supplement company will send you a notice each year before November 15 telling you how your drug coverage compares to Medicare Part D. See **Part D: The Medicare Prescription Drug Benefit** on p. 271 to do your own comparison.

Confused About Plan Selection?

You're probably wondering how you can possibly decide which Medicare supplement plan to choose. You also may be wondering what others have done with this decision. I can tell you that Plan F has been the most popular choice as it was held by more than 50 percent of Medicare supplement policyholders through July 2006.[12]

Plan F covers all of the deductibles and co-payments charged under the original Medicare program, plus it pays for the excess doctor charges. Plan C has the second-highest share of policyholders as it covers everything Plan F does, except for the excess doctor charges. If you live in a state that won't permit doctors to charge more than the Medicare-approved amount, Plan C may be the best choice.

However, a trend may be changing with plan selection. Since Plan J covers the full range of Medicare supplement benefits, it is the most desirable, but until the prescription drug benefit was eliminated from Plan J on January 1, 2006, it was the most expensive. Now Plan J costs less and some new policyholders are finding it affordable.

Whichever Medicare supplement plan you select, you also will need to select a Medicare prescription drug plan to cover your prescription drug costs.

Claims—Medicare supplements usually can't pay unless Medicare pays first. This means that the Medicare supplement insurance company needs to see a copy of the Medicare Summary Notice (MSN) before processing the claim.

If your doctor participates in the Medicare program (accepts assignment of benefits) and you have assigned the benefits of a qualified Medicare supplement policy to your doctor, the company that processes Medicare claims for your state will automatically send your physician's claim to the Medicare supplement insurance company for processing. You don't have to handle the paperwork of claims filing if your doctor accepts Medicare assignment.

If your doctor does not accept assignment, you may be solely responsible for filing your Medicare supplement claims. Some insurance companies provide electronic claims filing whether or not the doctor accepts assignment. Your insurance professional can tell you how each company works that you are considering.

Appeals—If you are not satisfied with how the Medicare supplement policy handled your claim, contact the insurance company or your insurance adviser. If you are still not satisfied, you can call the Department of Insurance in your state for help. (See *Appendix B* for a list of insurance departments by state.)

Managed Care for Medicare Supplements

∿∿∿∿∿∿∿∿∿∿∿∿∿∿∿∿∿∿∿∿∿∿∿∿∿

Medicare Select—A new way of handling Medicare supplement insurance was introduced in 1992 in 15 states. In 1995 it was authorized to be sold nationally for three years and approved indefinitely in 1998.

The original Medicare Select states were Alabama, Arizona, California, Florida, Illinois, Indiana, Kentucky, Massachusetts, Minnesota, Missouri, North Dakota, Ohio, Texas, Washington and Wisconsin.

The Medicare Select program allows policyholders to pay a lower premium in return for using a list of hospitals and doctors, called "preferred providers," specified by the insurance company or health maintenance organization (HMO) that underwrites the supplemental policy. The benefits when you use the designated providers are the same as the 12 standard Medicare supplement plans (A–L).

Emergency health care furnished by providers not on the list is covered. If it's not an emergency and you use a doctor or hospital not on the list, your Medicare supplement claim can be denied or the payment can be reduced. The Medicare benefit is paid as usual, so whether or not you use a health care provider on the list only affects your Medicare supplement benefit, not the Medicare payment.

Premiums for Medicare Select plans can be as much as 15% less than standard Medicare supplements but may or may not be available in your state.

How Do I Find a Medicare Supplement?

There are two ways:

1) To telephone for help, you can either call the insurance counseling number listed for your state in *Appendix B* or call 1-800-MEDICARE (1-800-633-4227). TTY users should call 1-877-486-2048. A counselor will help you get information on all your health plan options, including the Medicare supplement policies available in your area.

2) If you use a computer, go to www.medicare.gov. Scroll down to "Search Tools", then select "Compare Health Plans and Medigap Policies in Your Area". You can choose to look at only Medicare supplement policies (Medigap) or you can look at all the Medicare plans available in your area, such as Medicare Advantage plans and Medicare prescription drug plans which we will cover in the next two sections.

Medicare Advantage (Part C)

~~~~~~

Because of the necessity to contain health care costs, 97 percent of employees are in some type of managed health care plan.[13] With the Medicare population, that ratio is only 20%.[14] Why such a disparity? It's not that the government hasn't tried. Medicare Health Maintenance Organizations (HMOs) have been around since the 1970's, but their success has been marginal. In fact, after reaching an all-time high of 346 plans in 1998 and a 16% market penetration in 2000, many of them closed their doors and the number plummeted to only 247 in 2005.[15] What happened? First, let's review a couple of basic concepts about HMOs.

The most common HMO model is a local network of hospitals and doctors that delivers the services of Medicare Part A and B to the members who are on Medicare. The government gives the HMO a flat amount of dollars each year per member to provide those services. This model was supposed to create a winning situation for all three parties (the HMO, the member and the government) as follows:

For the HMO: By limiting the provider network to providers who would accept the HMO's payment schedule and managed care requirements, the HMO had the opportunity to manage the care in such a way that the member was served, but the HMO had money left over at the end of the year – yes, a profit – after providing necessary services. To woo members, HMOs typically offered services not covered by Medicare, such as prescription drugs, vision and hearing exams, routine physicals, etc. and many HMOs did not charge a monthly premium. The member still had to pay Part B premium but did not pay a separate premium to the HMO.

For the member: The member usually had a simpler plan with fewer deductibles and co-payments vs. the original Medicare program, and the care delivery system was much easier to understand because it closely resembled the care people were used to before they turned 65. Zero-premium plans with extra benefits made the HMO seem like a real deal.

For the government: The government had a budgetable figure for the Medicare program because each year the amount paid by the government to the HMO was not based on a fee for each service performed, but rather on a pre-determined amount per member.

Two things went wrong with this arrangement:

1) The government paid the same amount for all of the members in the geographical area with no regard to each member's health status. The result was that HMOs found

it difficult to provide adequate care to those members who were in poor health. When these members appeared for frequent treatment, the HMO was slow to approve some procedures. A number of these "frequent users" simply returned to the original fee-for-service Medicare program which allowed them to choose doctors and hospitals without going through the referral system and the overall gatekeeper model as a whole.

2) Compounding the lack of inadequate reimbursement for sicker members was the additional benefits which were not offset by additional premium. Just the opposite, the zero-premium plan really made it difficult for HMOs to survive, and many didn't.

It soon became apparent that the government would have to consider the member's health status when determining the funding method. After several years of phasing in this change, 100% of payments to Medicare managed-care organizations were "risk-adjusted" in 2007, which means they take into consideration demographic risk factors such as age, health conditions and sex, as well as geographic area. Add this change to an additional $46 billion in subsidies to Medicare Advantage plans provided by the same law that gave us the new Medicare drug program, and we can expect to see managed care for Medicare beneficiaries grow significantly in the next decade.[16]

Now for the detail. What exactly is Medicare Advantage?

Medicare Advantage Defined

Originally implemented in November, 1999 as Medicare+ Choice by the Balanced Budget Act of 1997 and sometimes called Part C of Medicare, Medicare Advantage is made up of Medicare plans operated by the private sector vs. the government. In 2007, all of the Medicare population had access to a Medicare Advantage plan.[17] These plans contract with specific health care providers (hospitals, doctors, skilled nursing facilities, physical therapists, etc.) to provide all the services covered by Medicare. People enrolled in these plans don't need a Medicare supplement because instead of being responsible for the Medicare deductibles and co-payments, the patient pays small co-payments (i.e., $5–$15 per doctor visit) and a small monthly premium. You still must pay the monthly Part B premium, unless the plan in which you are enrolled chooses to pay part or all of it.

Depending on the type of plan, the patient either has to receive all non-emergency services from the health care providers on the list to be covered at all or else expect a lower benefit to be paid to providers not on the list. You may hear the second type referred to as a "point-of-service" option, which just means you pay more out of your pocket to go to a provider outside the network. HMOs also require you to select a primary care doctor who controls your access to specialists. Some people don't mind these restrictions, as HMOs typically pay for additional services not covered by Medicare, such as eye and ear exams, dental care, foot care, routine checkups, and so forth.

What Kind of Choices Will You Have?

There are many private plans besides HMOs for you to choose from in addition to the traditional Medicare program. Some of these require you to use a specific list of providers to receive any benefits, but the benefits you receive will be at little or no cost to you. Others with the "Point of Service" option mentioned above will allow you to use providers not on the list if you pay more out of your pocket.

Other choices include:

Preferred Provider Organizations—You will be given a list of doctors and hospitals to choose from, but you are allowed to use providers not on the list and simply receive lower benefits. The federal government divided the country into 26 coverage areas to create regional PPOs that became available in 2006.[18] PPOs are less restrictive than HMOs because they don't require you to see a specialist without going through a primary care doctor. The new regional PPOs are required to offer a single deductible for Medicare Part A and B services and a cap on out-of-pocket spending to protect you from catastrophic medical expenses.

Private fee-for-service plans—These plans do not limit your choice of providers. You may go to any Medicare-approved doctor or hospital that accepts the plan's payment. There are no networks. You just have to ask if the doctor or hospital agrees to accept the plan's payment before you start using them. It's an easy process for the medical provider to agree to accept payment from a PFFS. Private fee-for-service plans can charge you a premium amount above the Medicare Part B premium and can charge deductible and coinsurance amounts that are different than those under the original Medicare Plan. In other words, the insurance company, rather than the Medicare program, decides how much you pay for the services you receive. Generally, however, the premium is lower for these plans and they include additional services not covered by Medicare. They also may provide worldwide coverage for emergency care and urgently needed care, which is something the original Medicare program does not do. Urgently needed is defined as care needed due to a sickness or injury of sudden and unexpected onset.

Medicare Special Needs Plans – These are plans that specialize in handling people with

1) chronic or disabling conditions like diabetes or end stage renal disease;
2) people who are in nursing homes; or
3) people who are eligible for both Medicare and Medicaid.

It's likely that you will be assigned a care coordinator who will develop a personal care plan for you to help you achieve the best overall health possible for your condition.

Medicare Medical Savings Accounts – Another exciting choice is a Medical Savings Account (MSA). An MSA is an exciting choice because it allows people to take more control over how their Medicare benefits are used. Here's how it works.

A Medicare Medical Savings Account has two parts: a high-deductible health insurance plan *with zero premium* and a Medical Savings Account that can be used to pay for any IRS-approved medical expense, including expenses that count toward your high deductible. After the deductible is met, the health plan pays 100% of all Medicare-covered services other than prescription drugs *(see note at the end of this section)*. The high-deductible plan is a Medicare Advantage plan, like an HMO or PPO.

The maximum deductible in 2007 was $9,500, indexed to increase annually. However, an MSA provider can offer a lower deductible. (A national plan that is approved as of this writing offers three deductibles: $2,500, $3,500 and $4,500.)[19] As we have already discussed, Medicare pays a set amount of money for your health care each year to the Medicare Advantage plan you have selected. In a Medicare MSA Plan, the Plan deposits the difference between the amount it thinks it needs to provide your care (the "bid amount") and the amount it receives from Medicare into your Medical Savings Account at the beginning of each calendar year, tax-free. The amount of the deposit for each Plan is published in the CMS publication *Your Guide to Medicare Medical Savings Account Plans* at www.medicare.gov. Here's an example using a Medicare allowance of $600 a month:

Medicare's annual allowance ($600 x 12):	$7,200
Medicare Advantage Plan's bid amount:	- $5,200
Amount the Medicare Advantage plan deposits into an account for you	$2,000

This deposit will be made in a lump sum in the first month of your enrollment in the program. Neither the initial deposit nor the growth will be taxable income to you, as long as you use the money for "qualified medical expenses," according to the IRS. This means you can use the money for medical expenses beyond what the traditional Medicare program covers such as eyeglasses, hearing aids, etc. (Eventually the Medicare Advantage plan may provide extra benefits like this.)

You aren't allowed to put any of your own money into your MSA and you aren't allowed to purchase a Medicare supplement to cover the expenses that count toward your deductible. However, if you have relatively few medical expenses and have money left over at the end of the year, the money is yours. It stays in your account and can be used for expenses in the following year. The healthier you are, the more money will accumulate in your Medical Savings Account because once a year, the Medicare Advantage Plan will make another lump sum deposit into your account.

The really exciting news is that tax-qualified long-term care insurance premium is considered an IRS-approved medical expense! Therefore, if you are in good health and don't use all of your MSA for medical expenses, there will be money left over which you may choose to use for the age-based amount of your long-term care insurance premium. Depending on your age and how much your premium is, you might be able to pay all of it out of your MSA. (See Chapter 2, *Features of a Good Long-Term Care Insurance Policy* for the definition of a tax-qualified policy and the allowable premium based on your age in 2008.)

A note about prescription drugs for MSA holders: Since the high-deductible plan doesn't cover prescription drugs, you will want to purchase a Medicare Part D prescription drug plan, which is explained in the next section. You can't pay Part D premium out of it; however, you can pay Part D co-payments, coinsurance and deductible from your MSA tax-free. These withdrawals just won't count toward your Medicare Advantage plan deductible, because only expenses covered by Medicare Part A or B count toward your deductible.

Benefits

All of the Medicare Advantage plans must provide at least the same benefits as Part A and Part B of the traditional Medicare program, including flu shots and pneumonia vaccines and preventive mammograms. Medicare Advantage plans also must:

▲ offer female beneficiaries direct access to specialists for pelvic exams, Pap smears and mammograms without first obtaining a referral from a primary physician;

▲ assess new enrollees to see if they need immediate medical attention of any kind;

▲ allow for direct access to specialists for complex medical conditions; and

▲ pay for diagnostic testing at emergency centers to determine if you need immediate attention and then pay for emergency treatment to stabilize your medical condition for a maximum co-pay of only $50 that you will be responsible for if you need emergency services outside of your plan's provider network. ("Severe pain" is an accepted medical reason to seek emergency help outside the provider network.)

As mentioned earlier, Medicare Advantage plans are allowed to include additional benefits that aren't covered by traditional Medicare such as prescription drugs, dental and foot care, and preventive services such as routine physicals and eye and ear exams.

Since 2003, Medicare Advantage plans have been allowed to waive the three-day prior hospital stay requirement for skilled nursing facility care if it is cost-effective. This means a patient could be admitted to a skilled nursing facility after a one or two-day hospital stay or directly from home.

Enrollment and Disenrollment

Medicare Advantage plans are required to accept people when they first become eligible for Medicare, no questions asked. This includes people who qualify for Medicare due to a disability. They can join a Medicare Advantage plan from three months before to three months after their 25th month of Social Security Disability Income payments. The exception to this rule is that end-stage renal disease patients usually can't join a Medicare Advantage plan unless they have a successful kidney transplant. If they are already in a Medicare Advantage plan, they can stay in it or join another plan offered by the same insurance company.

If you don't join one when you are first eligible, you are allowed to join from November 15th through December 31st each year and your coverage will be effective January 1st. If you don't like it and you want to switch to another Medicare Advantage plan, you can do so within the first three months of each calendar year.

What If I'm Afraid to Leave
the Original Medicare Program?

Congress passed safety nets in the Balanced Budget Act of 1997 to help people try Medicare Advantage plans. If you try one for the first time and don't like it, you can go back to the original Medicare program within one year of your enrollment, and you can get a Medicare supplement policy "guaranteed issue." This means you can't be turned down or made to wait for pre-existing conditions. People who try a Medicare Advantage plan as soon as they are eligible for Medicare get the same deal. However, just buying a Medicare supplement policy isn't enough. You have to disenroll from your Medicare Advantage plan; otherwise, your Medicare supplement plan won't be allowed to pay any of the Medicare deductibles or co-payments.

What if My Medicare Advantage Plan Withdraws From My Area?

This can happen. If it does, your Medicare Advantage plan is required to notify you at least 90 days before your coverage ends. You can enroll in another Medicare Advantage plan in your area if there is one available or return to original Medicare. If you return to original Medicare, you will have the right to buy at least a Plan A, B, C, F, K or L Medicare Supplement policy with no health questions if you apply within 63 days after your Medicare Advantage coverage ends. Whatever happens, there's a really good chance you can keep your doctor, as most Medicare Advantage doctors participate in original Medicare.

You Do Not Have to Switch At All

Congress is hoping many more people will give the new private plans a chance because they promote cost containment of health care costs. That's why they usually have lower premium and pay for more services than the original Medicare program. In fact, the Center for Medicare and Medicaid Services has reported that Medicare Advantage members are saving an average of $82 per month compared to what they would pay if they were still in the original Medicare program.[20] To make it even easier to try Medicare Advantage plans, a new law passed in December, 2006 that allows people who are in the original Medicare program to switch to a Medicare Advantage plan **without prescription drug coverage** anytime in 2007 and 2008.[21] This could be a Health Maintenance Organization, a Preferred Provider Organization or a Private Fee-for-Service Plan. However, you do not have to switch to any of these new programs. You may remain in traditional Medicare if you like.

Want to Know More?

For more information on the Medicare Advantage plans available in your state, you can either call the "insurance counseling" number listed for your state in *Appendix B* or may call 800-633-4227 (TDD-1-877-486-2948). A counselor will help you get information on all your health plan options, including the Medicare Advantage policies available in your area.

You can also visit the official Medicare website (www.medicare.gov) to download the publication *Medicare & You,* 2008. In addition to listing a number of valuable publications that you can order or print out to educate yourself thoroughly on the Medicare Advantage program, the website even allows you to enter your zip code and view a list of Medicare Advantage plans available in your area. You can even visit areas like "Home Health Compare" and "Nursing Home Compare", which allows you to review quality ratings and many other characteristics of the home health agencies and nursing homes in your area.

Medicare Prescription Drug Benefits (Part D)

∿∿∿∿∿∿∿∿∿∿∿∿∿∿∿∿∿∿∿∿∿∿∿∿∿∿∿∿∿∿∿∿

Next to long-term care, the second largest out-of-pocket expense for older Americans until recently has been prescription drugs.[22] Now all but 10% of the 43 million people on Medicare have drug coverage, thanks to the new Medicare Prescription Drug Program (Part D of Medicare) which insures half of them. The others are insured mainly by employer-provided health plans, both for people who are still working as well as those who are covered under retiree health plans, and people who are covered by other government programs such as the Federal Employees Health Plan, TRICARE and the Veterans Administration. [23]

Authorized by The Medicare Prescription Drug, Improvement and Modernization Act of 2003 (MMA), the first drug plans were effective January 1, 2006 and by the end of the year, almost 2000 standalone prescription drug plans (PDPs) were available and over 400 drug plans were available as part of a Medicare Advantage plan.[24] In fact, there are at least 50 standalone PDPs and Medicare Advantage/Prescription Drug plans to choose from in most states.[25] This way, people who remain in the original Medicare program have access to a standalone drug plan, and people who want a Medicare Advantage plan with embedded drug coverage can have that.

Who is Eligible?

Anyone who has Medicare is eligible for the new drug program. However, certain individuals may not choose to enroll in Medicare Part D because they have "creditable coverage", which means coverage that is better than that provided by a Medicare Part D plan. As mentioned above, there are mainly three types of people who fall into this category:

1) people who are covered by an employer or former employer's drug plan. Employers should have sent a letter to these policyholders by November 15, 2005 saying their coverage is "creditable coverage" which means it is as good as or better than Medicare Part D coverage. If they sign up for Medicare Part D, they will lose their employer/former employer's drug plan forever, and they might even lose the medical plan as well, so you can see why these people wouldn't enroll in Part D. If that coverage ever ends, the employee or retiree has 63 days to enroll in Part D without a penalty;

2) people who are entitled to drug coverage through the Veterans Administration health care plan. They can enroll in Medicare Part D later without a penalty if they want to; and

3) federal retirees who are enrolled in the Federal Employee Health Benefit Plan (FEHB) or military retirees who are enrolled in TRICARE as both of these plans are considered "creditable coverage".

Enrollment Periods

The initial enrollment period for anyone without creditable coverage was November 15 – May 15, 2006. People who missed that enrollment period will have to pay a 1% premium penalty for each month they wait to enroll after May 15, 2006 and they will pay that additional premium the rest of their lives.

Anyone who becomes eligible for Medicare now will have the same seven month open enrollment period as for Part B – three months before the month the person becomes eligible for Medicare, the month of eligibility, and the three months after that month. If the person doesn't enroll during that seven month period, the premium penalty will kick in.

Even people who currently get their drugs from Canada will probably want to sign up for Medicare Part D, because Canada could decide to not allow drugs to be exported to the U.S. at some point. Also Medicare Part D's catastrophic coverage (see **Premiums** below) offers far greater protection than lower foreign prices if the policyholder's drug needs escalate in the future.

Premiums

Like Part B of Medicare, the government subsidizes the premium heavily, so the new drug program is a good deal. Enrollees' premium funds 25.5 percent of the program and the government subsidizes the rest. [26]

The government initially predicted that monthly premium would average about $38, but in 2008, the average has fallen to $28, according to The Henry J. Kaiser Family Foundation. [27] Monthly premiums range from $9.80 to $107.50, however, and you won't be surprised to know that the specific benefit package has everything to do with the premium.[28]

The MMA established a minimum benefit package, but thanks to private enterprise, insurance companies compete for your business by offering you better benefits than the minimum package. Consequently, only one out of five Medicare Part D enrollees have the standard plan and just over ten percent of the plans offer it.[29] The standard plan looks like this:

Your 2008 Out-of-Pocket Expense	Description
$ 275	Deductible
$ 558	25% of the next $2,235 in charges
$3,216	100% of the next $3,216 in charges
$4,050	Total based on $5,726 in charges
5% of each prescription	Charges above $5,726

The great news is that if you are one of the few enrollees who have more than $5,726 in charges for the year, Medicare will pay 95 percent for the rest of the year! Since your out-of-pocket expense is limited to only 5 percent after $5,726 in charges, you have true protection against catastrophic drug bills.

However, insurance companies can improve these benefits by eliminating the deductible, lowering the out-of-pocket in Line 2 of the chart from 25 percent to a per prescription co-pay, or even providing benefits during the gap between $2,510 and $5,726 in charges (Line 3 of the chart), which is also called the "doughnut hole". Here is what has actually happened:

- over half of the plans have no deductible;

- almost 90 percent charge co-payments per prescription instead of the 25 percent coinsurance that vary by the type of drug, with generic drugs having the lowest co-pay; and

- most plans still have a coverage gap in the "doughnut hole" and of those that do provide coverage, it's usually for generic drugs as very few plans cover brand-name drugs in that gap.[30]

Help for Low-Income/Low-Asset Medicare Beneficiaries

People with limited income and assets don't have to pay premium or the $275 deductible and don't have the coverage gap ("doughnut hole") between $2,510 and $5,726 in charges. Their co-pays are only $1 - $2 for generic drugs and $3 - $5 for brand-name drugs. People in this category have incomes below $15,600 (single) or $21,000 (married) and have assets less than $11,990 (single) or $23,970 (married). The asset calculation doesn't include the primary residence, automobiles or personal possessions such as furniture and jewelry. **However, an estimated 2.6 million people meet the income and asset criteria and haven't stepped forward to claim this help.**[31]

If you aren't receiving any government assistance now but fall within those income and asset guidelines, you can apply for this extra help through the Social Security Administration either by mail, phone,

Internet or in person at a Social Security office. Here is the contact information:

Social Security Administration
Wilkes-Barre Data Operations Center
P. O. Box 1020
Wilkes-Barre, PA 18767-9910
800-772-1213
www.socialsecurity.gov (no signature is required for an online application)

You can also call the state counseling number listed in *Appendix B.*

People who are already on Medicaid, including nursing home patients, or receiving government assistance such as Supplemental Security Income (SSI) or are part of a low income program as explained on the preceding page are already approved for this extra help. If they didn't enroll in Part D by December 31, 2005, they were automatically switched to one, as Medicaid stopped paying their drug bills after that date.

Special note about nursing home patients on Medicaid: Some Medicaid nursing home patients have a retiree plan that provides supplemental coverage to Medicare. How do I know? My Aunt Jeannette whom you read about in Chapter 2 is one of them. I didn't want her enrolled in a Part D plan because it could jeopardize her General Motors retiree health plan. As her family representative and Power of Attorney, I provided the nursing home with a copy of the "creditable coverage" letter from General Motors so they would keep billing that plan for her drugs. I called GM and made sure they knew she wants to keep their plan. However, Medicare kept putting her in one Part D plan after another, even though I called to disenroll her from each one.

I learned that I had to call 1-800-MEDICARE to let Medicare know she wants to stick with the GM health plan for her drug coverage. It took two calls to Medicare and faxing proof of my Power of Attorney to get a message into her Medicare file, but Medicare finally stopped enrolling her in Plan D. And this is just a microscopic view of my duties as a long-distance caregiver!

Choices, Choices, Choices

Now we get to the really important question. How do you decide which Part D plan to join? You can gather your medicines and call the "insurance counseling" number listed for your state in *Appendix B* or you may call Medicare at 1-800-633-4227 (TDD-1-877-486-2948). But the most precise way to select the best plan is to collect your medicines and enter them by name into a special program developed just for this purpose on the Medicare website at www.medicare.gov. If you don't use a computer, perhaps a friend or family member will help you.

Why do you need to have your medicines handy when you call or use the computer? Because the plans vary as far as which drugs they cover. For example, the Secretary of Health and Human Services reports that about a million veterans have enrolled in Part D even though they are entitled to keep their VA coverage with no penalty. Why? The VA's drug coverage excludes a number of new drugs covered by Medicare Part D, including the world's best-selling drug, Lipitor, which is commonly prescribed for high cholesterol.[32]

Here is the easy process to select a plan using a computer.

Go to www.medicare.gov and click on "Compare Medicare Prescription Drug Plans". You will be asked to enter your Medicare ID number along with the date your Medicare coverage was effective. This information is on your Medicare card. Then enter your birthday and zip code. The comparison program will ask you to enter the drugs you are taking and will show the plans in your area that cover those drugs. You will have the opportunity to indicate a preferred pharmacy. When the plans appear, you can sort them by any of these headings:

- your estimated annual drug cost with that plan;
- the monthly premium;
- the deductible if there is one;
- if there is any coverage in the gap (charges between $2,510 and $5,726 in 2008) and if so, is it for brand or just generic; or
- the number of pharmacies in your area that participate in that plan.

You will be able to compare details of up to three plans at a time. You can also check how other enrollees rank a plan's performance in five areas:

- telephone customer service
- complaints
- appeals
- how well the plan communicates enrollment information to pharmacies
- accuracy of drug pricing information

For people who have multiple residences in multiple states, there are some national plans that provide coverage in all states and the comparison will identify those for you. When you've selected a plan, you can enroll online.

The great news is that EVERYONE has the chance to change plans EVERY YEAR between November 15th and December 31st. This is important and necessary because as different medical conditions develop, it is quite likely that your prescriptions will change, and the Medicare Part D plan you choose now may or may not be the best fit anymore.

What About Scams?

Companies marketing Medicare Part D plans are allowed to market by telephone or through the mail, but not door to door. They also have to comply with the Do-Not-Call rules and abide by federal and state calling hours. Marketing representatives are not allowed to ask for Medicare ID numbers, Social Security, bank account or credit card numbers.

Now you know more than 99 percent of the people who are talking about Medicare Part D. To "seal in" the information in your brain, put it to practice immediately by checking for yourself or finding a family member or friend who needs your help. By entering the information as outlined above at www.medicare.gov, you can really help that person with the Medicare Part D "shopping" experience. It might not be as much fun as figuring out long-term care insurance but the gratitude of the person you help is PRICELESS.

The Silver Lining in the New Medicare Plans

OK – We've finished going over all four parts of Medicare. As you wade through the maze of Medicare changes in the next few years, please bear one thing in mind. **The real risk today is long-term care.** The average amount spent by Medicare beneficiaries in 2003 for all out-of-pocket health expenses plus Medicare supplement premium was only about $3,500. Members of Medicare Advantage plans only spent about half of that, because the government is using lower out-of-pocket costs to create incentives for you to switch from traditional

Medicare to the new private Medicare plans.[33] And, both of these numbers will be lower when the next study is done because Medicare Part D is protecting so many older Americans from high prescription drug costs. So the really good news is that the less you spend for your acute care coverage like hospital and doctor bills, the more money you have available to spend on long-term care insurance, which covers the greatest health care risk you face and for which you are not covered by Medicare, private health insurance or Medicare Advantage plans.

Appendix B:
Directory of State Insurance Departments, Medicaid and Aging Agencies

ALABAMA

Alabama Insurance Department
201 Monroe Street
Ste. 1700
Montgomery, AL 36104
(334) 269-3550
Insurance Counseling
1-800-243-5463

Alabama Medicaid Agency
501 Dexter Avenue
Montgomery, AL 36103
(334) 242-5600
(800) 362-1504

Commission on Aging
770 Washington Avenue
RSA Plaza
Ste. 470
Montgomery, AL 36130
1-877-425-2243

ALASKA

Alaska Division of Insurance
333 Willoughby Avenue
State Office Building
9th Floor
Juneau, AK 99801
(907) 465-2515
Insurance Counseling
1-800-478-6065

Alaska Medicaid Agency
P.O. Box 110660
Juneau, AK 99811-0660
(907) 465-3355

Alaska Commission on Aging
P.O. Box 110209
Juneau, AK 99811-0209
(907) 465-3250

AMERICAN SAMOA

Insurance Department
Office of Governor
Pago Pago, AS 96799
011-684-633-4116

Medicaid Agency
Department of Health
LBJ Tropical Medical Center
Pago Pago, AS 96799
011-684-633-4590

Territorial Administration on Aging
Government of American Samoa
Pago Pago, AS 96799
011-684-633-1252

ARIZONA

Arizona Insurance Department
2910 N. 44th Street
Ste. 210
Phoenix, AZ 85018-7256
(602) 912-8444
Insurance Counseling
1-800-432-4040

282

Medicaid Agency
801 East Jefferson Street
Phoenix, AZ 85034
(602) 417-4000

Aging and Adult Administration
1789 W. Jefferson Street, Site Code
    950A
Phoenix, AZ 85007
(602) 542-4446

ARKANSAS

Arkansas Insurance Department
1200 West Third Street
Little Rock, AR 72201
1-800-282-9134
Insurance Counseling
1-800-224-6330

Medicaid Agency
Division of Medical Services
Department of Health and Human
    Services
Donaghey Plaza South
P.O. Box 1437, Slot S-401
Little Rock, AR 72203-1437
(501) 682-8292

Division of Aging and Adult
    Services
P.O. Box 1437, Slot S-530
Little Rock, AR 72203-1437
(501) 682-2441

CALIFORNIA

California Department of Insurance
300 Capital Mall
Suite 1700
Sacramento, CA 95814
1-800-927-4357
Insurance Counseling
1-800-434-0222

Medicaid Agency
714 P Street, Room 1253
Sacramento, CA 95814
(916) 654-0391

California Commission on Aging
1300 National Drive
Suite 173
Sacramento, CA 95834
(916) 419-7591

COLORADO

Colorado Insurance Division
1560 Broadway
Ste. 850
Denver, CO 80202
(303) 894-7499
Insurance Counseling
1-800-544-9181

Medicaid Agency
Department of Health Care Policy
    & Financing
1570 Grant Street
Denver, CO 80203-1818
(303) 866-4416

Division of Aging and Adult
    Services
1575 Sherman Street
10th Floor
Denver, CO 80203
(303) 866-2800

**Commonwealth of the Northern
    Mariana Islands**
Department of Community &
    Cultural Affairs, Civic Center
    Commonwealth of the Northern
Mariana Islands
Caller Box 10007
Saipan, MP 96950
011-607-234-6011

Medicaid Agency
Department of Public Health
    & Environmental Services
    Commonwealth of the Northern
    Mariana Islands
P.O. Box 409 CK
Saipan, MP 96950
011-670-664-4884

CONNECTICUT
Connecticut Insurance Department
153 Market Street 7th Floor
Hartford, CT 06103
Insurance Counseling
1-800-203-3447

Medicaid Agency
Department of Social Services
25 Sigourney Street
Hartford, CT 06106-5116
(860) 424-5116

Elderly Services Division
25 Sigourney Street
Hartford, CT 06106
(806) 424-5277

DELAWARE
Delaware Insurance Department
841 Silver Lake Blvd.
Dover, DE 19904
(302) 674-7300
Insurance Counseling
1-800-366-9500

Medicaid Agency
Department of Health and Social
    Services
1901 North DuPont Highway,
    Main Bldg.
New Castle, DE 19720
(302) 255-9040

Division of Services for Aging &
    Adults with Physical Disabilities
1901 N. DuPont Highway, Main
    Bldg.
New Castle, DE 19720
(302) 255-9390

DISTRICT OF COLUMBIA
Insurance Department
810 First Street, NE
Ste. 701
Washington, DC 20002
(202) 727-8000
Insurance Counseling
(202) 676-3900
Medicaid Agency

Medical Assistance Administration
825 North Capital St., NE
5th Floor
Washington, DC 20002
(202) 442-5988

Office on Aging
441 4th Street, NW
Suite 900S
Washington, DC 20001
(202) 724-5622

FEDERATED STATES OF MICRONESIA
State Agency on Aging
Office of Health Services
Federated States of Micronesia
Ponape, ECI 96941

FLORIDA
Florida Department of Insurance
200 E. Gaines Street
Tallahassee, FL 32399-0300
(850) 413-3140
Insurance Counseling
1-800-963-5337

Medicaid Agency
Agency for Health Care
   Administration
2727 Mahan Drive, Mail Stop 8
Tallahassee, FL 32308
(850) 488-3560

Department of Elder Affairs
4040 Esplanade Way
Tallahassee, FL 32399-7000
(850) 414-2000

GEORGIA
Georgia Insurance Department
Two Martin L. King, Jr. Drive
West Tower, Ste. 704
Atlanta, GA 30334
(404) 656-2070

Medicaid Agency
Department of Community Health
2 Peachtree Street
Atlanta, GA 30303
(404) 656-4507

Division of Aging Services
Department of Human Resources
2 Peachtree Street
Ste. 9385
Atlanta, GA 30303-3142
(404) 657-5258

GUAM
Guam Insurance Department
P.O. Box 23607
FMF Barrigada, GU 96921
011-671-475-1825
Insurance Counseling
(808) 586-7299

Medicaid Agency
Bureau of Health Care Financing
Department of Public Health &
   Social Services
P.O. Box 2816
Agana, GU 96910
011-671-735-7269

Division of Senior Citizens
Department of Public Health &
Social Services
P.O. Box 2816
Agana, GU 96932
011-671-477-2930

HAWAII
Hawaii Department of Commerce
& Consumer Affairs
Insurance Division
P.O. Box 3614
Honolulu, HI 96811
(808) 586-2790
Insurance Counseling
(808) 586-0100

Medicaid Agency
Department of Human Services
P.O. Box 339
Honolulu, HI 96809-0339
(808) 586-4996

Executive Office on Aging
No. 1 Capital District
250 S. Hotel Street
Rm. 406
Honolulu, HI 96813-2831
(808) 586-0100

IDAHO
Idaho Insurance Department
700 W. State Street, 3rd Floor
Boise, ID 83720-0043
(208) 334-4250
Insurance Counseling
1-800-247-4422

Medicaid Agency
Division of Medicaid
Department of Health and Welfare
Americana Building
P.O. Box 83720
Boise, ID 83720-0036
(208) 364-1802

Commission on Aging
3380 Americana Terrace, Ste. 120
Boise, ID 83706
(208) 334-3833

ILLINOIS
Dept. of Finance and Professional
Regulation
Division of Insurance
320 W. Washington St.
4th Floor
Springfield, IL 62767-0001
(217) 785-5516
Insurance Counseling
1-800-548-9034

Medicaid Agency
Department of Public Aid
201 South Grand Avenue, East
3rd Floor
Springfield, IL 62763-0001
(217) 782-2570

Department on Aging
421 E. Capitol Avenue, Suite 100
Springfield, IL 62701-1789
(217) 785-3356

INDIANA

Indiana Insurance Department
311 W. Washington Street
Ste. 300
Indianapolis, IN 46204-2787
(317-232-2385)
Insurance Counseling
1-800-452-4800

Medicaid Agency
Medicaid Policy and Planning
   Family & Social Services
   Administration
P.O. Box 7083
402 W. Washington Street
Indianapolis, IN 46207-7083
(317) 233-4454

Bureau of Aging & In-Home
   Services
402 W. Washington St., #W454
P.O. Box 7083
Indianapolis, IN 46207-7083
(317) 232-7020

IOWA

Iowa Insurance Department
330 Maple Street
Des Moines, IA 50319-0065
(515) 2181-5705
Insurance Counseling
1-800-452-4800

Medicaid Agency
Department of Human Services
Iowa Hoover State Office Bldg.
5th Floor
Des Moines, IA 50319
(515)-327-5121

Department of Elder Affairs
Jessie M Parker Building
510 E. 12th Street, Suite 2
Des Moines, IA 50319-9025
(515) 725-3333

KANSAS

Kansas Insurance Department
420 S.W. 9th Street
Topeka, KS 66612-1678
(785) 296-3071
Insurance Counseling
1-800-860-5260

Medicaid Agency
Suite 900-N
Landon State Office Building
900 SW Jackson Street
Topeka, KS 66612

Department of Aging
New England Bldg.
503 South Kansas Ave.
Topeka, KS 66603-3404
(785) 296-4986

KENTUCKY
Kentucky Insurance Department
215 W. Main Street
Frankfort, KY 40601
1-800-595-6053
Insurance Counseling
(502) 564-7372

Medicaid Agency
Department of Medicaid Services
275 East Main Street
6th Floor
Frankfort, KY 40621
(502) 564-4321

Office of Aging Services
Cabinet for Families and Children
275 East Main Street
Frankfort, KY 40601
(502) 564-6930

LOUISIANA
Louisiana Insurance Department
1702 North 3rd Street
Baton Rouge, LA 70802
Insurance Counseling
1-800-259-5301

Medicaid Agency
Bureau of Health Services
   Financing
1201 Capitol Access Road
P.O. Box 91030
Baton Rouge, LA 70821-9030
(225) 342-5774

Office of Elderly Affairs
PO Box 80374
Baton Rouge, LA 70802-0374
(225) 342-7100

MAINE
Maine Bureau of Insurance
#34 State House Station
Augusta, ME 04333-0034
(207) 624-8475
Insurance Counseling
1-800-750-5353

Medicaid Agency
Office of MaineCare Services
442 Civic Center Drive
State House Station 11
Augusta, ME 04333-0011
(207) 287-0215

Bureau of Elder and Adult Services
Department of Human Services
35 Anthony Avenue
Augusta, ME 04333
(207) 624-5335

MARYLAND
Maryland Insurance Administration
525 St. Paul Place
Baltimore, MD 21202-2272
(410) 468-2000

Medicaid Agency
Department of Health and Mental
   Hygiene
201 West Preston Street
Baltimore, MD 21201
(410) 767-4664

Department on Aging
State Office Building, Room 1007
301 West Preston Street
Baltimore, MD 21201-2374
(410) 767-1100

MASSACHUSETTS
Massachusetts Insurance Division
One South Station, 5th Floor
Boston, MA 02210-2208
(617) 521-7794

Medicaid Agency
Division of Medical Assistance
600 Washington Street
Boston, MA 02111
(617) 210-5690

Executive Office of Elder Affairs
One Ashburton Place
5th Floor
Boston, MA 02108
(617) 727-7750

MICHIGAN
Office of Financial and Insurance
   Services
Ottawa Bldg. 3rd Floor
Lansing, MI 48933
(517) 373-0220

Medicaid Agency
Medical Services Administration
Department of Community Health
Sixth Floor
Lewis Cass Bldg.
320 South Walnut St.
Lansing, MI 48913

(517) 373-3573
Office of Services to the Aging
611 W. Ottawa, N. Ottawa Tower
3rd Floor
PO Box 30676
Lansing, MI 48909
(517) 373-8230

MINNESOTA
Minnesota Insurance Department
85 Seventh Place East
Ste. 500
St. Paul, MN 55101-2198
(612) 296-4026

Medicaid Agency
Minnesota Department of Human
   Services
444 Lafayette Rd.
St. Paul, MN 55155-3852
(651) 297-3933

Board on Aging
444 Lafayette Rd.
St. Paul, MN 55155-3843
(651) 296-2770

MISSISSIPPI
Mississippi Insurance Department
501 N. West St.
1001 Woolfolk State Office Bldg.,
   10th Floor
Jackson, MS 39201
(601) 359-3569
Insurance Counseling
1-800-562-2957

Medicaid Agency
Division of Medicaid
Office of Governor
Suite 801, Robert E. Lee Bldg.
239 N. Lamar St.
Jackson, MS 39201-1399
(601) 359-6050

Council on Aging & Adult Services
750 N. State St.
Jackson, MS 39202
1-800-948-3090

MISSOURI

Missouri Department of Insurance
301 West High St
Room 530.
Jefferson City, MO 65101
Insurance Counseling
1-800-726-7390

Medicaid Agency
Division of Medical Services
Department of Social Services
615 Howerton Court
P.O. Box 6500
Jefferson City, MO 65102-6500
(573) 751-3425

Division of Senior Services
Department of Health and Senior
  Services
615 Howerton Court
P.O. Box 1337
Jefferson City, MO 65102-1337
(573) 751-3082

MONTANA

Montana Insurance Department
126 N. Sanders
Mitchell Bldg., Rm. 270
Helena, MT 59620
(406) 444-2040
Insurance Counseling
(402) 471-2201

Medicaid Agency
Department of Public Health and
  Human Services
1400 Broadway, Cogswell Bldg,
  Room A116
PO Box 202951
Helena, MT 59620-2951
(406) 444-4540

Senior & Long-Term Care Division
Department of Public Health and
  Human Services
P.O. Box 4210
111 N. Sanders Street, Rm. 211
Helena, MT 59620
(406) 444-4077

NEBRASKA

Nebraska Insurance Department
Terminal Bldg, Ste. 400
941 "O" Street
Lincoln, NE 68508
(402) 471-2201

Medicaid Agency
Medicaid Division
Nebraska Dept. of HHS
P.O. Box 95044
Lincoln, NE 68509-5044
(402) 471-2306

State Unit on Aging
State Office Bldg. 5th Floor
301 Centennial Mall South
Lincoln, NE 68509-5044
(402) 471-4623

NEVADA
Nevada Division of Insurance
788 Fairview Drive
Ste. 300
Carson City, NV 89701-5753
(775) 687-4270
Insurance Counseling
(775) 687-4270

Medicaid Agency
Nevada State Welfare Division
505 East King St.
Rm. 600
Carson City, NV 89710-3708
(775) 684-4000

Division for Aging Services
3416 Goni Rd.
Bldg. D
Ste. 132
Carson City, NV 89706
(775) 687-4210

NEW HAMPSHIRE
New Hampshire Insurance
   Department
21 South Fruit St. Ste 14
Concord, NH 03301
(603) 271-2261
Insurance Counseling
1-800-852-3416

Medicaid Agency
NH DHHS Office of Medicaid
   Business & Policy
Medicaid Program
129 Pleasant St.
Concord, NH 03301-3857
(603) 271-5254

NH DHHA Division of
   Community Based Care Services
Bureau of Elderly & Adult Services
129 Pleasant St.
Concord, NH 03301-3857
(603) 271-4680

NEW JERSEY
Department of Banking &
   Insurance
P.O. Box 325
Trenton, NJ 08625-0325
(609) 292-5360
Insurance Counseling
1-800-792-8820

Medicaid Agency
Department of Health and Senior
   Services
P.O. Box 360
Trenton, NJ 08625-0360
(609) 292-7837

Division of Senior Affairs
P.O. Box 807
Trenton, NJ 08625-0807
(609) 943-3437

NEW MEXICO
New Mexico Insurance Department
P.E.R.A. Building
1120 Paseo de Peralta
P.O. Box 1269
Santa Fe, NM 87504-1269
(505) 827-4601
Insurance Counseling
1-800-432-2080

Medicaid Agency
Medical Assistance Division
New Mexico Human Services
    Department
P.O. Box 2348
Santa Fe, NM 87504-2348
(505) 827-3100

State Agency on Aging
La Villa Rivera Building
228 East Palace Avenue, Ground
    Floor
Santa Fe, NM 87501
(505) 827-7640

NEW YORK
New York Insurance Department
25 Beaver Street
New York, NY 10004
(212) 480-6400
Insurance Counseling
1-800-333-4114

Medicaid Agency
NYS Department of Health
Office of Medicaid Management
Empire State Plaza
Rm. 1466, Corning Tower Bldg.
Albany, NY 12237
(518) 474-3018

State Office for the Aging
2 Empire State Plaza
Albany, NY 12223-1251
1-800-342-9871

NORTH CAROLINA
North Carolina Insurance
    Department
Dobbs Building
430 N. Salisbury St.
Raleigh, NC 27603-5926
(919) 733-2032
Insurance Counseling
(919) 807-6900
1-800-443-9354 (in state only)

Medicaid Agency
Division of Medical Assistance
Department of Health and Human
    Services
1985 Umstead Drive
2501 Mail Service Center
Raleigh, NC 27626-2501
(919) 857-4017

Division of Aging
2101 Mail Service Center
Raleigh, NC 27699-2101
(919) 733-3983

NORTH DAKOTA
North Dakota Insurance
    Department
State Capital, Fifth Floor
600 East Blvd.
Bismarck, ND 58505-0320
1-800-247-0560
Insurance Counseling
1-800-247-0560

Medicaid Agency
Medical Services Division
600 E Boulevard Ave., Dept. 325
Bismarck, ND 58505-0250
(701) 328-2321

Department of Human Services
Aging Services Division
600 E Boulevard Avenue Dept. 325
Bismarck, ND 58505-0250
(701) 328-3480

OHIO

Ohio Insurance Department
2100 Stella Court
Columbus, OH 43215-1067
(614) 644-2658
Insurance Counseling
1-800-686-1578

Medicaid Agency
Office of Medicaid
Department of Human Services
30 East Broad Street
31st Floor
Columbus, OH 43215-3414
(614) 644-0140

Department of Aging
50 W. Broad Street
9th Floor
Columbus, OH 43215-3362
(614) 466-5500

OKLAHOMA

Oklahoma Insurance Department
2401 NW 23rd Street, Suite 28
Oklahoma City, OK 73107
(405) 521-2828
Insurance Counseling
1-800-522-0071

Medicaid Agency
Oklahoma Health Care Authority
4545 North Lincoln Blvd.
Ste. 124
Oklahoma City, OK 73105
(405) 522-7300

Department of Human Services
Aging Services Division
2400 N. Lincoln Blvd.
Oklahoma City, OK 73105
(405) 521-2281

OREGON

Oregon Insurance Division
350 Winter Street NE
Rm. 440
Salem, OR 97301-3883
(503) 947-7980
Insurance Counseling
1-800-722-4134

Medicaid Agency
Department of Human Services
Office of Medical Assistance
    Programs
500 Summer Street, NE
Salem, OR 97310-1079
(503) 945-5772

Department of Human Resources
Senior & Disabled Services
  Division
500 Summer Street, NE
3rd Floor
Salem, OR 97301-1073
(503) 945-5811

PALAU
State Agency on Aging
Department of Social Services
Republic of Palau
P.O. Box 100
Koror, Palau 96940

PENNSYLVANIA
Pennsylvania Insurance Department
1326 Strawberry Square
Harrisburg, PA 17120
(717) 787-0442
Insurance Counseling
1-877-881-6388

Medicaid Agency
Medical Assistance Programs
Health and Welfare Bldg.
Rm 515
P.O. Box 2675
Harrisburg, PA 17105-2675
(717) 787-1870

Department of Aging
555 Walnut St.
5th Floor
Harrisburg, PA 17101-1919
(717) 783-1550

PUERTO RICO
Office of the Commissioner of
  Insurance
P.O. Box 8330
Fernandez Juncos Station
Sancturce, PR 00910-8330
(787) 722-8686
Insurance Counseling
(809) 721-8590

Medicaid Agency
Office of Economic Assistance
  to the Medically Indigent
  – Department of Health
Call Box 70184
San Juan, PR 00936
(787) 250-7429

Governor's Office of Elderly Affairs
P.O. Box 50063
San Juan, PR 00902
(787) 721-5710

*REPUBLIC OF THE
  MARSHALL ISLANDS*
State Agency on Aging
Department of Social Services
Republic of the Marshall Islands
Marjuro, Marshall Islands 96960

RHODE ISLAND
Rhode Island
233 Richmond Street
Providence, RI 02903-4233
(401) 222-2246
Insurance Counseling
1-800-322-2880

Medicaid Agency
Division of Medical Services
Department of Human Services
600 New London Avenue
Cranston, RI 02920
(401) 462-6500

Department of Elderly Affairs
160 Pine Street
Providence, RI 02903
(401) 222-2858

SOUTH CAROLINA
South Carolina Department of
    Insurance
300 Arbor Lake Dr.
Ste. 1200
Columbia, SC 29223
(803) 737-6160
Insurance Counseling
1-800-868-9095

Medicaid Agency
Department of Health and Human
    Services
P.O. Box 8206
Columbia, SC 29202-8206
(803) 898-2500

Lieutenant Governor's Office on
    Aging
1301 Gervais
Suite 200
Columbia, SC 29201
(803) 734-9900

SOUTH DAKOTA
South Dakota Division of Insurance
445 East Capitol
Pierre, SD 57501
(605) 773-3563
Insurance Counseling
1-800-822-8804

Medicaid Agency
Department of Social Services
700 Governors Drive
Pierre, SD 57501
(605) 773-3165

Office of Adult Services and Aging
700 Governors Drive
Pierre, SD 57501
(605) 773-3165

TENNESSEE
Tennessee Department of
    Commerce & Insurance
500 James Robertson Pkwy
Davy Crockett Tower
Nashville, TN 37243-0565
(615) 741-2241

Medicaid Agency
Bureau of TennCare
310 Great Circle Rd.
Nashville, TN 37243
1-866-311-4282

Commission on Aging & Disability
Andrew Jackson Bldg.
500 Deadrick Street
8th Floor
Nashville, TN 37243-0860
(615) 741-2056

TEXAS
Texas Department of Insurance
333 Guadalupe Street
Austin, TX 78701
(512) 463-6169
Insurance Counseling
1-800-252-3439

Medicaid Agency
Texas Health and Human Services
  Commission
Office of the Ombudsman, MC
  H-700
P.O. Box 13247
Austin, TX 78711-3247
(512) 424-6500

Department on Aging and
  Disability Services
701 W. 51st St.
Austin, TX 78751
(512) 438-3011

UTAH
Utah Insurance Department
State Office Bldg. Suite 3110
PO Box 146901
Salt Lake City, UT 84114-6901
1-800-538-3800
Insurance Counseling
1-800-439-3805

Medicaid Agency
Department of Health
Division of Health Care Financing
P.O. Box 143106
Salt Lake City, UT 84114-3106
(801) 538-6155

Aging Services Administration
  Office
120 North 200 West
Rm. 325
Salt Lake City, UT 84103
(801) 538-3910

VERMONT
Vermont Department of Banking
  & Insurance
89 Main Street, Drawer 20
Montpelier, VT 05620-3101
(802) 828-3301
Insurance Counseling
1-802-828-3302

Medicaid Agency
Office of Health Access
Department of Social Welfare
312 Hurricane Lane
Suite 201
Williston, VT 05495
(802) 879-5900

Department of Disabilities, Aging
  and Independent Living
Division of Disability & Aging
  Services
103 South Main Street
Weeks Building
Waterbury, VT 05671
(802) 241-2388

VIRGINIA
Virginia Bureau of Insurance
1300 E. Main Street
Richmond, VA 23219
(804) 371-9741
Insurance Counseling
1-877-310-6560

Medicaid Agency
Department of Medical Assistance
  Services
600 East Broad Street
Richmond, VA 23219
(804) 786-7933

Department for the Aging
1610 Forest Avenue
Suite 100
Richmond, VA 23229
(804) 662-9333

VIRGIN ISLANDS
Virgin Islands Insurance
  Department
St. Thomas
Kongens Gade No. 18
Charlotte Amalie
St. Thomas, VI 00802
(340) 774-7166
St. Croix
1131 King Street, Ste. 101
St. Croix, VI 00820
(340) 773-6459
Insurance Counseling
1-800-552-3402

Medicaid Agency
Bureau of Health Insurance and
  Medical Assistance
210-3A Altona
Suite 302 Frostco Center
St. Thomas, VI 00802
(340) 774-4624

Senior Citizen Affairs Division
Department of Human Services
19 Estate Diamond Fredericksted
St. Croix, VI 00840
(809) 774-0930

WASHINGTON
Washington Insurance Department
P.O. Box 40255
Olympia, WA 98504-0255
(360) 725-7000
Insurance Counseling
1-800-397-4422

Medicaid Agency
Medical Assistance Administration
P.O. Box 45080
Olympia, WA 98504-5080
(360) 725-1867

Aging & Adult Services
  Administration
Department of Social & Health
  Services
P.O. Box 45050
Olympia, WA 98504-5050
(360) 902-7797

WEST VIRGINIA
West Virginia Insurance
   Commission
1124 Smith Street
Charleston, WV 25301
(304) 558-3354
Insurance Counseling
1-800-642-9004

Medicaid Agency
Bureau of Medical Services
Department of Health & Human
   Resources
7011 MacCorkle Avenue SE
Charleston, WV 25304
(304) 926-1703

WV Bureau of Senior Services
1900 Kanawha Blvd. East
Holly Grove Bldg. 10
Charleston, WV 25305-0160
(304) 558-3317

WISCONSIN
Wisconsin Office of the
   Commissioner of Insurance
125 South Webster Street
Madison, WI 53702
(608) 266-3585
Insurance Counseling
1-800-242-1060

Medicaid Agency
Division of Health Care Financing
Department of Health & Social
   Services
One West Wilson Street
Room 350
Madison, WI 53701

(608) 266-8922
Wisconsin Division of Health Care
   Financing
Department of Health and Family
   Services
One West Wilson Street
Madison, WI 53707-7850
(608) 266-2536

WYOMING
Wyoming Insurance Department
Herschler Bldg.
3rd Floor East
122 West 25th Street
Cheyenne, WY 82002
(307) 777-7401
Insurance Counseling
1-800-856-4398

Office of Medicaid
6101 Yellowstone Rd.
Suite 210
Cheyenne, WY 82002
(307) 772-8403

Division on Aging
Wyoming Department of Health
6101 Yellowstone Rd.
Rm. 259B
Cheyenne, WY 82002-0710
(307) 777-7986

Appendix C:
Partnership Documents

It occurred to me that readers of this book might wish to see the instructions from the government which explain how Long-Term Care Partnerships are to be implemented. "The government" in this situation is the Centers for Medicare and Medicaid Services (CMS), the governing body that oversees Medicare and Medicaid.

Exhibit A is the document that defines the Long-Term Care Partnership. It explains the requirements that must be met in order for a long-term care insurance policy be labeled a Partnership policy and therefore qualify for the asset offset in the Medicaid eligibility process as explained in Asset Eligibility Criteria in Chapter 5, The Medicaid Benefit for Long-Term Care.

I was particularly pleased to see the inflation benefit requirement in Appendix 1 for purchasers under 61 years old. Unfortunately, the rule doesn't stipulate what kind of compound inflation. While I believe the intent was the standard 5% compound that is found in almost all policies, some insurance carriers believe a lower percentage meets this requirement; e.g. 2%, 3% or 4%. Another carrier believes that the annual compounding factor may be based on the Consumer Price Index for all items, which averages around 3.5% compound. The result of this confusion is that each state is interpreting the type of compounded inflation benefit that will meet the requirement for purchasers under age 61. I hope 5% compound wins.

Exhibit B is the language that CMS has provided to the states to use when requesting amendments to their Medicaid rules that will allow the asset offset both in the Medicaid eligibility process and in the estate recovery process. See Chapter 4, *The Partnership for Long-Term Care*, to refresh your memory on these points.

EXHIBIT A

Qualified Long-Term Care Partnerships
Under the
Deficit Reduction Act of 2005

Centers for Medicare & Medicaid Services
Center for Medicaid and State Operations

July 27, 2006

Enclosure Highlights—Section 6021

Deficit Reduction Act of 2005

I. **Expansion of State Long-Term Care (LTC) Partnership Program**

Section 6021(a)(1)(A) of the Deficit Reduction Act of 2005 (DRA), Pub. L. 109-171, expands State LTC Partnership programs, which encourage individuals to purchase LTC insurance. Prior to enactment of the DRA, States could use the authority of section 1902(r)(2) of the Social Security Act (the Act) to disregard benefits paid under an LTC policy when calculating income and resources for purposes of determining Medicaid eligibility. However, under section 1917(b) of the Act, only States that had State plan amendments approved as of May 14, 1993, could exempt the LTC insurance benefits from estate recovery.

The DRA amends section 1917(b)(1)(C)(ii) of the Act to permit other States to exempt LTC benefits from estate recovery, if the State has a State plan amendment (SPA) that provides for a qualified State LTC insurance partnership (Qualified Partnership). The DRA then adds section 1917(b)(1)(C)(iii) in order to define a "Qualified Partnership." States that had State plan amendments as of May 14, 1993, do not have to meet the new definition, but in order to continue to use an estate recovery exemption, those States must maintain consumer protections at least as stringent as those they had in effect as of December 31, 2005. We refer to both types of States as "Partnership States."

II. **Definition of "Qualified State LTC Partnership" and Requirements**

A. Definition

Section 6021(a)(1)(A) of the DRA adds several new clauses to section 1917(b)(1)(C) of the Act. The new clause (iii) defines the term "Qualified State LTC Partnership" to mean an approved SPA that provides for the disregard of resources, when determining estate recovery obligations, in an amount equal to the LTC insurance benefits paid to, or on behalf of, an individual who has received medical assistance. A policy that meets all of the requirements specified in a Qualified State LTC Partnership SPA is referred to as a "Partnership policy."

The insurance benefits upon which a disregard may be based include benefits paid as direct reimbursement of LTC expenses, as well as benefits paid on a per diem, or other periodic basis, for periods during which the individual received LTC services. The DRA does not require that benefits available under a Partnership policy be fully exhausted before the disregard of resources can be applied. Eligibility may be determined by applying the disregard based on the amount of benefits paid to, or on behalf of, the individual as of the month of application, even if additional benefits remain available under the terms of the policy. The amount that will be protected during estate recovery is the same amount that was disregarded in the eligibility determination.

It should be noted that while an approved Partnership SPA may enable an individual to become eligible for Medicaid by disregarding assets or resources under the authority of section 1902(r)(2) of the Act, the use of a qualified Partnership policy will not affect an individual's ineligibility for payment for nursing facility services, or other LTC services, when the individual's equity interest in home property exceeds the limits set forth in section 1917(f) of the Act, as amended by the DRA.

B. Requirements

The new clause (iii) also sets forth other requirements that must be met in order for a State plan amendment to meet the definition of a Qualified Partnership. These include the following:

1. The LTC insurance policy must meet several conditions, which are listed in Appendix I of this enclosure. These conditions include meeting the requirements of specific portions of the National Association of Insurance Commissioners' (NAIC) LTC Insurance Model Regulations and Model Act (see Appendices II and III).

    The Qualified Partnership SPA **must** provide that the State Insurance Commissioner, or other appropriate State authority, certify to the State Medicaid agency that the policy meets the specified requirements of the NAIC Model Regulations and Model Act. The State Medicaid agency may also accept certification from the same authority that the policy meets the Internal Revenue Code definition of a qualified LTC insurance policy, and that it includes the requisite inflation protections specified in Appendix I. If the State Medicaid agency accepts the certification of the Commissioner or other authority, it is not required to independently verify that policies meet these requirements. Changes in a Partnership policy after it is issued will not affect the applicability of the disregard of resources as long as the policy continues to meet all of the requirements referenced above.

    If an individual has an existing LTC insurance policy that does not qualify as a Partnership policy due to the issue date of the policy, and that policy is exchanged for another, the State Insurance Commissioner or other State authority must determine the issue date for the policy that is received in exchange. To be a qualified Partnership policy, the issue date must not be earlier than the effective date of the Qualified Partnership SPA.

2. The State Medicaid agency must provide information and technical assistance to the State insurance department regarding the Partnership and the relationship of LTC insurance policies to Medicaid. This information must be incorporated into the training of individuals who will sell LTC insurance policies in the State.

3. The State insurance department must provide assurance to the State Medicaid agency that anyone who sells a policy under the Partnership receives training and

demonstrates an understanding of Partnership policies and their relationship to public and private coverage of LTC.

4. The issuer of the policy must provide reports to the Secretary, in accordance with regulations to be developed by the Secretary, which include notice of when benefits are paid under the policy, the amount of those benefits, notice of termination of the policy, and any other information the Secretary determines is appropriate.

5. The State may not impose any requirement affecting the terms or benefits of a Partnership policy unless it imposes the same requirements on all LTC insurance policies.

III.   "Grandfather" Clause

A State that had a LTC insurance Partnership SPA approved as of May 14, 1993, is considered to have satisfied the requirements in section II above if the Secretary determines that the SPA provides consumer protections no less stringent than those applied under its SPA as of December 31, 2005. Under this provision California, Connecticut, Indiana, Iowa, and New York would continue to be considered Partnership States.

IV.   Effective Dates

A SPA that provides for a Qualified State LTC Insurance Partnership under the amended section 1917(b)(1)(C) of the Act may be effective for policies issued on or after a date specified in the SPA, but not earlier than the first day of the first calendar quarter in which the SPA is submitted.

The DRA requires the Secretary to develop standards regarding the portability of Partnership policies by January 1, 2007. These standards will address reciprocal treatment of policies among Partnership States. The Secretary is also required to develop regulations regarding reporting requirements for issuers of Partnership policies and related data sets. It is not necessary for States to wait for these standards and rules to be promulgated before submitting a Partnership SPA. A State may submit a Partnership SPA at any time after the effective date of the DRA.

Appendix I

Requirements for a Long-Term Care Insurance Policy under a Qualified Long-Term Care Insurance Partnership

order for a State Plan Amendment to meet the definition of a "Qualified Partnership," owing the State to disregard assets or resources equal to the amount paid on behalf of an lividual, the long-term care insurance policy, including a group policy, must meet the llowing conditions:

1. The policy must cover a person who was a resident of the Qualified Partnership State when coverage first became effective. If a policy is exchanged for another, the residency rule applies to the issuance of the original policy.
2. The policy must meet the definition of a "qualified long-term care insurance policy" that is found in section 7702B(b) of the Internal Revenue Code of 1986.
3. The policy must not have been issued earlier than the effective date of the SPA.
4. The policy must meet specific requirements of the National Association of Insurance Commissioners (NAIC) Long Term Care Insurance Model Regulations and Model Act. These are listed in Appendices II and III.
5. The policy must include inflation protection as follows:
   - For purchasers under 61 years old, compound annual inflation protection;
   - For purchasers 61 to 76 years old, some level of inflation protection; or
   - For purchasers 76 years or older, inflation protection may be offered but is not required.

Appendix II

NAIC Model Regulations

The following is a list of the NAIC Model regulations that are referenced in Appendix I, item 4:

Model Regulations

1. Section 6A, with a certain exception, relating to guaranteed renewal or non-cancellability;
2. Section 6B of the Model Act, as it relates to 6A;
3. Section 6B, with certain exceptions, relating to prohibitions on limitations and exclusions;
4. Section 6C, relating to extension of benefits;
5. Section 6D, relating to continuation or conversion of coverage;
6. Section 6E, relating to discontinuance and replacement of policies;
7. Section 7, relating to unintentional lapse;
8. Section 8, with certain exceptions, relating to disclosure;
9. Section 9, relating to disclosure of rating practices to the consumer;
10. Section 11, relating to prohibitions against post-claims underwriting;
11. Section 12, relating to minimum standards;
12. Section 14, relating to application forms and replacement coverage;
13. Section 15, relating to reporting requirements;
14. Section 22, relating to filing requirements for marketing;
15. Section 23, with certain exceptions, relating to standards for marketing, with the exception of specific paragraphs;
16. Section 24, relating to suitability;
17. Section 25, relating to prohibition against pre-existing conditions and probationary periods in replacement policies or certificates;
18. Section 26, relating to contingent non-forfeiture benefits;
19. Section 29, relating to standard format outline of coverage; and
20. Section 30, relating to the requirement to deliver the NAIC publication *"A Shopper's Guide to Long-Term Care Insurance"*.

Appendix III

NAIC Model Act

ıe following is a list of the requirements of the NAIC Model Act that are referenced in ɔpendix I, item 4:

1. Section 6C, relating to pre-existing conditions;
2. Section 6D, relating to prior hospitalization;
3. Section 8, the provisions relating to contingent non-forfeiture benefits;
4. Section 6F, relating to right to return;
5. Section 6G, relating to outline of coverage;
6. Section 6H, relating to requirements for certificates under group plans;
7. Section 6J, relating to policy summary;
8. Section 6K, relating to monthly reports on accelerated death benefits; and
9. Section 7, relating to incontestability period.

EXHIBIT B

Language for Cover Note for DRA Long-Term Care Partnership Preprint Templates from Centers for Medicare and Medicaid Services

Attached are two State Plan Preprint templates for States to use, if they wish to do so, when amending their State Medicaid Plans to implement a Long-Term Care Insurance Partnership as provided for in Section 6021 of the Deficit Reduction Act of 2005 (DRA), P.L. 109-171. These templates deal with the disregard of assets under a State Long-Term Care Partnership and the corresponding exception for estate recoveries. Long-Term Care Partnerships are optional for States, therefore only those States that choose to implement a Partnership program should submit these State Plan Amendments (SPAs).

Prior to enactment of the DRA five States had Long-Term Care Partnerships which were approved no later than May 14, 1993. These States are California, Connecticut, Indiana, Iowa and New York. Under the provisions of the DRA, these States are not required to submit new State Plan Amendments, but may continue to operate their Partnerships as described in their existing approved State Plans. For all other States that choose to provide a disregard of assets based on a Partnership program, SPAs must be submitted and must comply with the new requirements of section 1917(b)(1)(C) of the Social Security Act as amended by section 6021 of the DRA. States that do choose to implement a Partnership should submit the amendment regarding the disregard of assets and the amendment regarding estate recoveries simultaneously.

States should direct any questions they may have about these draft templates to their CMS regional office.

309

State Long-Term Care Insurance Partnership

This template introduces a new Supplement 8c to Attachment 2.6-A. This template provides for a disregard of resources in the eligibility determination under section 1902(r)(2) of the Social Security Act, and stipulates that the disregard will be based on benefits paid by long-term care insurance policies that meet the requirements of 1917(b)(1)(C) of the Act.

SUPPLEMENT 8c TO ATTACHMENT 2.6-A

STATE PLAN UNDER TITLE XIX OF THE SOCIAL SECURITY ACT

State:_____

STATE LONG-TERM CARE INSURANCE PARTNERSHIP

1902(r)(2)   The following more liberal methodology applies to individuals who are 1917(b)(1)(C)   eligible for medical assistance under one of the following eligibility groups:

> An individual who is a beneficiary under a long-term care insurance policy that meets the requirements of a "qualified State long-term care insurance partnership" policy (partnership policy) as set forth below, is given a resource disregard as described in this amendment. The amount of the disregard is equal to the amount of the insurance benefit payments made to or on behalf of the individual. The term "long-term care insurance policy" includes a certificate issued under a group insurance contract.

310

_____ The State Medicaid Agency (Agency) stipulates that the following requirements will be satisfied in order for a long-term care policy to qualify for a disregard. Where appropriate, the Agency relies on attestations by the State Insurance Commissioner (Commissioner) or other State official charged with regulation and oversight of insurance policies sold in the state, regarding information within the expertise of the State's Insurance Department.

- The policy is a qualified long-term care insurance policy as defined in section 7702B(b) of the Internal Revenue Code of 1986.

- The policy meets the requirements of the long-term care insurance model regulation and long-term care insurance model Act promulgated by the National Association of Insurance Commissioners (as adopted as of October 2000) as those requirements are set forth in section 1917(b)(5)(A) of the Social Security Act.

- The policy was issued no earlier than the effective date of this State plan amendment.

- The insured individual was a resident of a Partnership State when coverage first became effective under the policy. If the policy is later exchanged for a different long-term care policy, the individual was a resident of a Partnership State when coverage under the earliest policy became effective.

- The policy meets the inflation protection requirements set forth in section 1917(b)(1)(C)(iii)(IV) of the Social Security Act.

- The Commissioner requires the issuer of the policy to make regular reports to the Secretary that include notification regarding when benefits provided under the policy have been paid and the amount of such benefits paid, notification regarding when the policy otherwise terminates, and such other information as the Secretary determines may be appropriate to the administration of such partnerships.

- The State does not impose any requirement affecting the terms or benefits of a partnership policy that the state does not also impose on non-partnership policies.

- The State Insurance Department assures that any individual who sells a partnership policy receives training, and demonstrates evidence of an understanding of such policies and how they relate to other public and private coverage of long-term care.

- The Agency provides information and technical assistance to the Insurance Department regarding the training described above.

Estate Recoveries

This template introduces a revised page 53b to Attachment 4.17, which replaces the current page 53b as it was issued in a May 1995 Program Memorandum. States that elect a Long-Term Care Partnership program must submit the new page in order to exclude from estate recoveries those assets that were disregarded in the eligibility determination under the Partnership.

Revised Page 53b

STATE PLAN UNDER TITLE XIX OF THE SOCIAL SECURITY ACT

State:_____

1917(b)1(C)   (4) _____   If an individual covered under a long-term care insurance policy received benefits for which assets or resources were disregarded as provided for in Attachment 2.6-A, Supplement 8c (State Long-Term Care Insurance Partnership), the State does not seek adjustment or recovery from the individual's estate for the amount of assets or resources disregarded.

Appendix D:
What Your State Lets You Keep - 2008 Medicaid Eligibility Asset/Income Requirements and Penalty Period Divisors for 50 States

State	Your asset allowance	Your spouse's minimum asset allowance	Your personal monthly needs allowance	Your spouse's monthly income allowance	Divestment Penalty Divisor (Monthly)
Alabama*	$2,000	$25,000	$30	$1,750	$4,400
Alaska*	$2,000	$104,400	$75	$2,610	Varies by area $10,000 in Anchorage
Arizona*	$2,000	$20,880	$93.45	$1,750	$,5119 Maricopa, Pima & Pinal Counties, $4,759 All other counties
Arkansas*	$2,000	$20,880	$40	$1,750	$3,801
California	$2,000	$104,400	$35	$2,610	$5,101
Colorado*	$2,000	$104,400	$50	$1,750	$5,546
Connecticut	$1,600	$20,880	$63	$1,750	$9,096
Delaware*	$2,000	$25,000	$50	$1,750	$4,905
District of Columbia	$2,600	$104,400	$70	$2,610	Nursing home actual cost where the applicant is seeking benefits
Florida*	$2,000	$104,400	$35	$1,750	$3,300
Georgia	$2,000	$104,400	$30	$2,610	$4,258
Hawaii	$2,000	$104,400	$30	$2,610	$7,314
Idaho*	$2,000	$20,880	$40	$1,750	$5,213
Illinois	$2,000	$104,400	$30	$2,610	Daily benefit x 30
Indiana	$1,500	$20,880	$52	$1,750	$4,249
Iowa*	$2,000	$24,000	$50	$2,610	$3,698
Kansas	$2,000	$20,880	$50	$1,750	$4,000 for transfers prior to 2/8/06; on/after that date, $136.60 per day

State	Your asset allowance	Your spouse's minimum asset allowance	Your personal monthly needs allowance	Your spouse's monthly income allowance	Divestment Penalty Divisor (Monthly)
Kentucky	$2,000	$22,000	$40	$1,750	$4,585
Louisiana*	$2,000	$104,400	$38	$2,610	$3,000
Maine	$2,000	$104,400	$40	$1,750	$6,778
Maryland	$2,500	$20,880	$66	$1,750	$4,300
Massachusetts	$2,000	$20,880	$72.80	$1,750	$7,680
Michigan	$2,000	$20,880	$60	$1,750	$6,191
Minnesota	$3,000	$29,389	$84	$1,750	$4,198
Mississippi*	$2,000	$104,400	$44	$2,610	$4,600
Missouri	$1,000	$20,880	$30	$1,750	$3,859
Montana	$2,000	$20,880	$50	$1,750	$4,512
Nebraska	$4,000	$20,880	$50	$2,610	No calculated average. Based on individual cost of care.
Nevada*	$2,000	$20,880	$35	$1,750	$7,034
New Hampshire	$2,500	$20,880	$56	$1,750	$6,814
New Jersey	$2,000	$20,880	$35	$1,750	$6,655
New Mexico*	$2,000	$31,290	$58	$1,750	$4,551
New York	$4,150	$74,820	$50	$2,610	Varies by region: NYC: $9,636; Long Island: $10,555; N. Metro: $9,316; NE: $7,431; Central: $6,696; Rochester: $8,089; Western: $7,066

State	Your asset allowance	Your spouse's minimum asset allowance	Your personal monthly needs allowance	Your spouse's monthly income allowance	Divestment Penalty Divisor (Monthly)
North Carolina	$2,000	$20,880	$30	$1,750	$4,800
North Dakota	$3,000	$104,400	$60	$2,610	$4,633
Ohio	$1,500	$20,880	$40	$1,750	$4,806
Oklahoma*	$2,000	$25,000	$50	$2,610	$2,000
Oregon*	$2,000	$20,880	$30	$1,750	$4,700
Pennsylvania	$2,400	$20,880	$45	$1,750	$6,942
Rhode Island	$4,000	$20,880	$50	$1,750	$7,031
South Carolina*	$2,000	$66,480	$30	$2,610	$4,852
South Dakota*	$2,000	$20,880	$60	$1,750	$4,026
Tennessee	$2,000	$20,880	$40	$1,750	$3,874
Texas*	$2,000	$20,880	$60	$2,610	$3,713
Utah	$2,000	$20,880	$45	$1,750	$3,618
Vermont	$2,000	$104,400	$47.66	$1,750	$5,921
Virginia	$2,000	$20,880	$30	$1,750	$6,654 in Northern Virginia; $4,954 elsewhere in state
Washington	$2,000	$41,493	$41.62	$1,750	$5,763
West Virginia	$2,000	$20,880	$50	$1,750	$3,380
Wisconsin	$2,000	$50,000	$45	$2,282	$5,584
Wyoming*	$2,000	$104,400	$50	$2,610	$4,956

Appendix E:
Deficit Reduction Act of 2005 Medicaid LTC and Partnership Provisions

Public Law 109-171
109th Congress
Enacted February 8, 2006

S.1932

Deficit Reduction Act of 2005 (Enrolled as Agreed to or Passed by Both House and Senate)

CHAPTER 2--LONG-TERM CARE UNDER MEDICAID

Subchapter A--Reform of Asset Transfer Rules

SEC. 6011. LENGTHENING LOOK-BACK PERIOD; CHANGE IN BEGINNING DATE FOR PERIOD OF INELIGIBILITY.

(a) Lengthening Look-Back Period for All Disposals to 5 Years- Section 1917(c)(1)(B)(i) of the Social Security Act (42 U.S.C. 1396p(c)(1)(B)(i)) is amended by inserting `or in the case of any other disposal of assets made on or after the date of the enactment of the Deficit Reduction Act of 2005' before `, 60 months'.

(b) Change in Beginning Date for Period of Ineligibility- Section 1917(c)(1)(D) of such Act (42 U.S.C. 1396p(c)(1)(D)) is amended--

  (1) by striking `(D) The date' and inserting `(D)(i) In the case of a transfer of asset made before the date of the enactment of the Deficit Reduction Act of 2005, the date'; and

  (2) by adding at the end the following new clause:

`(ii) In the case of a transfer of asset made on or after the date of the enactment of the Deficit Reduction Act of 2005, the date specified in this subparagraph is the first day of a month during or after which assets have been transferred for less than fair market value, or the date on which the individual is eligible for medical assistance under the State plan and would otherwise be receiving institutional level care described in subparagraph (C) based on an approved application for such care but for the application of the penalty period, whichever is later, and which does not occur during any other period of ineligibility under this subsection.'.

(c) Effective Date- The amendments made by this section shall apply to transfers made on or after the date of the enactment of this Act.

(d) Availability of Hardship Waivers- Each State shall provide for a hardship waiver process in accordance with section 1917(c)(2)(D) of the Social Security Act (42 U.S.C. 1396p(c)(2)(D))--

>(1) under which an undue hardship exists when application of the transfer of assets provision would deprive the individual--

>>(A) of medical care such that the individual's health or life would be endangered; or

>>(B) of food, clothing, shelter, or other necessities of life; and

>(2) which provides for--

>>(A) notice to recipients that an undue hardship exception exists;

>>(B) a timely process for determining whether an undue hardship waiver will be granted; and

>>(C) a process under which an adverse determination can be appealed.

(e) Additional Provisions on Hardship Waivers-

>(1) APPLICATION BY FACILITY- Section 1917(c)(2) of the Social Security Act (42 U.S.C. 1396p(c)(2)) is amended--

>>(A) by striking the semicolon at the end of subparagraph (D) and inserting a period; and

>>(B) by adding after and below such

subparagraph the following:

`The procedures established under subparagraph (D) shall permit the facility in which the institutionalized individual is residing to file an undue hardship waiver application on behalf of the individual with the consent of the individual or the personal representative of the individual.'.

(2) Authority to make bed hold payments for hardship applicants- Such section is further amended by adding at the end the following: `While an application for an undue hardship waiver is pending under subparagraph (D) in the case of an individual who is a resident of a nursing facility, if the application meets such criteria as the Secretary specifies, the State may provide for payments for nursing facility services in order to hold the bed for the individual at the facility, but not in excess of payments for 30 days.'.

SEC. 6012. DISCLOSURE AND TREATMENT OF ANNUITIES.

(a) In General- Section 1917 of the Social Security Act (42 U.S.C. 1396p) is amended by redesignating subsection (e) as subsection (f) and by inserting after subsection (d) the following new subsection:

`(e)(1) In order to meet the requirements of this section for purposes of section 1902(a)(18), a State shall require, as a condition for the provision of medical assistance for services described in subsection (c)(1)(C)(i) (relating to long-term care services) for an individual, the application of the individual for such assistance (including any recertification of eligibility for such assistance) shall disclose a description of any interest the individual or community spouse has in an annuity (or similar financial instrument, as may be specified by the Secretary), regardless of whether the annuity is irrevocable or is treated as an asset. Such application or recertification form shall include a statement that under paragraph (2) the State becomes a remainder beneficiary under such an annuity or similar financial instrument by virtue of the provision of such medical assistance.

`(2)(A) In the case of disclosure concerning an annuity under subsection (c)(1)(F), the State shall notify the issuer of the annuity of the right of the State under such subsection as a preferred remainder beneficiary in the annuity for medical assistance furnished to the individual. Nothing in this paragraph shall be construed as preventing such an issuer from notifying persons with any other remainder interest of the State's remainder interest under such subsection.

`(B) In the case of such an issuer receiving notice under subparagraph (A), the State may require the issuer to notify the State when there is a change in the amount of income or principal being withdrawn from the amount that was being withdrawn at the time of the most recent disclosure described in paragraph (1). A State shall take such information into account in determining the amount of the State's obligations for medical assistance or in the individual's eligibility for such assistance.

`(3) The Secretary may provide guidance to States on categories of transactions that may be treated as a transfer of asset for less than fair market value.

`(4) Nothing in this subsection shall be construed as preventing a State from denying eligibility for medical assistance for an individual based on the income or resources derived from an annuity described in paragraph (1).'.

(b) REQUIREMENT FOR STATE TO BE NAMED AS A REMAINDER BENEFICIARY- Section 1917(c)(1) of such Act (42 U.S.C. 1396p(c)(1)), is amended by adding at the end the following:

`(F) For purposes of this paragraph, the purchase of an

annuity shall be treated as the disposal of an asset for less than fair market value unless--

　　　`(i) the State is named as the remainder beneficiary in the first position for at least the total amount of medical assistance paid on behalf of the annuitant under this title; or

　　　`(ii) the State is named as such a beneficiary in the second position after the community spouse or minor or disabled child and is named in the first position if such spouse or a representative of such child disposes of any such remainder for less than fair market value.'.

(c) INCLUSION OF TRANSFERS TO PURCHASE BALLOON ANNUITIES- Section 1917(c)(1) of such Act (42 U.S.C. 1396p(c)(1)), as amended by subsection (b), is amended by adding at the end the following:

`(G) For purposes of this paragraph with respect to a transfer of assets, the term `assets' includes an annuity purchased by or on behalf of an annuitant who has applied for medical assistance with respect to nursing facility services or other long-term care services under this title unless--

　　　`(i) the annuity is--

　　　　　`(I) an annuity described in subsection (b) or (q) of section 408 of the Internal Revenue Code of 1986; or

　　　　　`(II) purchased with proceeds from--

　　　　　　　`(aa) an account or trust described in subsection (a), (c), or (p) of section 408 of such Code;

　　　　　　　`(bb) a simplified employee pension (within the meaning of section 408(k) of such Code); or

　　　　　　　`(cc) a Roth IRA described in section 408A of such Code; or

　　　`(ii) the annuity--

`(I) is irrevocable and nonassignable;
`(II) is actuarially sound (as determined in accordance with actuarial publications of the Office of the Chief Actuary of the Social Security Administration); and
`(III) provides for payments in equal amounts during the term of the annuity, with no deferral and no balloon payments made.'.

(d) Effective Date- The amendments made by this section shall apply to transactions (including the purchase of an annuity) occurring on or after the date of the enactment of this Act.

SEC. 6013. APPLICATION OF `INCOME-FIRST' RULE IN APPLYING COMMUNITY SPOUSE'S INCOME BEFORE ASSETS IN PROVIDING SUPPORT OF COMMUNITY SPOUSE.

(a) In General- Section 1924(d) of the Social Security Act (42 U.S.C. 1396r-5(d)) is amended by adding at the end the following new subparagraph:

`(6) APPLICATION OF `INCOME FIRST' RULE TO REVISION OF COMMUNITY SPOUSE RESOURCE ALLOWANCE- For purposes of this subsection and subsections (c) and (e), a State must consider that all income of the institutionalized spouse that could be made available to a community spouse, in accordance with the calculation of the community spouse monthly income allowance under this subsection, has been made available before the State allocates to the community spouse an amount of resources adequate to provide the difference between the minimum monthly maintenance needs allowance and all income available to the community spouse.'.

(b) Effective Date- The amendment made by subsection (a)

shall apply to transfers and allocations made on or after the date of the enactment of this Act by individuals who become institutionalized spouses on or after such date.

SEC. 6014. DISQUALIFICATION FOR LONG-TERM CARE ASSISTANCE FOR INDIVIDUALS WITH SUBSTANTIAL HOME EQUITY.

(a) In General- Section 1917 of the Social Security Act, as amended by section 6012(a), is further amended by redesignating subsection (f) as subsection (g) and by inserting after subsection (e) the following new subsection:

`(f)(1)(A) Notwithstanding any other provision of this title, subject to subparagraphs (B) and (C) of this paragraph and paragraph (2), in determining eligibility of an individual for medical assistance with respect to nursing facility services or other long-term care services, the individual shall not be eligible for such assistance if the individual's equity interest in the individual's home exceeds $500,000.

`(B) A State may elect, without regard to the requirements of section 1902(a)(1) (relating to statewideness) and section 1902(a)(10)(B) (relating to comparability), to apply subparagraph (A) by substituting for `$500,000', an amount that exceeds such amount, but does not exceed $750,000.

`(C) The dollar amounts specified in this paragraph shall be increased, beginning with 2011, from year to year based on the percentage increase in the consumer price index for all urban consumers (all items; United States city average), rounded to the nearest $1,000.

`(2) Paragraph (1) shall not apply with respect to an individual if--

>`(A) the spouse of such individual, or
>`(B) such individual's child who is under age 21, or (with respect to States eligible to participate in the State program established under title XVI) is blind

or permanently and totally disabled, or (with respect to States which are not eligible to participate in such program) is blind or disabled as defined in section 1614,

is lawfully residing in the individual's home.

`(3) Nothing in this subsection shall be construed as preventing an individual from using a reverse mortgage or home equity loan to reduce the individual's total equity interest in the home.

`(4) The Secretary shall establish a process whereby paragraph (1) is waived in the case of a demonstrated hardship.'.

(b) Effective Date- The amendment made by subsection (a) shall apply to individuals who are determined eligible for medical assistance with respect to nursing facility services or other long-term care services based on an application filed on or after January 1, 2006.

SEC. 6015. ENFORCEABILITY OF CONTINUING CARE RETIREMENT COMMUNITIES (CCRC) AND LIFE CARE COMMUNITY ADMISSION CONTRACTS.

(a) Admission Policies of Nursing Facilities- Section 1919(c)(5) of the Social Security Act (42 U.S.C. 1396r(c)(5)) is amended--

(1) in subparagraph (A)(i)(II), by inserting `subject to clause (v),' after `(II)'; and

(2) by adding at the end of subparagraph (B) the following new clause:

`(v) TREATMENT OF CONTINUING CARE RETIREMENT COMMUNITIES ADMISSION CONTRACTS- Notwithstanding subclause (II) of subparagraph (A)(i), subject to subsections (c) and (d) of section

1924, contracts for admission to a
State licensed, registered, certified, or
equivalent continuing care retirement
community or life care community,
including services in a nursing facility
that is part of such community, may
require residents to spend on their care
resources declared for the purposes of
admission before applying for medical
assistance.'.

(b) Treatment of Entrance Fees- Section 1917 of such Act (42
U.S.C. 1396p), as amended by sections 6012(a) and 6014(a),
is amended by redesignating subsection (g) as subsection
(h) and by inserting after subsection (f) the following new
subsection:

`(g) Treatment of Entrance Fees of Individuals Residing in
Continuing Care Retirement Communities-

`(1) IN GENERAL- For purposes of determining
an individual's eligibility for, or amount of, benefits
under a State plan under this title, the rules specified
in paragraph (2) shall apply to individuals residing in
continuing care retirement communities or life care
communities that collect an entrance fee on admission
from such individuals.

`(2) TREATMENT OF ENTRANCE FEE- For
purposes of this subsection, an individual's entrance
fee in a continuing care retirement community or
life care community shall be considered a resource
available to the individual to the extent that--

`(A) the individual has the ability to use the
entrance fee, or the contract provides that
the entrance fee may be used, to pay for
care should other resources or income of the
individual be insufficient to pay for such care;

`(B) the individual is eligible for a refund of any remaining entrance fee when the individual dies or terminates the continuing care retirement community or life care community contract and leaves the community; and
`(C) the entrance fee does not confer an ownership interest in the continuing care retirement community or life care community.'.

SEC. 6016. ADDITIONAL REFORMS OF MEDICAID ASSET TRANSFER RULES.

(a) REQUIREMENT TO IMPOSE PARTIAL MONTHS OF INELIGIBILITY- Section 1917(c)(1)(E) of the Social Security Act (42 U.S.C. 1396p(c)(1)(E)) is amended by adding at the end the following:
`(iv) A State shall not round down, or otherwise disregard any fractional period of ineligibility determined under clause (i) or (ii) with respect to the disposal of assets.'.
(b) Authority for States To Accumulate Multiple Transfers Into One Penalty Period- Section 1917(c)(1) of such Act (42 U.S.C. 1396p(c)(1)), as amended by subsections (b) and (c) of section 6012, is amended by adding at the end the following:
`(H) Notwithstanding the preceding provisions of this paragraph, in the case of an individual (or individual's spouse) who makes multiple fractional transfers of assets in more than 1 month for less than fair market value on or after the applicable look-back date specified in subparagraph (B), a State may determine the period of ineligibility applicable to such individual under this paragraph by--
`(i) treating the total, cumulative uncompensated value of all assets transferred by the individual (or individual's spouse) during all months on or after

the look-back date specified in subparagraph (B) as 1 transfer for purposes of clause (i) or (ii) (as the case may be) of subparagraph (E); and

`(ii) beginning such period on the earliest date which would apply under subparagraph (D) to any of such transfers.'.

(c) INCLUSION OF TRANSFER OF CERTAIN NOTES AND LOANS ASSETS- Section 1917(c)(1) of such Act (42 U.S.C. 1396p(c)(1)), as amended by subsection (b), is amended by adding at the end the following:

`(I) For purposes of this paragraph with respect to a transfer of assets, the term `assets' includes funds used to purchase a promissory note, loan, or mortgage unless such note, loan, or mortgage--

`(i) has a repayment term that is actuarially sound (as determined in accordance with actuarial publications of the Office of the Chief Actuary of the Social Security Administration);

`(ii) provides for payments to be made in equal amounts during the term of the loan, with no deferral and no balloon payments made; and

`(iii) prohibits the cancellation of the balance upon the death of the lender.

In the case of a promissory note, loan, or mortgage that does not satisfy the requirements of clauses (i) through (iii), the value of such note, loan, or mortgage shall be the outstanding balance due as of the date of the individual's application for medical assistance for services described in subparagraph (C).'.

(d) INCLUSION OF TRANSFERS TO PURCHASE LIFE ESTATES- Section 1917(c)(1) of such Act (42 U.S.C. 1396p(c)(1)), as amended by subsection (c), is amended by adding at the end the following:

`(J) For purposes of this paragraph with respect to a transfer of assets, the term `assets' includes the purchase of a life estate interest in another individual's home unless the purchaser resides in the home for a period of at least 1 year after the date of the purchase.'.

(e) EFFECTIVE DATES-

    (1) IN GENERAL- Except as provided in paragraphs (2) and (3), the amendments made by this section shall apply to payments under title XIX of the Social Security Act (42 U.S.C. 1396 et seq.) for calendar quarters beginning on or after the date of enactment of this Act, without regard to whether or not final regulations to carry out such amendments have been promulgated by such date.

    (2) EXCEPTIONS- The amendments made by this section shall not apply--

        (A) to medical assistance provided for services furnished before the date of enactment;

        (B) with respect to assets disposed of on or before the date of enactment of this Act; or

        (C) with respect to trusts established on or before the date of enactment of this Act.

    (3) EXTENSION OF EFFECTIVE DATE FOR STATE LAW AMENDMENT- In the case of a State plan under title XIX of the Social Security Act (42 U.S.C. 1396 et seq.) which the Secretary of Health and Human Services determines requires State legislation in order for the plan to meet the additional requirements imposed by the amendments made by a provision of this section, the State plan shall not be regarded as failing to comply with the requirements of such title solely on the basis of its failure to meet these additional requirements before the first day of the first calendar quarter beginning after the close of the first regular session of the State legislature that begins after

the date of the enactment of this Act. For purposes of
the previous sentence, in the case of a State that has
a 2-year legislative session, each year of the session is
considered to be a separate regular session of the State
legislature.

Subchapter B--Expanded Access to Certain Benefits

SEC. 6021. EXPANSION OF STATE LONG-TERM CARE PARTNERSHIP PROGRAM.

(a) EXPANSION AUTHORITY-

(1) IN GENERAL- Section 1917(b) of the Social
Security Act (42 U.S.C. 1396p(b)) is amended--

(A) in paragraph (1)(C)--

(i) in clause (ii), by inserting `and which
satisfies clause (iv), or which has a State
plan amendment that provides for a
qualified State long-term care insurance
partnership (as defined in clause (iii))'
after `1993,'; and

(ii) by adding at the end the following
new clauses:

`(iii) For purposes of this paragraph, the term
`qualified State long-term care insurance partnership'
means an approved State plan amendment under
this title that provides for the disregard of any assets
or resources in an amount equal to the insurance
benefit payments that are made to or on behalf of an
individual who is a beneficiary under a long-term care
insurance policy if the following requirements are met:

`(I) The policy covers an insured who was
a resident of such State when coverage first
became effective under the policy.

`(II) The policy is a qualified long-term
care insurance policy (as defined in section

331

7702B(b) of the Internal Revenue Code of 1986) issued not earlier than the effective date of the State plan amendment.

`(III) The policy meets the model regulations and the requirements of the model Act specified in paragraph (5).

`(IV) If the policy is sold to an individual who--

>`(aa) has not attained age 61 as of the date of purchase, the policy provides compound annual inflation protection;

>`(bb) has attained age 61 but has not attained age 76 as of such date, the policy provides some level of inflation protection; and

>`(cc) has attained age 76 as of such date, the policy may (but is not required to) provide some level of inflation protection.

`(V) The State Medicaid agency under section 1902(a)(5) provides information and technical assistance to the State insurance department on the insurance department's role of assuring that any individual who sells a long-term care insurance policy under the partnership receives training and demonstrates evidence of an understanding of such policies and how they relate to other public and private coverage of long-term care.

`(VI) The issuer of the policy provides regular reports to the Secretary, in accordance with regulations of the Secretary, that include notification regarding when benefits provided under the policy have been paid and the amount of such benefits paid, notification regarding when the policy otherwise terminates, and such other information as the Secretary determines may be appropriate to the administration of such partnerships.

`(VII) The State does not impose any requirement affecting the terms or benefits of such a policy unless the State imposes such requirement on long-term care insurance policies without regard to whether the policy is covered under the partnership or is offered in connection with such a partnership.

In the case of a long-term care insurance policy which is exchanged for another such policy, subclause (I) shall be applied based on the coverage of the first such policy that was exchanged. For purposes of this clause and paragraph (5), the term `long-term care insurance policy' includes a certificate issued under a group insurance contract.

`(iv) With respect to a State which had a State plan amendment approved as of May 14, 1993, such a State satisfies this clause for purposes of clause (ii) if the Secretary determines that the State plan amendment provides for consumer protection standards which are no less stringent than the consumer protection standards which applied under such State plan amendment as of December 31, 2005.

`(v) The regulations of the Secretary required under clause (iii)(VI) shall be promulgated after consultation with the National Association of Insurance Commissioners, issuers of long-term care insurance policies, States with experience with long-term care insurance partnership plans, other States, and representatives of consumers of long-term care insurance policies, and shall specify the type and format of the data and information to be reported and the frequency with which such reports are to be made. The Secretary, as appropriate, shall provide copies of the reports provided in accordance with that clause to the State involved.

`(vi) The Secretary, in consultation with other appropriate Federal agencies, issuers of long-term care insurance, the National Association of Insurance Commissioners, State insurance commissioners, States with experience with long-term care insurance partnership plans, other States, and representatives of consumers of long-term care insurance policies, shall develop recommendations for Congress to authorize and fund a uniform minimum data set to be reported electronically by all issuers of long-term care insurance policies under qualified State long-term care insurance partnerships to a secure, centralized electronic query and report-generating mechanism that the State, the Secretary, and other Federal agencies can access.'; and

(B) by adding at the end the following:

`(5)(A) For purposes of clause (iii)(III), the model regulations and the requirements of the model Act specified in this paragraph are:

`(i) In the case of the model regulation, the following requirements:

`(I) Section 6A (relating to guaranteed renewal or noncancellability), other than paragraph (5) thereof, and the requirements of section 6B of the model Act relating to such section 6A.

`(II) Section 6B (relating to prohibitions on limitations and exclusions) other than paragraph (7) thereof.

`(III) Section 6C (relating to extension of

334

benefits).

`(IV) Section 6D (relating to continuation or conversion of coverage).

`(V) Section 6E (relating to discontinuance and replacement of policies).

`(VI) Section 7 (relating to unintentional lapse).

`(VII) Section 8 (relating to disclosure), other than sections 8F, 8G, 8H, and 8I thereof.

`(VIII) Section 9 (relating to required disclosure of rating practices to consumer).

`(IX) Section 11 (relating to prohibitions against post-claims underwriting).

`(X) Section 12 (relating to minimum standards).

`(XI) Section 14 (relating to application forms and replacement coverage).

`(XII) Section 15 (relating to reporting requirements).

`(XIII) Section 22 (relating to filing requirements for marketing).

`(XIV) Section 23 (relating to standards for marketing), including inaccurate completion of medical histories, other than paragraphs (1), (6), and (9) of section 23C.

`(XV) Section 24 (relating to suitability).

`(XVI) Section 25 (relating to prohibition against preexisting conditions and probationary periods in replacement policies or certificates).

`(XVIII) Section 29 (relating to standard format outline of coverage).

`(XIX) Section 30 (relating to requirement to deliver shopper's guide).

`(ii) In the case of the model Act, the following:
    `(I) Section 6C (relating to preexisting conditions).
    `(II) Section 6D (relating to prior hospitalization).
    `(III) The provisions of section 8 relating to contingent nonforfeiture benefits.
    `(IV) Section 6F (relating to right to return).
    `(V) Section 6G (relating to outline of coverage).
    `(VI) Section 6H (relating to requirements for certificates under group plans).
    `(VII) Section 6J (relating to policy summary).
    `(VIII) Section 6K (relating to monthly reports on accelerated death benefits).
    `(IX) Section 7 (relating to incontestability period).
`(B) For purposes of this paragraph and paragraph (1)(C)--
    `(i) the terms `model regulation' and `model Act' mean the long-term care insurance model regulation, and the long-term care insurance model Act, respectively, promulgated by the National Association of Insurance Commissioners (as adopted as of October 2000);
    `(ii) any provision of the model regulation or model Act listed under subparagraph (A) shall be treated as including any other provision of such regulation or Act necessary to implement the provision; and
    `(iii) with respect to a long-term care insurance policy issued in a State, the policy shall be deemed to meet applicable requirements of the model regulation or the model Act if the State plan amendment under paragraph (1)(C)(iii) provides that the State insurance commissioner for the State certifies (in a manner

satisfactory to the Secretary) that the policy meets such requirements.

`(C) Not later than 12 months after the National Association of Insurance Commissioners issues a revision, update, or other modification of a model regulation or model Act provision specified in subparagraph (A), or of any provision of such regulation or Act that is substantively related to a provision specified in such subparagraph, the Secretary shall review the changes made to the provision, determine whether incorporating such changes into the corresponding provision specified in such subparagraph would improve qualified State long-term care insurance partnerships, and if so, shall incorporate the changes into such provision.'.

(2) STATE REPORTING REQUIREMENTS- Nothing in clauses (iii)(VI) and (v) of section 1917(b)(1)(C) of the Social Security Act (as added by paragraph (1)) shall be construed as prohibiting a State from requiring an issuer of a long-term care insurance policy sold in the State (regardless of whether the policy is issued under a qualified State long-term care insurance partnership under section 1917(b)(1)(C)(iii) of such Act) to require the issuer to report information or data to the State that is in addition to the information or data required under such clauses.

(3) EFFECTIVE DATE- A State plan amendment that provides for a qualified State long-term care insurance partnership under the amendments made by paragraph (1) may provide that such amendment is effective for long-term care insurance policies issued on or after a date, specified in the amendment, that is not earlier than the first day of the first calendar quarter in which the plan amendment was submitted to the Secretary of Health and Human Services.

(b) STANDARDS FOR RECIPROCAL RECOGNITION

AMONG PARTNERSHIP STATES- In order to permit
portability in long-term care insurance policies purchased
under State long-term care insurance partnerships, the
Secretary of Health and Human Services shall develop, not
later than January 1, 2007, and in consultation with the
National Association of Insurance Commissioners, issuers
of long-term care insurance policies, States with experience
with long-term care insurance partnership plans, other States,
and representatives of consumers of long-term care insurance
policies, standards for uniform reciprocal recognition of such
policies among States with qualified State long-term care
insurance partnerships under which--

> (1) benefits paid under such policies will be treated the
> same by all such States; and
> (2) States with such partnerships shall be subject to
> such standards unless the State notifies the Secretary in
> writing of the State's election to be exempt from such
> standards.

(c) ANNUAL REPORTS TO CONGRESS-

> (1) IN GENERAL- The Secretary of Health and
> Human Services shall annually report to Congress on
> the long-term care insurance partnerships established
> in accordance with section 1917(b)(1)(C)(ii) of the
> Social Security Act (42 U.S.C. 1396p(b)(1)(C)(ii))
> (as amended by subsection (a)(1)). Such reports
> shall include analyses of the extent to which such
> partnerships expand or limit access of individuals to
> long-term care and the impact of such partnerships
> on Federal and State expenditures under the Medicare
> and Medicaid programs. Nothing in this section shall
> be construed as requiring the Secretary to conduct an
> independent review of each long-term care insurance
> policy offered under or in connection with such a
> partnership.

(2) APPROPRIATION- Out of any funds in
the Treasury not otherwise appropriated, there is
appropriated to the Secretary of Health and Human
Services, $1,000,000 for the period of fiscal years
2006 through 2010 to carry out paragraph (1).

(d) NATIONAL CLEARINGHOUSE FOR LONG-TERM
CARE INFORMATION-

(1) ESTABLISHMENT- The Secretary of Health
and Human Services shall establish a National
Clearinghouse for Long-Term Care Information. The
Clearinghouse may be established through a contract
or interagency agreement.

(2) DUTIES-

(A) IN GENERAL- The National
Clearinghouse for Long-Term Care
Information shall--

(i) educate consumers with respect
to the availability and limitations of
coverage for long-term care under the
Medicaid program and provide contact
information for obtaining State-specific
information on long-term care coverage,
including eligibility and estate recovery
requirements under State Medicaid
programs;

(ii) provide objective information
to assist consumers with the
decisionmaking process for determining
whether to purchase long-term care
insurance or to pursue other private
market alternatives for purchasing
long-term care and provide contact
information for additional objective
resources on planning for long-term

care needs; and

(iii) maintain a list of States with State long-term care insurance partnerships under the Medicaid program that provide reciprocal recognition of long-term care insurance policies issued under such partnerships.

(B) REQUIREMENT- In providing information to consumers on long-term care in accordance with this subsection, the National Clearinghouse for Long-Term Care Information shall not advocate in favor of a specific long-term care insurance provider or a specific long-term care insurance policy.

(3) APPROPRIATION- Out of any funds in the Treasury not otherwise appropriated, there is appropriated to carry out this subsection, $3,000,000 for each of fiscal years 2006 through 2010.

Appendix F:
Useful Websites

Useful Web Sites

Assisted Living and Nursing Home Resources
American Association of Homes and Services for the Aging:
    www.aahsa.org
American Health Care Association: www.ahca.org
Assisted Living Facilities for Seniors: www.helpguide.org/elder/
    assisted_living_facilities.htm
Assisted Living Federation of America: www.alfa.org
Assisted Living Info: www.assistedlivinginfo.com
Consumer Consortium on Assisted Living: www.ccal.org
National Academy for State Health Policy (state assisted living
    practices) www.nashp.org
National Center for Assisted Living: www.ncal.org
Nursing Home Compare: www.medicare.gov

Caregiving Resources
Alzheimer's Association: www.alz.org
Caregiver information: www.caregiver.com
Family Caregiver Alliance: www.caregiver.org
National Alliance for Caregiving: www.caregiver.org
National Family Caregivers Association: www.nfcacares.org
Well Spouse Foundation: www.wellspouse.org

Elder Law Resources
ElderLaw: www.elderlawanswers.com
Elder Law Bulletinwww.tn-elderlaw.com
National Academy of Elder Law Attorneys: www.naela.org
National Senior Citizen's Law Center: www.nsclc.org

Geriatric Care Management and Social Service Resources
National Association of Professional Geriatric Care Managers:
    www.caremanager.org
National Association of Social Workers: www.socialworkers.org

Government Websites and Statistics
Medicare & Medicaid Info: www.cms.hhs.gov and
    www.medicare.gov
National Center for Health Statistics (national nursing home,
home care and hospice surveys): www.cdc.gov/nchs
National Conference of State Legislators:
    www.ncsl.org/programs/health/forum/caregiversupport.htm
Thomas Library of Congress (legislation website):
    http://thomas.loc.gov
Urban Institute (long-term care government research):
    http://www.urban.org/health/index.cfm
U.S. Administration on Aging: www.aoa.gov
U.S. Census Bureau: www.census.gov
U.S. Government Accountability Office: www.gao.gov

Health Care
Agency for Health Care Research and Quality: www.ahrq.gov
American Psychological Association: www.apa.org
Kaiser Family Foundation: www.kff.org

Health Insurance and Benefits
America's Health Insurance Plans: www.ahip.net
Benefits Checkup: www.benefitscheckup.org
Blue Cross of California (Medicare MSA in California):
    www.bluecrossca.com
Unicare Life and Health Insurance (Medicare MSA Provider)
    www.unicare.com or 888-211-9813

Home Care and Hospice Resources
Home Care Compare: www.medicare.gov
National Association for Home Care and Hospice: www.nahc.org
Right at Home: www.rightathome.net
Visiting Nurse Associations of America: www.vnaa.org

Life Settlements
Life Insurance Settlement Association: www.lisassociation.org
Life and Viatical Settlements: The Heritage Group –
    www.HeritageGroup.us
Life Settlements: Ashar Group, LLC- www.ashargroupllc.com

Long-Term Care
MetLife Mature Market Institute: www.maturemarketinstitute.com
National Clearinghouse for Long-Term Care: www.longtermcare.gov
"Own Your Future" Federal Long-Term Care Consumer
    Education Campaign: http://www.aoa.gov/ltc/
    awareness_campaign.asp

Long-Term Care Insurance
LTC Consultants: www.ltcconsultants.com
Center for Long-Term Care Financing: www.centerltc.com
Long-Term Care Rate & History Guide: www.insurance.
    ca.gov/0100-consumers/0060-information-guides/0050-
    health/ltc-rate-history-guide/index.cfm
American Association for Long-Term Care Insurance:
    www.aaltci.org/consumer/started.html

Prescription Drug Information and Assistance
American Medical Pharmaceutical Outlet: ww.medshelp4u.com
The Medicine Program: www.themedicineprogram.com
Prescription Assistance Programs:
    www.disabilityresources.org/RX.html
Medicare Part D Information: www.medicare.gov

Print Publications
Health Affairs (health policy journal): www.healthaffairs.org
Long-Term Care Provider Newsletter: www.longtermcareprovider.com
USA Today: www.usatoday.com
Wall St. Journal: www.wsj.com

Reverse Mortgage Resources
National Reverse Mortgage Lenders Association:
  www.reversemortgage.org
Reverse Mortgage information: www.reversemortgagenation.com

Senior/Elder Care Information
AARP Public Policy Institute: www.aarp.org/research
Careguide: www.careguide.com
ElderCare Online: www.ec-online.net
Eldercare Facilities: www.eldercarelink.com
Eldercare Locator: www.eldercare.gov
ElderWeb Online Eldercare Sourcebook: ww.eldercareweb.com
Gerontological Society of America: www.geron.org
National Council on Aging: www.ncoa.org
PACE (Program for All Inclusive Care for the Elderly):
  http://www.cms.hhs.gov/pace/

Appendix G:

Sources for **Introduction**

Sources for **Long-Term Care and Your Financial Security**

Sources for **Features of a Good Long-Term Care Insurance Policy**

Sources for **Long-Term Care Insurance: The New Employee Benefit**

Sources for **The Partnership for Long-Term Care**

Sources for **The Medicaid Benefit for Long-Term Care**

Sources for **Alternatives for Financing Long-Term Care**

Sources for **Appendix A: Senior Benefits**

Introduction:

1. *Caregiving in America,* The Schmieding Center and The International Longevity Center-USA, November 25 2006, p. 3.

2. Genworth Financial Cost of Care Survey, April 2008.

3. Dychtwald, Ken, PhD and Daniel J. Kadlec. **The Power Years**, John Wiley & Sons, Inc., 2005, p. 12

Sources for Chapter 1:
Long-Term Care and Your Financial Security

1. Quote given to Phyllis Shelton on May 18, 2006 by Terry Savage, *Chicago Sun-Times* Financial Columnist, Author of **The Savage Number: How Much Money Do You Need to Retire?**, John Wiley & Sons, Inc., 2005.

2. "An Employer's Guide to Long-Term Care Insurance", America's Health Insurance Plans (formerly Health Insurance Association of America), June 2002, p. 2.

3. Genworth Financial Cost of Care Survey, April 2008.

4. *Ibid*

5. *Ibid*

6. Based on an average 6.2% compound growth rate between $56 daily cost in 1987 compared to $187 in 2007. Source for 1987 cost: Medical Expenditure Panel Survey (MEPS) Chartbook #6, "Nursing Home Expenses 1987-1996", Agency for Research

and Quality, p. 6. Source for 2007 cost of care: Genworth Financial Cost of Care Survey, April 2008

7. Based on a Nashville, Tennessee annual cost survey for 1990 provided by John Hancock Financial Services, Nashville, Tennessee and the MetLife Market Survey of Nursing Home and Assisted Living Costs, October 2007.

8. National Alliance for Caregiving and AARP: *Caregiving in the U.S.,* April 2004, p. 33.

9. Unpublished data from *The National Nursing Home Survey: 2004,* National Center for Health Statistics, obtained December 7, 2006.

10. *Caregiving in America,* The Schmieding Center and The International Longevity Center-USA, November 25, 2006, p. 10.

11. "Statistical Data on Alzheimer's Disease," Alzheimer's Association, 2008.

12. *The MetLife Study of Alzheimer's Disease: The Caregiving Experience*, MetLife Mature Market Institute in conjunction with LifePlans, Inc., August 2006, p. 6.

13. National Alliance for Caregiving and AARP: *Caregiving in the U.S.,* April 2004, p. 32.

14. *Wall St. Journal Online/Harris Interactive Personal Finance Poll,* Vol. 2, Issue 1, February 1, 2006.

15. "John Hancock Survey Finds Many Americans Affected by Caregiving for Aging Friends and Family", John Hancock Press Release, November 16, 2006.

16. Kemper et al. "Long-Term Care Over an Uncertain Future: What Can Current Retirees Expect?" *Inquiry* 42: Winter 2005/2006, p. 342.

17. Dychtwald, Ken, PhD. **The Power Years**, John Wiley & Sons, Inc., 2005, p. 13.

18. *Ibid*

19. U.S. Census Bureau, www.census.gov.

20. *Ibid*

21. Friend, Tim. "Science Finds No Limit on Life Span," *USA Today,* March 17, 1999.

22. Lane, Harriet. *The Observer*, posted on *Smiler* magazine website, November 28, 2002.

23. Shellenbarger, Sue. "Gray is Good: Employers Make Efforts To Retain Older, Experienced Workers," Wall St. Journal, "Work & Family," December 1, 2005.

24. Brendle, Anna. "102-Year-Old Professor Hailed as Oldest U.S. Worker," *National Geographic News*, September 26, 2002.

25. "Old, Smart, Productive," *Business Week* cover story, June 27, 2005.

26. Skatssoon, Judy. "Baby Boomers to Reach 120," *The Australian*, November 15, 2002.

27. Wells, Sandy. "This is My Life," *The Charleston Gazette*, September 14, 2003.

28. "2005 Disability Status Reports," Rehabilitation Research and Training Center on Disability Demographics and Statistics, Ithaca, NY: Cornell University, 2005, p. 12; Spillman, Brenda C. and, Kirsten J. Black. "Staying the Course: Trends in Family Caregiving," The Urban Institute, November 2005, p. 9; "2004 National Nursing Home Survey," National Center of Health Statistics, 2007.

29. Unpublished data from *The National Nursing Home Survey: 2004,* National Center for Health Statistics, obtained December 7, 2006.

30. Burton, Thomas M. *"Cognitive Dissonance* - Why Some Patients Get No Help After Brain Injury", *Wall St. Journal,* January 8, 2007, p. A-14.

31. Traumatic Brain Injury: Hope Through Research," National Institute of Neurological Disorders and Stroke, Page 1, published February 2002, updated September 13, 2006, p. 1

32. Burton, Thomas M. "Two Simple Tests Can Prevent Stroke, But Few Get Them," *Wall St. Journal,* September 24, 2004.

33. National Alliance for Caregiving and AARP: *Caregiving in the U.S.,* April 2004, pp. 10, 33.

34. Dychtwald, Ken, PhD. **AgePower,** Penguin Putnam, Inc. Publishers, 1999, p. 146 and **The Power Years**, John Wiley & Sons, Inc., 2005, p. 13.

35. Pew Research Center, "Baby Boomers Approach Age 60: From the Age of Aquarius to the Age of Responsibility," December 8, 2005.

36. "A Profile of Older Americans: 2005," Administration of Aging, 2006, p. 5.

37. Carter, Jessica. "Workshop to Help Those Who Care for Loved Ones," *Daily News Journal*, Murfreesboro, Tennessee, April 18, 2000, p. 1B.

38. "CMS OSCAR Data Current Surveys, Medical Condition – Mental Status," American Health Care Association, June 2006 (almost half of nursing home patients have some type of dementia).

39. *Contra Costa Times*, Walnut Creek, California, March 29, 1996, Reporter: Julie Appleby.

40. *Parade Magazine*, March 1, 1998.

41. "Women-Owned Businesses in the United States, 2006 Fact Sheet," Center for Women's Business Research, September 2006, p. 2.

42. National Alliance for Caregiving and AARP: *Caregiving in the U.S.,* April 2004, pp. 10, 33.

43. National Alliance for Caregiving and AARP: *Caregiving in the U.S.,* April 2004, pp. 21, 65.

44. Burton, Thomas M. "Screening for Artery Disease if Good Idea for People Over 60," *Wall St. Journal,* September 24, 2004, p. B3.

45. Centers for Medicare and Medicaid Services, 2005 statistics, Released January 2007.

46. *Contra Costa Times*, Walnut Creek, California, March 29, 1996, Reporter: Julie Appleby.

47. CMS, Office of Information Services: 2001 Data from the Medicare Support Access Facility; data development by the Office of Research, Development, and Information, 2004 Statistical Supplement.

48. Spillman, Brenda C. and Kirsten J. Black. "Staying the Course: Trends in Family Caregiving," The Urban Institute, November 2005, p. v.

49. Centers for Medicare and Medicaid Services, 2005 statistics, Released January 2007, Table 3, "National Health Expenditures, by Source of Funds and Type of Expenditure: Calendar Years 2000-2005, and Burwell, Brian, Kate Sredi, and Steve Eiken. "Medicaid Long-Term Care Expenditures in FY 2005," MedStat, Cambridge, MA, July 7, 2006.

50. Burwell, Brian, Kate Sredi, and Steve Eiken. "Medicaid Long-Term Care Expenditures in FY 2005," MedStat, Cambridge, MA, July 7, 2006.

51. Walker, David M. (U.S. Comptroller General). "GAO's Strategic Plan 2004-2009," Government Accountability Office, March 2004, p. 23.

52. Based on average 6% compounded growth rate between $56 daily cost in 1987 compared to $187 in 2007. Source for 1987 cost of care: Medical Expenditure Panel Survey (MEPS) Chartbook #6 "Nursing Home Expenses 1987-1996", Agency for Healthcare Research and Quality, p. 6. Source for 2007 cost of care: Genworth Financial Cost of Care Survey, April 2008.

53. Walker, David M. (Comptroller General of the U.S.). "Better Transparency, Controls, Triggers and Default Mechanisms Would Help to Address our Large and Growing Long-Term Fiscal Challenge," GAO-06-761T, May 25, 2006.

54. Spillman, Brenda C. and Kirsten J. Black. "Staying the Course: Trends in Family Caregiving," The Urban Institute, November 2005, p. v.

55. 2005 LTCI Buyer Non-Buyer Survey, America's Health Insurance Plans, 2007.

56. A conservative estimate based on historical growth and number of existing groups documented in 2001 – 2007 studies, *U.S. Group Long-Term Care Insurance Sales and In Force*, Life Insurance Market Research Association (LIMRA), 2008.

57. Centers for Medicare and Medicaid Services, 2005 statistics, Released January 2007, Table 3, "National Health Expenditures, by Source of Funds and Type of Expenditure Calendar Years 2000-2005, and Burwell, Brian, Kate Sredi, and Steve Eiken. "Medicaid Long-Term Care Expenditures in FY 2005," MedStat, Cambridge, MA, July 7, 2006.

58. According to the Economist Intelligence Unit, Sweden's income tax burden is one of the heaviest among the world's industrialized economies: a 60 percent top income tax rate. The 2006 Index of Economic Freedom, The Economist Intelligence Unit.

59. Cohen, Marc A., PhD. "Buyers and Non-Buyers of LTC Insurance: Fifteen Years of Innovation, Change and Shifting Market Challenge," Presented to AHIP 2006 Long-Term Care Workshop, September 12, 2006.

60. *Ibid*

61. Ruffenach, Glenn (ENCORE editor, *Wall St. Journal*). "Cracks in the Nest Egg," October 22, 2001.

62. Caplan, Craig and Normandy Brangan. "Out-of-Pocket Spending on Health Care by Medicare Beneficiaries Age 65 and Older in 2003," AARP Public Policy Institute, Data Digest #101, September 2004, p. 4.

63. Elswick, Jill. "Retirement Needs Outpace Americans' Savings Habits," Employee Benefit Research Institute study, *BenefitNews.com*, VOLUME 18, NUMBER 2, February 1, 2004.

64. Gordon, Harley, J.D. **"Financial Planners Risk Lawsuits for Failing to Recommend Realistic Plans for Long-Term Care,"** *Financial Planning Association Journal*, August 2005.

65. Arno, Peter S. "Economic Value of Informal Caregiving," presented at the Care Coordination and the Caregiving Forum, Dept. of Veterans Affairs, NIH, Bethesda, MD, January 25-27, 2006.

Chapter 2:
Features of a Good Long-Term Care Insurance Policy

1. **People receiving care with ADL deficiency under age 65 at home:** "2005 Disability Status Reports," Rehabilitation Research and Training Center on Disability Demographics and Statistics, Ithaca, NY: Cornell University, 2005, p. 12.

   People receiving care in a nursing home under age 65: "2004 National Nursing Home Survey," National Center of Health Statistics, 2007.

People receiving formal or informal care at home over age 65: Spillman, Brenda C. and Kirsten J. Black. "Staying the Course: Trends in Family Caregiving," November 2005, p. 9.

People receiving care in a nursing home over age 65: Spillman, Brenda C. and Kirsten J. Black. "The Size and Characteristics of the Residential Care Population: Evidence from Three National Surveys," The Urban Institute, January 4, 2006, p. 28.

2. Alexich, Lisa. "Nursing Home Use by 'Oldest Old' Sharply Declines," The Lewin Group, National Press Club, November 21, 2006, p. 3.

3. Okrent, David R. "Medical Deductions for the Elderly, Part II, Expenses and Premiums Related to Long-Term Care," *The ElderLaw Report*, Panel Publishers, March 2002, p. 2.

4. "Report: Shortage of Adult Day Services in Most U.S. Counties," Robert Wood Johnson Foundation, 2006.

5. *Ibid* (Adult day care costs are trended forward from $56 per day in 2002)

6. Genworth Financial Cost of Care Survey, April 2008.

7. *Ibid*

8. Wright, Bernadette. "Assisted Living in the United States," AARP Public Policy Institute, October 2004.

9. Unpublished data from the 2004 National Nursing Home Survey, National Center of Health Statistics, received January 8, 2007.

10. Genworth Financial Cost of Care Survey, April 2008.

11. *Ibid*

12. Internal Revenue Service Rev. Proc. 2006-53.20 and 2006-53.41.

13. Alexich, Lisa. "Nursing Home Use by 'Oldest Old' Sharply Declines," The Lewin Group, National Press Club, November 21, 2006 (The Lewin Group tabulations of the 2004 National Nursing Home Survey).

14. Unpublished data from the 2004 National Nursing Home Survey, National Center of Health Statistics, received December 7, 2006.

15. Kemper et al. "Long-Term Care Over an Uncertain Future: What Can Current Retirees Expect?" *Inquiry* 42: Winter 2005/2006, p. 342.

16. "The Impact of Long-Term Care on Women," Genworth Financial, July 14, 2006, p. 1.

17. Cohen, Marc A., PhD. "Benefits of Long-Term Care Insurance: Enhanced Care for Disabled Elders, Improved Quality of Life for Caregivers, and Savings to Medicare & Medicaid," prepared for Health Insurance Association of America by LifePlans, Inc., September 2002, p. 3.

18. Helwig, Dawn and Deborah Grant. "Long-Term Care Claims, How Long Do Claims Really Last?" Milliman Consultants and Actuaries, April 2005, Chart G.

19. "Costs are growing about 5.6 percent a year, according to estimates from the Centers for Medicare and Medicaid Services" – Mara, Janis. "Preparing for Illness in Old Age," *ContraCostaTimes*, November 6, 2006.

20. *Ibid*

21. Alexich, Lisa. "Nursing Home Use by 'Oldest Old' Sharply Declines," The Lewin Group, National Press Club, November 21, 2006, p. 3.

22. Thau, Claude. "Eighth Annual Individual Long Term Care Insurance Survey", *Broker World*, July 2006.

23. Chevreau, Jonathan. "Live the Good Life, But Save for the Worst: Health Scares Force a Reassessment of Priorities", *Financial Post,* December 23, 2006 www.canada.com/nationalpost/financialpost.

24. Life Insurance Market Research Association (LIMRA), 2008.

25. Genworth Financial Cost of Care Survey, April 2008.

26. Genworth Financial Cost of Care Survey, April 2008.

27. Cohen, Marc A., PhD. "Buyers and Non-Buyers of LTC Insurance: Fifteen Years of Innovation, Change and Shifting Market Challenge," Presented to AHIP 2006 Long-Term Care Workshop, September 12, 2006.

28. Helwig, Dawn and Deborah Grant. "Long-Term Care Claims, How Long Do Claims Really Last?" Milliman Consultants and Actuaries, April 2005, Chart G.

Sources for Chapter 3:
Long-Term Care: The New Employee Benefit

1. *Caregiving in America,* The Schmieding Center and The International Longevity Center-USA, p. 2.

2. Fisherkeller, Karen. "Group LTC Insurance, Annual Review 2007", LIMRA International, March, 2008.

3. Dychtwald, Ken PhD and Daniel J. Kadlec. "The Power Years," John Wiley & Sons, Inc., 2005, p. 12.

4. "Caregiving in the U.S." National Alliance for Caregiving AARP, April 2004, p. 8.

5. "An Employer's Guide to Long-Term Care Insurance," America's Health Insurance Plans (formerly Health Insurance Association of America), June 2004, p. 2 and *U.S. Group Long-Term Care Insurance: 2005 Sales and In Force*, Life Insurance Market Research Association (LIMRA), 2006.

6. "Study of Employee Benefits: 2006 & Beyond", Prudential, August 2006, p. 11.

7. "What's Hot and What's Not in Voluntary Benefits," Aon Consulting Study, Press Release January 31, 2006.

8. "The MetLife Study of Employee Benefits Trends," 2006, p. 42.

9. *Ibid*

10. *Caregiving in the U.S.*, National Alliance for Caregiving/ AARP, April 2004, p. 26.

11. Stucki, Barbara, PhD. "Passing the Trust to Private LTC Insurance," January 2003.

12. Family Caregiver Alliance as reported in "Moving Creates Boom in Long-Distance Care," Michael Hill, *The Miami Herald.com*, Posted March 14, 2005.

13. "John Hancock Survey Finds Many Americans Affected by Caregiving for Aging Friends and Family" – John Hancock Press Release November 16, 2006.

14. Life Insurance Market Research Association (LIMRA), 2006.

15. *LTC Consultants* Online Policy Comparison.

16. *Caregiving in the U.S.,* National Alliance for Caregiving/ AARP, 2004, p. 31.

17. "The MetLife Study of Sons at Work: Balancing Employment and Eldercare," National Alliance for Caregiving/Towson University, MetLife Mature Market Institute, June 2003, p. 2.

18. "The MetLife Study of Employee Benefits Trends," 2006, p. 42.

19. *Caregiving in the U.S.,* National Alliance for Caregiving/AARP, 2004, p. 65.

20. *Ibid,* p. 64

21 Pavalko, Eliza and Kathryn Henderson. "Combining Care Work and Paid Work: Do Workplace Policies Make a Difference?" *Research on Aging,* Vol. 28, May 2006, pp. 359-374.

22. "The MetLife Caregiving Cost Study: Productivity Losses to U.S. Business," MetLife Mature Market Institute National Alliance for Caregiving, July 2006, p.6.

23. "Miles Away: The MetLife Study of Long-Distance Caregiving," MetLife Mature Market Institute with Zogby International, July 2004, pp. 3, 11.

24. *Caregiving in the U.S.,* National Alliance for Caregiving/ AARP, 2004, p. 33.

25. *Ibid,* p. 32

26. "The MetLife Caregiving Cost Study: Productivity Losses to U.S. Business," MetLife Mature Market Institute/ National Alliance for Caregiving, July 2006, "The Impact of Long Term Care on Women", Genworth Financial; *Caregiving in the U.S.,* National Alliance for Caregiving AARP, 2004.

27. "*Caregiving in the U.S.,* National Alliance for Caregiving AARP, 2004, p.64.

28. "The MetLife Caregiving Cost Study: Productivity Losses to U.S. Business," MetLife Mature Market Institute National Alliance for Caregiving, July 2006, p. 4.

29. "The MetLife Study of Alzheimer's Disease: The Caregiving Experience," MetLife Mature Market Institute/LifePlans, Inc., August 2006, p. 6.

30. Telephone call from *LTC Consultants* to Megan Lamison, Director of "Lancaster Generations," the adult day care center provided by Lancaster Labs, December 20, 2006.

31. National Family Caregivers Association Fact Sheet, www.ngca.org.

32. "Suzanne Minta, Co-Founder of Nation's Largest Caregiver Advocacy Group, Honored with 2004 Lifetime Achievement Welcome Back Award," National Family Caregivers Association Press Release, April 30, 2004.

33. "How Do Family Caregivers Fare?" Center on an Aging Society, Georgetown University, June, 2005, p. 3.

34. "John Hancock Survey Finds Many Americans Affected by Caregiving for Aging Friends and Family" – John Hancock Press Release November 16, 2006.

35. "The Impact of Long Term Care on Women," Genworth Financial, p. 14.

36. "Women-Owned Businesses in the United States, 2006 Fact Sheet," Center for Women's Business Research, September 2006, p. 2.

37. *Caregiving in the U.S.,* National Alliance for Caregiving/AARP, 2004, p. 14.

38. *Ibid,* pp. 20, 21.

39. Spillman, Brenda C. and Kirsten J. Black. "Staying the Course: Trends in Family Caregiving", November 2005, p. 24.

40. "Financial Commitments to Family Members Especially Prevalent Among Surveyed Hispanics," Second Annual "Retirement Reality Check" survey, Allstate, November 14, 2002.

41. *Caregiving in the U.S.,* National Alliance for Caregiving/ AARP, 2004, p. 15.

42. *The Breakthrough Intercessor*, an intercessory prayer ministry founded by Catherine Marshall, author of **Christy**, Lincoln, Virginia.

43. *Caregiving in the U.S.,* National Alliance for Caregiving/ AARP, 2004, p. 68.

44. Kemper et al. "Long-Term Care Over an Uncertain Future: What Can Current Retirees Expect?" *Inquiry* 42: Winter 2005/2006, p. 342.

45. "2005 Disability Status Reports," Rehabilitation Research and Training Center on Disability Demographics and Statistics, Ithaca, NY: Cornell University, 2005, p. 12.

46. Unpublished data from *The National Nursing Home Survey: 2004*, National Center for Health Statistics, obtained December 7, 2006.

47. Tatum, Cheryl. *"Letters to My Daughter* is ALS Patient's Legacy," *The Hendersonville Star News*, November 30, 2005, p. 1 and personal interview by Phyllis Shelton with Dr. Yarbrough, January 2007.

48. Personal interview with Kristi and David Denton by Phyllis Shelton, 2002.

49. Personal interview with Denny Eckels (President of First Financial Group, Towson, Maryland) by Phyllis Shelton, December 21, 2006.

50. Written testimony from David C. Sharp, Montgomery Village Care and Rehabilitation Center, Montgomery Village, Maryland to Phyllis Shelton, January 22, 2003.

51. Interview conducted by Phyllis Shelton with attorney's father who prefers to remain anonymous (January 2007).

52. Statement from Jennifer Douglas, LIMRA, January 2007, February 2, 2007

53. Mara, Janis, "Preparing for Illness in Old Age," *ContraCosta Times*, November 6, 2006.

54. "2005 Disability Status Reports," Rehabilitation Research and Training Center on Disability Demographics and Statistics, Ithaca, NY: Cornell University, 2005, p. 12; "2004 National Nursing Home Survey" National Center of Health Statistics, 2007; Spillman, Brenda C. and Kirsten J. Black. "Staying the Course: Trends in Family Caregiving", November 2005, p. 9; Spillman, Brenda C. and Kirsten J. Black. "The Size and Characteristics of the Residential Care Population: Evidence from Three National Surveys," The Urban Institute, January 4, 2006, p. 28.

55. Gilcrest, Laura. "Analysis: The New 'Old-Folks Home,' " UPI.com, November 21, 2006.

56. Sweden website, http://www.sweden.gov.se.

57. Stucki, Barbara. "Passing the Trust to Long-Term Care Insurance," American Council of Life Insurers, January 2003, p. 10.

58. "The SeniorBridge Family Study of Home Caregivers," May 2004, p. 3.

Sources for Chapter 4: The Partnership for Long-Term Care

1. Smith, Vernon Smith, PhD, et al. "Low Medicaid Spending Growth Amid Rebounding State Revenues: Results from a 50-State Medicaid Budget Survey State Fiscal Years 2006 and 2007," Kaiser Commission on Medicaid and the Uninsured, October 2006, p. 70.

2. Genworth Financial Cost of Care Survey, April 2008

3. *Ibid*

4. *Ibid*

5. Burwell, Brian, Kate Sredi, and Steve Eiken. "Medicaid Long Term Care Expenditures in FY 2006," The MEDSTAT Group, Cambridge, Massachusetts, August 10, 2007.

6. Flowers, Lynda, Leigh Gross, Patricia Kuo, and Shelly-Ann Sinclair. "State Profiles 2005: Reforming the Health Care System," AARP Public Policy Institute, 2005, pp. 140, 142.

7. Burwell, Brian, Kate Sredi, and Steve Eiken. "Medicaid Long Term Care Expenditures in FY 2006," The MEDSTAT Group, Cambridge, Massachusetts, August 10, 2007.

8. Houser, Ari, Wendy Fox-Grage, and Mary Jo Gibson. "Across the States: Profiles of Long-Term Care and Independent Living," AARP Public Policy Institute, 2006, p. 217.

9. Guttchen, David. Third Quarter 2007 Statistics for The Connecticut Partnership for Long-Term Care, released 12/07.

10. California, Connecticut, Indiana and New York Third Quarter 2007 Statistics.

Sources for Chapter 5:
The Medicaid Benefit for Long-Term Care

1. "The Long-Term Care Outlook for Health Care Spending: Sources of Growth in Projected Federal Spending on Medicare and Medicaid", Congressional Budget Office, November, 2007, p. 19.

2. Burwell, Brian, Kate Sredi and Steve Eiken. "Medicaid Long-Term Expenditures in FY 2006", MedStat, Cambridge, Massachusetts, August 10, 2007

3. "A Report on Shortfalls in Medicaid Funding for **Nursing Home Care**," prepared by BDO Seidman, LLP, accountants and consultants for the American Health Care Association, June 2006, p. 6.

4. *Ibid,* p. 8

5. The Deficit Reduction Act of 2005, Public Law 109-171, enacted February 8, 2006, Section 6013.

6. *Wisconsin Dept. of Health and Family Services v. Blumer,* Supreme Court of the United States, 00-952, February 20, 2002.

7. The Deficit Reduction Act of 2005, Public Law 109-171, enacted February 8, 2006, Section 6014.

8. The Deficit Reduction Act of 2005, Public Law 109-171, enacted February 8, 2006, Section 6012.

9. *Ibid*

10. Tax Relief and Health Care Act of 2006, H.R. 6111, enacted December 20, 2006, Section 405, CERTAIN MEDICAID DRA TECHNICAL CORRECTIONS, "Clarifying Treatment of Certain Annuities (Section 6012)."

11. "Medicaid Estate Recovery," U.S. Department of Health and Human Services, Office of the Assistant Secretary for Planning and Evaluation, www.cms.hhs.gov/MedicaidEligibility/08 Estate_Recovery.asp.

12. Karp, Naomi, Charles P. Sabatino, Erica F. Wood. "Medicaid Estate Recovery: A 2004 Survey of State Programs and Practices," by ABA Commission on Law and Aging for the AARP Public Policy Institute, June 2005, Table 12, p. 37.

13. "Recipient's Assets Conveyed to Wife Are Recoverable from Her Estate," June 2000, pp. 5–6 (In the Matter of the Estate of Wirtz, N.D. Sup. Ct., No. 990275, 2000 WI, 291154, March 21, 2000).

14. Karp, Naomi, Charles P. Sabatino, Erica F. Wood. "Medicaid Estate Recovery: A 2004 Survey of State Programs and Practices," by ABA Commission on Law and Aging for the AARP Public Policy Institute, June 2005, Table 12, p. 59.

15. "Nevada Class Action Seeks to Block Liens on Homes of Spouses," *ElderLaw Answers.com*, April 29, 2002.

16. Request for Release by the Bureau of TennCare, as required by *T.C.A. §71-5-116(c)(2)* (http://tennessee.gov tenncare/members/estaterecovery1.htm).

17. Karp, Naomi, Charles P. Sabatino, Erica F. Wood. "Medicaid Estate Recovery: A 2004 Survey of State Programs and Practices," by ABA Commission on Law and Aging for the AARP Public Policy Institute, June 2005, Table 1, p. 49 and Burke, Sheila. "Families Lose Their Homes to TennCare: State Intensifies Efforts to Recoup Costs for Care," *The Tennessean*, October 23, 2006.

18. Pear, Robert. "Health Secretary Calls for Medicaid Changes," *The New York Times,* February 2, 2005.

19. "Table 8-Nursing Home Care Expenditures Aggregate, Per Capita Amounts, and Percent Distribution, by Source of Funds: Selected Calendar Years 1970-2005, Centers for Medicare and Medicaid Services, Released January 2007.

20. Houser, Fox-Grage, Gibson. "Across the States: Profiles of Long-Term Care and Independent Living," AARP Public Policy Institute, 2006.

21. Walker, David M. (Comptroller General of the U.S.). "Better Transparency, Controls, Triggers and Default Mechanisms Would Help to Address our Large and Growing Long-Term Fiscal Challenge," GAO-06-761T, May 25, 2006.

22. Crowley, Jeffrey S. "Medicaid Long-Term Care Services Reforms in the Deficit Reduction Act," Health Policy Institute, Georgetown University, prepared for the Kaiser Commission on Medicaid and the Uninsured, Kaiser Family Foundation, April 2006, p. 2.

23. Summer, Laura. "Strategies to Keep Consumers Needing Long-Term Care in the Community and Out of Nursing Facilities," Georgetown University Health Policy Institute for Kaiser Commission on Medicaid and the Uninsured, October 2005, p. 23.

24. "A Report on Shortfalls in Medicaid Funding for Nursing Home Care," prepared by BDO Seidman, LLP, accountants and consultants for the American Health Care Association, June 2006, p. 2.

25. Franklin, Mary Beth. "Medicaid Gets Tough," *Kiplinger's Personal Finance Magazine*, May 2006.

26. "Review and Outlook: Medicaid for Millionaires," *Wall St. Journal*, February 24, 2005 (no author listed).

27. Cohen, Marc A., PhD. "Buyers and Non-Buyers of LTC Insurance: Fifteen Years of Innovation, Change and Shifting Market Challenge," Presented to America's Health Insurance Plans (AHIP) 2006 Long-Term Care Workshop, September 12, 2006.

Sources for Chapter 6: Alternatives for Financing Long-Term Care

1. Viatical Settlements Model Regulation #698, National Association of Insurance Commissioners, 2006, p. 698-5.

2. *Ibid,* p. 698-6

3. Viatical Settlements Model Act with LISA Amendments 2006, National Association of Insurance Commissioners, Section 9C.

4. Case study provided by The Heritage Group, Oklahoma City, OK, a firm that specializes in life and viatical settlements.

5. "Cashing in on Unneeded Life Insurance Policies: *How Seniors Are Benefiting From Life Settlements*", Life Insurance Settlement Association, 2006, p. 10.

6. "NAIC Committee Adopts Amendments to Viatical Settlements Model Regulation" NAIC Press Release, December 11, 2006 on NAIC website (www.naic.org).

7. Pension Protection Act of 2006, Public Law 109-280, Section 844.

8. Baskies, Jeffrey A. and Slafsky, Neal A., *Trusts & Estates*, June 1997.

9. "Statistical Data on Alzheimer's Disease," Alzheimer's Association's website, 2008.

10. Mara, Janis. "Preparing for Illness in Old Age", *ContraCostaTimes*, November 6, 2006 ("Costs are growing about 5.6% a year, according to estimates from the Centers for Medicare and Medicaid Services").

11. Helwig, Dawn and Grant, Deborah. "Long-Term Care Claims, How Long Do Claims Really Last?" Milliman Consultants and Actuaries, April 2005, Chart G.

Sources for Appendix A: Senior Benefits

1. "An Employer's Guide to Long-Term Care Insurance",
    America's Health Insurance Plans (formerly Health Insurance
    Association of America), June 2004, p. 2

2. "The Long-Term Outlook for Health Care Spending",
    Congressional Budget Office, November 2007, Appendix A

3. "The Medicare Prescription Drug Benefit", The Henry J. Kaiser
    Family Foundation, February 2008, p. 2

4. "A Survey of Medigap Enrollment Trends, July 2006", America's
    Health Insurance Plans (AHIP) Center for Policy and Research,
    October 2006, p. 1

5. Neuman, Patricia et al. "How Much 'Skin in the Game' Do
    Medicare Beneficiaries Have? The Increasing Financial Burden
    of Health Care Spending, 1997-2003", Health Affairs, November-
    December 2007, p. 1694

6. Douglas, Jennifer, "Individual LTC Insurance, Annual Review
    2005", LIMRA International, Inc., 2006, p. 4

7. "2008 Choosing a Medigap Policy: A Guide to Health
    Insurance for People with Medicare", Centers for Medicare
    and Medicaid Services, p. 33

8. *Ibid,* p. 61

9. *Ibid,* p. 19

10. *Ibid,* p. 28

11. Bankers Life & Casualty Vice President, Product Development and Management, January 20, 2007

12. "A Survey of Medigap Enrollment Trends, July 2006", America's Health Insurance Plans (AHIP) Center for Policy and Research, October 2006, p. 6

13. "Employer Health Benefits 2006 Annual Survey", The Kaiser Family Foundation and Health Research and Educational Trust, p. 60

14. "Medicare Advantage Fact Sheet", The Henry J. Kaiser Family Foundation, June 2007

15. "Medicare Advantage Fact Sheet", The Henry J. Kaiser Family Foundation, September 2005, p. 1

16. "Comparing Bush and Kerry on Issues Important to the Elderly", ElderLawAnswers.com, reviewing the Medicare Prescription Drug, Improvement, and Modernization Act of 2003, September 13, 2004

17. "Medicare Chartpack", Kaiser Family Foundation, May 8, 2007

18. "Medicare Advantage Fact Sheet", The Henry J. Kaiser Family Foundation, September 2005, p. 1

19. *Your Guide to Medicare Medical Savings Account Plans*, Centers for Medicare & Medicaid Services, p. 30

20. "Ignagni: Critics Continue to Ignore the Evidence – Medicare Advantage Plans Providing Beneficiaries Better Benefits at Lower Out-of-Pocket Costs", America's Health Insurance Plans (AHIP) Press Release, November 30, 2006

21. HR 6111, "Tax Relief and Health Care Act of 2006", Section 206 of Division B, *Medicare and Other Health Provisions*, Title II – *Medicare Beneficiary Protections*, p. 69

22. "Medicare Chart Book, The Henry J. Kaiser Family Foundation, 2005, p. 32

23. "The Medicare Prescription Drug Fact Sheet", The Henry J. Kaiser Family Foundation, Feburary 2008, p. 2

24. "Medicare Part D Plan Characteristics, 2007", The Henry J. Kaiser Family Foundation

25. "The Medicare Prescription Drug Fact Sheet", The Henry J. Kaiser Family Foundation, February 2008, p. 1

26. *Ibid*, p. 2

27. Ibid, p. 1 and Leavitt, Mike. "Medicare and the Market", *Washington Post*, January 11, 2007

28. "The Medicare Prescription Drug Fact Sheet", The Henry J. Kaiser Family Foundation, February 2008, p. 1

29. Hoadley, Jack, et al. "Benefit Design and Formularies of Medicare Drug Plans: A Comparison of 2006 and 2007

Offerings, A First Look", Georgetown University Health Policy Institute, The Henry J. Kaiser Family Foundation, November 2006, p. 1

30. "The Medicare Prescription Drug Fact Sheet", The Henry J. Kaiser Family Foundation, February 2008, p. 1

31. *Ibid,* p. 2

32. Leavitt, Mike. "Medicare and the Market", *Washington Post*, January 11, 2007

33. Caplan, Craig and Normandy Brangan. "Out-of-Pocket Spending on Health Care by Medicare Beneficiaries Age 65 and Older in 2003", AARP Public Policy Institute, September 2004, p. 4

ACKNOWLEDGMENTS

We gratefully acknowledge receiving help from the following publications and groups: *Medicare and You, Choosing a Medigap Policy: A Guide to Health Insurance for People with Medicare,* and *Your Guide to Medicare Medical Savings Accounts Plans.* The National Association of Insurance Commissioners, the State of Tennessee Department of Commerce and Insurance (Howard Magill), the following organizations and individuals who are there for you when you need them, and most of all, to the wonderful staff of *LTC Consultants* without whom nothing would ever be printed!

The Urban Institute: Brenda Spillman, PhD

Centers for Medicare and Medicaid Services: Monica Radcliffe, Anna Long, Roy Trudel

National Center for Health Statistics: Genevieve Strahan

United States Office of Personnel Management: John Cutler, Laura Lawrence and Holly Schumann

Phil Sullivan, SellingLTC, LLC

LifePlans, Inc. Marc Cohen, Ph.D., Jessica Miller

Life Insurance Market Research Association (LIMRA): Jennifer Douglas

Long-Term Care Group: Eileen Tell

MedStat: Brian Burwell

Center for Health Policy Research and Ethics, George Mason University: Mark Meiners, PhD

Department of Health and Human Services: Hunter McKay

Connecticut Partnership for Long-Term Care: David Guttchen

Visiting Nurse Service of New York: Christopher M. Murtaugh, PhD

Osborne & Co., PC, Certified Public Accountants - Tim Osborne, CPA

Centennial Adult Care Center – Nashville, Tennessee: Stephen Zagorski

Corporation for Long-Term Care Certification: Harley Gordon, Attorney-at-Law

Center for Long-Term Care Financing: Steve Moses

Elder Law Attorney: Harry Margolis, Esq.

Insurance Companies:
AEGON: Bob Glowacki
Bankers Life & Casualty: Pat Fleming
Blue Cross of California: Karen A. Brown, Chau Le (Medicare MSA)
Blue Cross Blue Shield of Tennessee: John Sellers
Coventry CareLink: Bob Clement
John Hancock: Gene Arsenault, Evelyn Fox
MedAmerica: Gail Holubinka
MetLife: Kim Purnell, Denny Joe, John Sherman
MetLife Mature Market Institute: Sandra Timmerman, Barbara Howard, Kathy O'Brien
OneAmerica (Combo LTC Plans): Bruce Moon
Mutual of Omaha: John Ferroni
Sterling Plans (Private Fee-For-Service Provider): Faye Karpman
United Health Care: Joyce Ruddock

Milliman and Robertson: Dawn Helwig

Avon Long Term Care Consultants, LLC: Gary Korliss

Next Generation Financial Services (Reverse Mortgage Lenders, First Mariner Bank) Valerie Van Booven, RN, BSN, PGCM

The Ark Group (Critical Illness Specialists): Don Hansen

Martin Bayne (Mr. LTC)

Asher Group LLC (Life Settlement Specialists): Paul Bowen and
Kristine Kugler

Association of Health Insurance Advisors: Diane Boyle

National Association of Health Underwriters: John Greene

American Council of Life Insurers: Lynn Boyd

*and the biggest thanks of all goes to my wonderful spouse who
endures my annual research and writing cycle!!*